Keys to the Kingdom 2

Sins of the Father

KEYS TO THE KINGDOM 2

SINS OF THE FATHER

TY MARSHALL

KEYS TO THE KINGDOM 2

For information contact :

www.tymarshallbooks.com

Cover design by Josh Wirth

ISBN: 978-0-9984419-3-1

First Edition: December 2016

10 9 8 7 6 5 4 3 2 1

DEDICATION

This book is dedicated to Trentavious "Bankroll Fresh" White. We miss you nephew. Long Live Bankroll. Streeeeet!

CHAPTER 1

"The Sins of the father will be visited upon the children." — Unknown

THIS WAS NEVER SUPPOSED TO HAPPEN. Sin could still feel the aftershock from the blast. The ground of the cemetery still trembling beneath him, the scent of charred flesh and metal lingering in the air. He had completely misjudged his enemies. It wasn't their power he had underestimated but their proximity. They were closer to him than he thought; too close and now tragedy was once again at his doorstep. A rhythmic recurrence of thuds filled his head as his pulse quickened into a frenzy of activity. Sin winced in agony, pain shooting through his body, causing him to let out a low, muffled grunt as he sat up. Every bone in his body ached from being hurled through the air and slammed to the ground. Sin squinted his eyes from the sun, trying to bring the chaotic scene playing out around him into focus. Things seemed to move in slow motion, a bunch of vague images appearing in blurred flashes. Sin shook his head trying to gain some clarity. Finally, he was able to recognize the mob of grief stricken mourners as his vision began to improve. It was then he saw the panic, the look of terror on the faces of the people scrambling around in a mass of confusion. He also saw the bodies. A few of his men were sprawled out all over the place with their leg or an arm missing. The cemetery resembled a battlefield. An uneasy feeling swept over him as he examined the crowd. Some people had long, fixed stares of shock on their faces. While other's faces were painted with fear, their screams muted by the loud ringing occurring in his ears. Which face amongst them belonged to the person responsible for this?

Sin swept the debris from his slacks then wiped the trickles of blood coming from the swelling on his forehead. Then at once it hit him. Where's Ariane? he thought as he looked around frantically then attempted to get to his feet without any further concern for his own well-being. The excruciating pain that shot through him pulled him back to the ground. Once again he attempted to get to his feet but suddenly things grew dark. A large shadow began to cast over him, blocking the sun from view. When Sin looked up, his eyes were met by a hand gripping a gun.

Case seemed so imposing as he loomed into clear view,

bearing down on Sin, his gun within a distance not much more than an arm's length away. Something ominous hung in the air between the two men as their eyes locked. It was as if they were the only ones in the cemetery, the way they stared into each-others souls. The expression Case wore was decidedly hostile and there was a ruthless gleam in his eyes as his finger rested on the trigger. For all of Sin's power in the street, his fate now lied in the hands of an unknown enemy with a deep rooted hatred for him. The playing field had been leveled. The gun in Case's hands was the ultimate equalizer and now he held all the power.

Sin had dealt in death enough to recognize Case's murderous intentions. He broke eye contact long enough to scan for his gun, catching a glimpse of it out the corner of his eye. It was laying on the ground just a few feet away. Where it had landed after the explosion. Without giving it a second thought Sin went for it, lunging with the quickness of a black mamba but the distance exceeded his outreached hands. Damn, he thought to himself.

Case smiled for just a moment, his stone face almost softened. He had Sin right where he wanted him. Without ever saying a word, he squeezed the trigger causing his gun to bark with a menacing boom that echoed throughout the massive cemetery.

* * *

The howling rumble of an engine caught everyone's attention just before they heard the shots from Case's gun. A darkly tinted vehicle fishtailed from one side of the road to the other weaving its way through the cemetery. The screeching tires sent a harsh, ear piercing sound through the air as bullets pinged against the car. Case stepped around Sin into the street repeatedly firing at the car, the rest of Sin's crew all followed suit, sending a serenade of gunshots in the fleeing car's direction. The car zoomed recklessly through the gates of the cemetery, disappearing out of sight.

"What the fuck just happened!" Beans shouted in frustration, while pacing back and forth, staring in the direction where the car had disappeared. Suddenly he turned his attention back to where Sin laid on the ground.

The group of men raced back towards Sin, who was finally lifting himself up. Case was the first to reach him and extended a helping hand. Beans totally disregarded the gesture, stepping in front of Case and shooting him an unwelcoming glare before pulling Sin to his feet. The animosity between Beans and Case could be felt immediately. The tension thickened as the two men faced off like bulls preparing to clash with one another.

"Who the fuck is this nigga?" Beans asked to nobody in particular.

"Who the fuck is you?" Case replied. His eyes were piercing, glistening with hatred as he spoke.

"No Beans please," Cassie said as he went to lift his gun. She placed her hand on his wrist stopping him. She could feel the intensity in Beans' hand as he gripped the gun. Cassie knew he would kill Case without much of a second thought. "This ain't the time or place for that. He's cool," she insisted.

"He ain't cool with me," Beans said.

Cassie felt a great sense of relief as his hand began to relax at her request, easing the tension a bit. Cassie turned toward Sin and hugged him around the neck, squeezing him tight. "Are you okay?"

"Yeah I'm good," he answered in a raspy tone.

"Oh my God!" a terrified Ashleigh shouted following close behind Cassie. But when she reached the group, she noticed the looks on Beans and Case's faces and placed her hand on Case's chest. Ashleigh could feel it raging up and down. She wrapped an arm around his waist, hugging him, trying to bring calm to the escalating tension between the men. When Beans ice cold glare landed on her, Ashleigh turned her head, avoiding eye contact by burying her face into Case's chest.

Case's eyes were full of malice as he smirked and nodded at Beans while embracing Ashleigh. The look on both men's faces made it clear to one another that they would surely continue this at another time.

"Ariane!" Sin shouted finally seeing the wreckage.

Heartache rapidly filled his chest and grief ripped through him like a jagged blade. The hurt was much greater than any physical suffering he had felt before. He pushed his way through the group and raced towards the untamable flames, hoping to find some signs of life. The raging blaze had devoured the entire Range Rover, belching out flames that leaped into the air. Flashes of red and yellow sparks twirled in a fiery dance creating a wall of intense heat. Sin tried fighting the flames off as he frantically circled the car. He could feel his lungs burning with every breath as thick, black clouds of smoke choked the air. He covered his mouth and nose with his hand. refusing to give up, calling Ariane's name over the loud crackles of the fire.

A voice calling out to him, rekindling the hope that was slowly receding like the ocean's tide. It was like a rush of new energy came over him and Sin began searching the wreckage more intensively. Ariane was a survivor, she would fight to live not giving up and he wasn't going to give up on her either.

"Sin, c'mon!" the voice called out again.

This time he felt a tug on his shirt, forcefully pulling him away from the fire as he fought to get towards it. Then reality kicked him in the stomach. The voice that had given Sin a glimmer of hope, belonged to Beans not Ariane. Sin felt his knees weaken. It was like he had been blindsided on the chin. His heart exploded in his chest. He had never experienced the level of pain and heartache he felt. When he lost his mother to her battle with cancer, he had time to prepare himself but this was different, this was so sudden. His mind couldn't process what was happening fast enough. Normally, he was in strict control of his emotions. Sin took great pride in keeping his composure in the most extreme situations. The inability to reign in the grief was foreign to him and he found it increasingly harder to keep it together with each passing moment. His eyes were next to fail him. They began to cloud with tears but the hurt in his eyes quickly turned to pure rage. Sin reached out towards the flames. "Why?" This time his voice cracked as tears ran down his face. His normally handsome face grew ugly with sorrow and his lips quivered.

Cassie had tears in her eyes as she watched from a far, in pain, covering her mouth in shock. She never thought she'd see her brother so broken, that in itself was heartbreaking enough.

Jewlz, the youngest Holloway sibling, had a blank stare on his face and his head had remained on a swivel, still unsure of what he had just witnessed. Death was all around him. He had once viewed his family as untouchable, that was now a faded picture. Jewlz had always thought of his father and then his brother as protection from the world they lived in. That was no longer the case. Jewlz felt the need to step up. He himself would now have to guard against these same enemies. After all, he was a Holloway, which made his life worth taking.

Ashleigh was at a lost too and couldn't stand to watch it any longer. She turned her face, wiping away tears. Her heart bleeding for her brother as she held on to Case, who felt nothing but joy. He found pleasure in all the suffering. His thirst for revenge made him incapable of having sympathy for anyone in her family, especially Sin. All he saw was weakness around him, a crumbling empire. A chink in Sin's armor that he planned to exploit and finish what the other enemies had started. Sin had the ability to love. That was an emotion Case wasn't capable of. He didn't care about a soul in the whole world. That made him a dangerous enemy.

"We need to back up. This shit gonna blow again," Beans informed Sin as he continued to pull at him trying to get them away from the blaze.

"I gotta save her," Sin continued to repeat trying to break away from Beans grasp.

"She gone my nigga. She gone," Beans told him in an apologetic tone, hating to be the bearer of bad news. At that instant, he could feel all Sin's weight collapse on to him in defeat, finally accepting that there was nothing more he could do. Beans pulled Sin away moments before another explosion went off, rocking the cemetery again causing more screams to fill the air.

Staring back as flickers from the inferno danced in the

reflection of his watery eyes, Sin didn't say it but he knew in his heart that he would do whatever had to be done, kill whoever had to be killed to make those responsible for Ariane's death pay. He trusted God would understand the things a man must do sometimes to protect his family.

CHAPTER 2

A WEEK LATER, IN THE front of a funeral home in Brooklyn, a half dozen Muslim men in dark suits were talking to a group of women dressed in tight fitted dresses not suitable for a funeral. The women looked more ready for the club instead of being there to pay their last respects to the dead. Although the outfits may have been their only dressy clothes, the group of men protecting Sheik's wake still had denied them entry. Sin also thought it was tasteless the way they were dressed but didn't show it as he approached the group. Originally, most of the crew thought it was safer if they all stayed away due to what happened at Marion's service. They didn't want the same to happen at Sheik's funeral but Sin disagreed. He knew they couldn't send flowers or money without making an appearance. They all owed Sheik more than that. Sin felt it necessary that the crew all paid their proper respects to Maleekah and the kids. He took the necessary precautions to guarantee not only his but everyone in attendance safety, placing his henchmen all over the block. Nothing was going to happen and nothing was going to keep him away. He was also carrying fifty thousand dollars in an envelope, tucked in his suit jacket that he wanted to personally deliver to Maleekah. She needed to know he would be there for them in their time of loss. He had lost a close and dear friend in Sheik but she had lost the head of her household, her husband and the kids had lost their father. Their suffering was unmatched by anyone in attendance.

Sin inhaled a deep breath. He was on edge but feeling the hug of the bullet proof vest he wore under his suit jacket, put his mind at ease. In the midst of war, he could never be too safe. Beans walked side by side with him, Ali and Barkim following as Kyrie and the twins, Cairo and Egypt brought up the rear. It didn't seem right to any of them that Sheik wasn't striding up the sidewalk with them and as they walked, personal memories of him played in each one of their minds.

As they approached, a young man noticed Sin and disappeared inside the funeral home. By the time the group had made it to the door, the young man had returned along with Maleekah and she was waiting on them, holding her newborn son in her arms.

Sheik had left a young, beautiful widow behind but Maleekah appeared to have aged ten years overnight. Her eyes were bloodshot red, swollen from crying and surrounded by dark circles. She looked like she hadn't slept in days as she stood there in a black Kaftan Abaya dress and Hijab covering her head, traditional of her Muslim faith. The streets had not only claimed her husband's life but seemingly hers too. The light in her eyes was gone, forever dimmed and Sin could see that she would never be the same again.

"Sorry I'm late," Sin greeted somberly then instantly felt a lump form in his throat making it impossible to say anything else. Truth was, he had been so consumed by Ariane's death that he hadn't allowed himself to think about Sheik much. For that he felt guilty and seeing Maleekah made it all hit him at once, as soon as he spoke, he felt a flood of emotions inside. On the outside, Sin remained firm, hoping his show of strength would be contagious to the rest of the crew. He leaned in to hug Maleekah but she rejected him.

"You shouldn't be here," Maleekah announced as tears raced down her face.

"Nothing was gonna keep me away," Sin assured her.

"Yeah, but you still shouldn't be here," she said in a

more assertive tone making her intention clear.

"Huh?" Sin asked a bit confused by her reaction to his presence.

"You heard me. I don't want you here. None of you, but especially you," she expressed through tears. "I don't want you around me or my children. I never want to see your face again." All the pain and hurt she felt inside was spilling out as anger directed at Sin.

Maleekah's cold demeanor caught him off guard. He paused before speaking just to let what she said sink in. He had known Maleekah for years and never seen her so much as raise her voice but he understood she was suffering. Sin looked down at Sheik's young daughter, who was standing beside Maleekah, hiding her face in her mother's dress while looking up at him. Sin wanted to pick the little girl up and embrace her. He wanted to explain to her how much Sheik loved her, how she meant the world to her father. He could see that the little girl wanted to reach out to him like she had always done before but Maleekah held her tightly at bay. Sin knew then that a line had been drawn.

"C'mon Maleekah, this is foul," Ali chimed in causing the Muslim bodyguards to step forward.

"Be easy," Sin spoke sternly, holding up his hand quieting Ali's objection. "I completely understand," he said to Maleekah. Although he was crushed on the inside, there was no way he was going to disobey her wishes, purely out of respect. Sin operated on a strict set of principles, family and loyalty above anything else. He believed in honoring and protecting the women in his circle like they were his own wife. He would never disrespect any of them or let them be disrespected. So in his mind, Ali was out of line more than Maleekah. Reaching inside his jacket, he pulled out the envelope and extended it to her. "I wanted to give you this. For you and the kids—."

"I don't want or need any of your blood money. Allah will provide for us," Maleekah said immediately turning her face away from him, rejecting the offer.

Sin pulled the envelope away and the rest of the crew didn't even bother to reach for theirs. "I'll respect your wishes for now but if you—."

"Good," Maleekah cut him off, raising her voice as tears rolled down her face. She stepped closer to Sin, looking as though she wanted to take a swing at him, only to stop herself. "What were you thinking coming here? Have you no shame? This is all your fault. Why did you let this happen to my husband? Why Sin?" she spoke with so much hurt, more of a pleading cry truly hoping Sin would have an answer for her but he didn't. He felt the chill of her pain in his bones.

"I must be dreaming. That's what this is, all just a really bad dream—" she stopped herself mid-sentence and took a deep sigh that sounded more like a whimper. Maleekah took a step back towards the door, her eyes still fixed on Sin, the focal point of her tirade. "My faith won't allow me to hate you but I curse the day my husband ever met you," she spewed with a cold vengeance in her voice then turned her back on him, walking back inside the building.

"She don't mean that shit. She just fucked up in the head right now. That's the pain talking," Beans whispered to him.

Another man in front of the funeral home spoke up as the door closed behind Maleekah. He felt the need to explain her actions. "Everybody in this hood knows how close you and Sheik were. Y'all were like brothers. I know that and she knows that too," he said as smoke oozed from his nostrils. He took the last drag of the cigarette before tossing it to the ground.

Sin didn't need any explanation from anyone, he understood Maleekah's emotional outburst. "You her brother right?" he asked, recognizing the man's face. When the man confirmed, Sin extended the envelope to him but didn't let it go immediately. "Make sure she gets this some kind of way," he expressed the seriousness of his tone with a look to match. There was no need though, the man knew Sin's reputation and had no plans to disobey his wishes.

"Let her know anything her and the kids need, anything, I got em," Sin said before releasing his grip on the envelope. He headed back towards the car without saying another word to anybody. As he walked Maleekah's words played over in his mind. They had cut him deep, mainly because she was right. It was all his fault. Sheik's murder, Ariane's death, maybe his father's too. Their deaths all laid at his feet and that burden weighed heavy on his shoulders. He could feel it with every step he took. He had fought many wars but this one had truly taken a toll on him. He had loss more than he had gained and it didn't sit well with him. His only hope was that in time he could make it right. Right with Maleekah, right with his crew and his siblings but most importantly right within himself. Because as of now he still hadn't forgiven himself.

* * *

Sin pulled into an alley between some abandoned buildings and parked. He exited the car, his Timberland's splashing in a puddle as he stepped out. He slammed the door behind him then pulled the hood of his coat over his head as he stood there in silence for a moment. The night was cold and pitch black. A thin layer of smog trapped the city's light and made the sky appear darker than usual. A beam of light from the street penetrated a small distance into the alley but beyond that it was all shadows. There was no movement out on the street this late at night and rarely was there in this part of town. It was where Sin came to let off some steam and release his pinned up frustrations. After not being allowed in Sheik's wake earlier that day, he had tons of it.

Sin followed the alley on foot until he came to a locked door between two dumpsters. He pulled a key from his pocket, struggling momentarily then finally opening the heavy door after pushing his weight into it. The place smelled like mildew and dust and hit him all at once. He removed the fitted hat he wore, and used it to cover his nose. The large abandoned space was once a nightclub, many years ago but now was a hollowed shell where rats roamed and pigeons perched high, painting the floors with their shit. Sin made his way over to a flight of steps that descended even further into the darkness. Reaching the bottom, he flipped on a light switch that lit up the entire basement. The floor of the basement was covered in plastic. That plastic was covered in dried blood and if the walls could speak, they would tell the stories of the many men that never made it out of there alive.

In the center of the room, two men dangled from a wooden beam in the ceiling. Both were badly beaten and bloody. Their hands and feet were bound with thick rope and their mouths were gagged in order to muffle their screams. One man began to moan and squirm when he spotted Sin. The fear in his eyes told the story of the torture he had already suffered at Sin's hands. The other man was barely conscious. He just hung there, clinging to what life he had left.

Sin's eyes were cold and his stoned face showed no

emotion. He was a man on a mission. The pain he felt inside fed his vengefulness, giving him a callous disregard for any of his enemy's lives. Sin picked up the machete that was propped up against the wall and covered in dry blood. The more conscious man of the two began sobbing, trying to speak through his gag as Sin approached. The men had suffered tremendously over the past twenty-four hours. Their battered bodies had been struck over and over again with a chain, leaving large tears in their flesh. Sin showed them no mercy, dishing out pain until they would pass out. The men went from begging for their lives to wishing he would just kill them. Tonight it all would all end, they were going to get their wish. Sin had had enough.

Now standing directly in front of both men, Sin viciously swung the blade towards one of them and hacked off the man's foot. Blood sprayed against the walls and spilled out onto the floor. Sin stood back as the man screamed and howled in agony. He took great pleasure in the man's pain.

"Oooh fuck, it hurts!" the man wailed as Sin removed the gag from his mouth.

"You ready to talk?" Sin asked him.

"Go fuck your mother. I hope they kill you and your whole family, especially the lil' bitch you're looking for. I hope they fuck her good before she dies too," he said then spit in Sin's direction.

Sin looked more amused than angry. He returned the gag into the man's mouth, again muffling the sounds of his screams. "I see you still prefer to do this the hard way," Sin said eerily calm and covered in blood splatter. "All I want to know is who kidnapped the little girl and where's she at?" Sin tightened his jaw as he swung the machete again, this time cutting off the man's hands at the wrists. The man's body made a thud as it sunk to the ground. He resembled a worm as he tried to wiggle away on his bloody stumps.

"Oh shit!" the man screamed as Sin removed the gag and stepped on his back, preventing him from moving any further. "Somebody help me!" he shouted at the top of his lungs as if someone could hear him deep in the bowels of an abandon nightclub, behind a darkened alleyway. He was miles away from anything or anybody.

"Nobody's coming to save you," Sin told him then pulled the gun from his waist and in one motion fired a shot into the back of his head, ending his life. He turned to the second man, who remained motionless as he floated in and out of this consciousness. "Time to wake up," Sin said repeatedly slapping the man in the face until he was alert. "How 'bout you, you ready to talk?'

"I swear to you on my kid's life. I don't know anything 'bout no missing girl, no bombs or who tried to kill you. I don't know nothing 'bout nothing," the man spoke with a slow drawl and a heavy accent that made him sound like

Rocky Balboa. "All I can tell you is that it wasn't us. I promise you," he said trying to clear his crime family of any wrongdoing. For the last twenty-four hours he continued to insist he had nothing to do with what happened to Bria or Ariane.

Sin pressed the gun to the man's forehead and demanded answers. "Then who? Give me a name."

"I don't know. I swear to you," the man sobbed almost like it hurt to cry. "Jesus A. Christ, if I knew I'd tell you. On my grandmother's grave. Please, I'm telling you the truth," the man pleaded for his life. "What else you wanna know, huh? Anything please. Just don't kill me."

Sin lowered his gun and put it in his waist. "What's your bosses address?" When the man hesitated momentarily Sin posed another question. "You wanna live or not?"

"Oh God, yes, please."

"Ok well, what's your bosses address? I need you to deliver a message for me," Sin said.

The man began jumbling his words together as he fired them off rapidly in order to save his life. The relief in his eyes was evident and the color slowly began to return to his face. He feared he would suffer the same fate as his partner who lay dead on the floor of the basement.

"I want you to tell that fat muthafucka, that for every one of mine he takes, I'm gonna take ten of his. You understand me?" he asked.

"Yes, I understand. I got it," the man answered nervously. He just wanted to get out of there alive. He would agree to anything, do and say whatever to achieve that. He had no intentions of delivering any messages only bullets. He would make his boss aware of what Sin had done immediately. Sin was as good as dead when he was let out of that basement. He would personally make sure of it. He didn't know who kidnapped the young girl Sin had been asking about but he hoped where ever she was, that she was being tortured the same way Sin had done him. He hoped she suffered great and experienced a brutal death.

Sin stared off into the distance for a moment, the wheels in his mind churning with deep thoughts. "On second thought," he said after reconsidering, pulling his gun out again. All the fear the man felt instantly returned and all the blood rush out of his face again. He looked pale and ghostly. "I'll deliver it myself," Sin said firing off one shot to the middle of the man's forehead. His head slumped as blood leaked from the hole in his head and ran down his face. Sin grabbed the machete, cutting the man's hands free from the ropes allowing the lifeless body to drop to the floor.

* * *

Fat Tony hadn't even budged when the doorbell rang, too engaged in the Thursday night football game and too comfortable to care who was at the door. But the blood curdling scream of his wife caused him to rise from his favorite chair in the living room and quickly waddle out into the impressive entrance way of his residence. When he reached his wife, he saw her gently backing away from the front door. One hand covering her mouth and the other covering her chest like she was holding her heart in place, keeping it from leaping through her shirt. She was pale with fear and her breathing was rapid. As she turned towards him, her eyes looked confused and she was visibly shaken, quivering like a leaf in the wind.

"What is it?" he asked full of concern, pulling her into his hug.

She remained silent, sinking into his embrace and pointing to the door. Fat Tony released her and cautiously stepped towards the front door. He was anxious to see what in the doorway had startled her. He immediately saw the ribbon trimmed box resting just outside on the porch. The top was slightly off and an odor so offensive to his senses was coming for the box, he had to stop himself from vomiting. Fat Tony hesitated while covering his mouth. He began looking around to see who had left the package. There wasn't anyone in sight and now Fat Tony wasn't sure if he even wanted to see the contents inside the box. His curiosity quickly got the better of him and he lifted the top but was forced to turn his head away immediately. Inside the box was the severed head of one of the men Sin had killed in the basement.

"Figlio di puttana," he cursed to himself in Italian then screamed out to his wife. "Hey. Go upstairs and pack a few things. We're not staying here tonight."

CHAPTER 3

"THAT FUCKIN' MOULINYAN HAS TO die," Fat Tony declared slamming his fist on the table. As the new head of the Martello family, he was holding court in the back dining room of an Italian restaurant in Manhattan. An area where no one who wasn't connected was ever allowed to be seated. "Who does that nigger think he is? After what he did, I say we bury all those cocksucking bastards," the fiery tempered, round faced man with the gravelly voice barked.

Joey Barboza leaned forward in his chair, still chewing the food in his mouth and began speaking. "I agree with Tony. Sin should suffer for his disrespect. You don't violate a man's home and scare his wife like that. He really thinks he's big shit. But he's crossed the line this time."

"His father thought he was big shit too. I always hated that smooth talking piece of shit Marion. I'm glad he's fucking dead. Good riddance," Fat Tony said pretending to spit on his grave. "But even he had morals. We need to put his bastard son in the ground with him. Before he can become big enough to cause any real trouble."

The men gathered around the table all nodded. They had all come together over a large Italian feast for one reason, to rid themselves of the Holloway organization once and for all. After Mike Di Toro's opportunistic attempt to seize total power and the bloodbath that had followed, their once mighty organization had been severely weakened. The war between Iron Mike and the old guard was over but it had taught the new regime of upstarts a valuable lesson. The old leaders had gotten soft over the years, relying too much on their political power and maneuvering and not enough on brute force. Individually The Five Families had been damaged, each family's boss had been murdered and manpower diminished but as a unit they were still strong. All it would take is some reorganizing, some rebuilding of the families and they would resemble the powerful Commission of old. That's what today's meeting was about, getting back to tradition and becoming unified. All members were present, except for Phil Catanzano, the last of the old dons, who had purposely not been made aware of the meeting.

Tommy Black poured himself another glass of wine before chiming in on the conversation. "The way Sin got rid of Mike Di Toro, makes me think he could be a serious problem moving forward. Someone like him has got to have an endgame."

"That's not gonna pan out well for him," Fat Tony assured them causing the men seated around the table to laugh.

Dom Brigandi was the youngest of all the new dons in the room and his family had had the longest business relationship with the Holloway family. In his opinion, killing Sin wasn't necessarily the best move but he had attended the meeting to hear the other families out. His family had made plenty of money with the Holloway organization. So the apprehension he felt was clear when he spoke. "What about the rest of his organization? Do you think they will just sit idle after Sin is killed?"

"Who gives a fuck? Fuck them," Fat Tony shouted. "Those niggers think they are untouchable. They can't just run around thinking they can do whatever the fuck they want to. If we hit them hard enough, they will get the message. Trust me."

Dom Brigandi lit a cigar, inhaling then blowing smoke into the air. "If you ask me, we all owe Sin a debt of gratitude. If it wasn't for him, we would still be losing a war with Mike Di Toro or have you all forgotten? Hell, he should have a seat in the Commission for the work he did," he joked half-heartedly.

No one else seemed to find his attempt at humor funny, especially Fat Tony. "As long as I sit on this Commission, that nigger never will," he shouted reaching across grabbing more bread. He ripped it apart, dipped it into his plate then stuffed it in his mouth. The way he scarfed down food it was easy to see how he had earned his nickname.

With Fat Tony's mouth full it gave Joey Barboza a chance to speak up. "He's right. It goes against everything we stand for Dom. Regardless of how we all felt about Mike Di Toro and his actions. He was a boss of a family. He was one of us. Sin is getting bolder with his moves. If this latest move goes unpunished, how long will it be before he comes after me, or you or even you," he said pointing around the table at all the men stopping at Dom Brigandi.

"The old bosses took too many of these upstarts lightly over the past few years. The Niggers, the Russians, the Columbians, the Chinese and look where it got us. We're weaker now than we've ever been at any time in the history of this thing of ours. Those other motherfuckers in this city are laughing at us. It's time to return to the old ways of doing business. No more politicking and fucking around. We need to restore the order in New York," Fat Tony declared. "I've contacted our friends in the Midwest and they're willing to provide us enough soldiers to make this war as quick and easy as possible."

Tommy Black pulled the cloth napkin from his neck and tossed it onto the empty plate in front of him. "So how long will it take to put this plan of yours in motion?" he asked.

"If everyone here is in agreeance. All I have to do is make the call," Fat Tony announced pulling out his phone.

All of the eyes at the table suddenly landed on Dom Brigandi. They all felt his angst and wanted to know where he stood. His family was in complete shambles after the death of his iconic grandfather. The once mighty Brigandi name didn't mean as much as it once had in the city. The young don had inherited a crumbling empire. He was in no position to do anything but go along with the rest of the group or risk losing it all.

"Who am I to get in the way of progress," he said with a shrug of the shoulders.

"Good, good. For a minute I thought you was a nigger lover like your grandfather was," Fat Tony said disrespectfully then laughed while pouring himself a fresh glass of wine. "You see that?" he said pointing to Dom with a smile on his round face. "You'd be walking funny for years if you let those moolies donut hole you the way Catanzano does."

The men gathered around the table all laughed then watched in silence as Fat Tony picked up his phone and made the call.

"Hello, paisan. Yes, everything is fine. Thanks for asking. So about that fishing trip we talked about. Yeah. I think it's time we go. Ok. Fine. No problem."

Fat Tony hung up the phone then leaned back in his chair. "It's done. Now we just wait for the call to say they caught that fish," he said with a big smile on his face.

The men all smiled with him as they raised their glasses to celebrate Sin's fate being sealed.

CHAPTER 4

AS DAWN BROKE, THE SUN ascended like a ball of flame, turning the sky from darkness to a burnt orange. Emma Holloway was settled into one of the European designed patio chairs watching as the sun rose above her beautiful home in Westchester County.

I created all of this, she thought to herself taking in the immaculate view. "Some happy life I've made for myself," she said snidely in a mocking tone before taking another sip of her morning mimosa.

From the private balcony attached to her bedroom, Emma could see the well-manicured landscape, the tennis court and the swimming pool on the massive Holloway Estate. It was truly her creation. Many years ago, she had falling in love with a Mediterranean-style home she and Marion had vacationed to in Morocco and couldn't stop talking about it for months after. Marion was never one to let his wife want for anything. He took great pleasure in providing for her, catering to her every whim every chance he got. So out of the blue, he purchased an oversized lot of land and had their home built in the exact same style. It was meant to be a dream home but to Emma it was merely another beautiful distraction. Something to mask all the hurt and pain he had caused over the years. Marion was a natural born leader of men, a great provider and he tried to be as good a man as possible. But he was still a man and wasn't without flaw. Most of which Emma learned to deal with over the years. The lifestyle he afforded her made a lot of things easier for Emma to deal with at times. But the truth was she had spent most of their years together simultaneously loving and hating the man she slept next to every night. It was an internal conflict she had dealt with every day.

The night before, Emma had slept sporadically, it had become routine since Marion's funeral. The see-saw of emotions swinging back and forth kept her from resting fully or peacefully. There were days she rejoiced in killing her husband, happy that he was finally gone. Then there were those like today when she missed him painfully. His signature scent that floated in a room when he entered. The way his tailored suits laid across his broad shoulders. His handsome face, magnetic smile and charm that had captured her heart all those years ago. Emma allowed her mind to wander back to better times between them, only to have her thoughts immediately interrupted by her housekeeper Etilda.

"Buenos Dias Senora Emma," said the stubby Hispanic woman, placing the covered tray down on the table and lifting the sterling silver lid. "Your breakfast," she said as the sweet smell of maple bacon and eggs filled the air. "Is everything okay?" the woman asked noticing the look on Emma's face and feeling the air of melancholy surrounding her.

"I'm fine Tilda. That would be all," Emma waved her hand, dismissively ignoring the woman's concerns and turning her attention towards the breakfast.

"Mason is here to see you," Etilda informed her. "Should I send him up or will you be coming downstairs?" she asked and waited for an answer with her hands clasped in front of her at the waist.

"No, send him up," Emma said before the woman disappeared into the house.

The world slowly grew brighter by the moment. The day had just begun to come alive and Emma couldn't help but wonder what her son, the newly elected Mayor, wanted with her so early in the morning.

"Senora Emma," Etilda called out once again causing her to turn in her chair to face the entryway as Mason step out onto the balcony.

"Good morning mother," he greeted her with a kiss on the cheek then sat down next to her.

"Should I bring another plate?" Etilda asked Mason.

He put his hand up to stop her. "That won't be necessary. I won't be staying long," he said offering a half-hearted smile as he waited for her to leave. Once she did, Mason turned his attention to his mother. Seeing the emptiness in her eyes, he could tell she had probably had another restless night. "So how have you been?"

"I'm holding up," she confessed. "Doing as well as I possibly can," she said sadly. Convincingly hiding behind her supposed grief, easily stringing him along like she had everyone else.

Mason understood fully, he was still hurting from the loss of his father as well. The man he had idolized his whole life and now he felt a major void in his world and in his heart. Mason had achieved an ultimate career goal. One of the things his father had always envisioned for him but he had lost so much in the process. He couldn't help but to wonder if it was karma that had claimed the life of his father. Although it was, Mason had no idea that it was his father's own karma from many years ago that had come back to collect. Mason assumed that it was his or his mother's karma that had cost his father his life.

"Ma," Mason began in a low, soft tone. "The election has been over for a few weeks now. The inauguration is quickly approaching. Don't you think it's time for Bria to come home?" he asked in a reluctant whisper. He peered over his shoulder not wanting anyone to overhear the fact that he had been in on his own daughter's abduction in an attempt to draw sympathy from voters and rig the election. He had been easily persuaded by Emma and her guaranteed plan of victory. His greed and lust for power ruled him as he aided Emma in orchestrating Bria's kidnapping but now he was having second thoughts.

"What are you having some sort of come to Jesus moment?" Emma questioned but didn't wait for him to answer before continuing. "Didn't I tell you I had everything under control and for you not to worry. Everything I told you would happen, has happened so far."

"Yes, but I really don't see a reason for her not to be home now. Where she belongs, with her mother and me. Back with family," he stressed. "Khari is getting worse by the day. She's losing her mind, talking to herself. She cries all the time. And she keeps asking questions, I feel like she knows I'm keeping something from her—."

Mason's ability to keep the secret about Bria was becoming harder and harder. It wasn't so much the lying to Khari that bothered him, that was now second nature. It was his own personal shame that was eating him alive. What kind of father uses his daughter as a sacrificial lamb for his own personal gain, he thought to himself constantly.

"Oh, she keeps asking questions," Emma mocked him in frustration. She could see the stress wearing on him. It was all over his face, even his clothes looked like he had just rolled out of bed and thrown them on. The whole ordeal was eating at him but Emma showed not an ounce of compassion. She had sacrificed everything and lost more than he could ever imagine, just for him to be in the position he was. So Mason would have to seek the sympathy he sought somewhere else. "What's wrong with you? For Christ sakes Mason grow a pair. You're the man of that house, start acting like it. Now I got you elected didn't I? I gave you exactly what you wanted. You knew what you were doing. You're far from a victim darling, you just play one on TV."

"But Bria is," he proclaimed.

"Means to an end," Emma stated coldly with a nonchalant shrug of the shoulders. She was willing to use anyone to get the things she wanted done. No one was exempt.

"That's my daughter!"

"Lower your voice!" Emma demanded. "I don't care if you're the mayor or not, I am still your Mother."

Mason followed her orders and lowered his tone. "That's your granddaughter we're talking about ma."

"Really," Emma snickered.

"What's that supposed to mean?" Mason asked sitting

up in the chair and placing his elbows on the table.

"Nothing at all," Emma insisted, not willing to play her hand just yet. Knowing that Sin was Bria's real father was a valuable piece of information and she was keeping her trump card in her pocket for now. "I'm just wondering where was all this when you thought she could get you elected? You didn't have a problem with my plan then."

Mason hung his head in shame. He knew she was speaking the truth. He would have cut off his right arm to become mayor. They both knew it. "Where is she ma? Where are you keeping her? Is she safe?" he asked all in one breath.

"Mason, Mason, Mason," Emma softened her tone a bit. "I have it all under control, no need to worry. You just get ready to run this city and let me handle everything else. Bria will be back where she belongs in due time."

"What about the men you used? I don't want to have to worry about this coming back to me in the future," he said.

"Trust me, you have nothing to worry about," she assured him. Emma wasn't one for loose ends. The men she used didn't know who they were working for. Besides they were of little significance, therefore they would be disposed of when they had served their purpose.

Mason didn't say another word. Enough was enough, he didn't care what his mother said. He was ready for his daughter to come home and since Emma didn't see it his way, he decided right there that he would take the situation into his own hands. He stood to his feet and started heading back into the house.

"Mason honey," Emma called out in a loving tone stopping him in his tracks. She stood, walked over to him and began straightening out his tie before brushing off his shoulders. "I'm proud of you and so was your father. You do know that, don't you?" she asked.

"Yes," Mason replied.

"Mmkay," she smiled. "Now go show this city why they elected you and have a great day. I love you." She kissed him on the cheek then smiled. He returned the gesture before turning and leaving her alone on the balcony.

Emma's phone began buzzing. She walked over, scooping it up off the table. A cunning look came into her eyes as she looked at the number. She gazed over her shoulder making sure she was completely alone before answering the phone.

"I haven't heard from you in quite a while. Why is Yasin still breathing?" she questioned.

"I can assure you, he won't be for long," the voice said on the other end. "You'll see."

"Ok." Emma said then hung up ending the brief conversation. A conniving smile creased her lips. Her plan was coming together. Sin would be dead soon and it wouldn't be long before what was rightfully hers was back in her possession. Her smile didn't last long, fading as quickly as the darkness in the sky had. Now alone and without distraction, Emma had only her thoughts to keep her company. A slight breeze blew through the balcony causing her to shiver some. She tightened up her robe and wrapped her arms around like she was hugging herself then began rubbing. It reminded her of the countless times she found warmth in her husband's embrace as they watched the sunrise together from that very spot. She could always find comfort in his arms and the look of unconditional love in his eyes. But those eyes held so many secrets. They had seen so much, they knew where all the bodies were buried and could hide his true intentions as well; good or bad.

Over the years Emma had learned to do the same thing with her eyes and her intentions, most of them cruel and self-serving. She mastered the ability to hide her wicked and devious ways behind a poisonous smile. The role of being the wife of such a powerful man had hardened her but the pain made her evil. She remembered being warned of this as a young girl. It was hard imagining someone like Emma as an innocent young girl, even harder imagining her going through the process of becoming a woman. Someone of her prestige and stature seemed like they had always been an adult. Her gorgeous face seemed like she had never had a blemish. The bourgeois way she carried herself, as if she had never experienced an awkward moment in her life, never had a broken heart or been completely helpless to the mercy of fate. Even she couldn't remember herself as that vulnerable teenage girl anymore, it had been so long ago.

Emma once thought she was the luckiest girl on earth. She was born to extraordinary parents, a Cuban mother who she had inherited her beauty from. A powerful father, who adored her and did all he could to protect her from the streets and keep her away from the game. Emma couldn't remember an unhappy moment in her young life but that all changed when she met Marion one summer afternoon in Harlem.

CHAPTER 5

THE SERVICES FOR ARIANE WERE much different than the grand event that was held in honor of Marion Holloway's home going, even Sheik's funeral had dwarfed hers. Sin preferred it that way, he guarded Ariane's memory in death the way he had hoped to protect her in life. She was a private person, so her services were conducted the same way. It was an intimate affair, held at a small, secluded church with only a handful in attendance. It was the church that Sin's mother had belonged to. He hadn't stepped foot in it since her funeral but he made sure the lights stayed on in the place with monthly donations.

There were more flowers in the church than people. The beautiful arrangements surrounded a large picture of

Ariane that sat at the front of the church. She looked angelic, with a bright smile on her face. The way those that knew her, would always remember her.

Sin sat at the very front of the church listening to the pastor speak about the lovely soul of the woman he loved. The control he had over his emotions had returned and to the untrained eye, he appeared tough as steel. Sin never once shed a tear, even as Ariane's best friend gave a heartfelt speech and reminisced about the close relationship they shared growing up. But to those that truly knew Sin, could see he was suffering on the inside, fighting hard to hold it all together. He was emotionally wounded, his chest felt empty and he could barely remember the last time he felt his heart beat. He was numb from loss, consumed by thoughts of revenge and his eagerness to shed blood. The cocktail of feelings racing through him threatening to bubble over at any moment but he refused to give in to them, at least not in public. In private was where he let the pain pour out of him.

Beans, like always, was right by his side, sitting to his right dressed in a dark blue suit. In the past few weeks, he had worn more suits than he did his entire life. Cassie was to Sin's left along with Elijah and her sons. She was the only member of the Holloway family in attendance. She had come to show her support for Sin in his time of need, she held onto his hand the entire time. In the back of the church, an unexpected guest sat quietly paying his respects.

After the services, in a now empty church Sin approached the man, who stood to greet him. "Dominic," Sin extended his hand.

"Sin," Dom Brigandi met his hand and shook it. The young crime boss had David Beckham good looks, shadow beard, steel blue eyes and style to match. His last name was mafia royalty to those in the circles of the underworld.

"I'm surprised to see you here," Sin said.

"Yeah, I know. I wish we were meeting under better circumstances but this couldn't wait," Dom admitted.

"I'm all ears," Sin told him as the two began to walk.

"The other night a few of the families had a meeting and you were the topic of discussion. They're not happy with some of the moves you've been making lately, especially Fat Tony." Both men smirked. The word had gotten around about the package he had received on his doorstep courtesy of Sin. "They're planning to come after you. Hard. All of them. They're even bringing in guys from out West to help get rid of you," Dom explained.

Sin flared his nostrils like a bull and ran his hand over his face. A war with Di Toro was one thing but to face the entire Commission was something else. He wasn't about to back down though. "I'll be ready when they come," Sin said confidently.

"My family is not as strong as it once was in the past,"

Dom painfully admitted. "But I believe in loyalty. So I personally came to let you know that the Brigandi family will stand with you in any war that takes place."

"That's good to hear," Sin acknowledged then the two men shook hands again.

Out on the steps of the church, Cassie's two boys played joyfully with one another, slap boxing. Suddenly, one of the boys landed a clean shot on the other and immediately noticed the change in his brother's playful mood, causing him to take off running down the steps as the other gave chase.

"I'ma kill you," the older one shouted.

Elijah and Beans laughed as they watched the boys play. Sin emerged from the church with Dom Brigandi at his side and bumped right into a waiting Faye, Ariane's best friend. Her swollen, tear filled eyes couldn't mask her undeniable beauty. Sin could tell by the look on her face that she had a bunch of questions she needed answers to. He knew how close she and Ariane were and he wanted to do his best to put the pieces of the puzzle together for her. But right now wasn't the time. He was still trying to figure them out for himself.

"I need to speak with you?" Faye asked, more of a demand than a request.

"Of course." Sin then nodded towards Cassie, who approached Dom and started up a conversation as Sin stepped away with Faye. Once they were alone Sin turned to her and asked, "How you holding up?"

"I'm not," she answered honestly. "This has been the hardest thing I've ever had to go through in my life. I just can't believe she's gone. I don't know what to do with myself. I don't know how to go on without her. She was more than my best friend. She was my sister." Faye broke down into tears.

Sin felt for her. "I understand. I wish I could bring her back somehow. I would do it. I would die right now if it would bring her back." He meant every word and Faye felt his passion.

"What happened to my friend, Sin? Why would someone wanna blow up her car," Faye asked, almost in a begging tone as she wiped away the tears on her face.

The bomb was meant for him but he wasn't about to tell her that. "I don't know but I'm gonna find out. I promise you that."

Faye begin to cry again, shaking her head back and forth. All she wanted was some answers about her friend's death and Sin was the person she believed should have them for her.

"It's going to be alright," he said rubbing her arm trying to calm her down.

"I know, I know," she repeated as she wiped her tears again. "I have to pull it together and be strong. I've been crying for days now. I have to stop it. Ariane wouldn't want that. She would've wanted me to be strong," she scolded herself.

"She definitely would've wanted that," he said more as a reminder to himself than to Faye.

"Oh my God, I'm so sorry," Faye said like she had suddenly realized a mistake. She could see the love Sin had for her friend in his eyes as they spoke. "Here I am rambling on about me and I never once stopped to think about you. How are you holding up?"

"I'm good," he replied.

"You've been through a lot lately, huh?" Faye rubbed his arm, now offering him comfort. "The last time I spoke to Ariane, she told me about your father. I'm sorry for your loss," she said.

"Thank you."

"I'm praying for you and your family," she said.

Sin nodded accepting her condolences but he wanted to tell her that whoever was responsible for needed the prayers more than he did. He decided against it though. Faye had no idea the caliber of man she was speaking with and he wanted to keep it that way.

Faye couldn't quite get a read on Sin. He was a total mystery but it was clear to her that he was much more than meets the eye. She had never seen someone that moved like him. The street in him couldn't hide from her under the expensive fabric of his tailor made suit. "I wanted to let you know that I'll be staying around for a little while. I have a few business opportunities here in New York and I want to explore them. I'm going be staying at Ariane's while I'm here."

Sin once again didn't reply, just nodding his head. He really didn't need Faye hanging around to meddle in his affairs. He would play along for now in hopes that she wouldn't cause any unwanted problems later on.

"Take my number," she said then paused as he took out his phone. "Promise me that you'll let me know, if you find out anything," she begged.

"I will. I promise," Sin said followed by a charming smile.

"Ok, thank you. I'll be in touch," she said before walking away.

Sin watched as she descended the steps of the church before his eyes landed on his two nephews playing at the bottom of the steps on the sidewalk. They were a handsome pair, sharply dressed in dark grey suits. He envied their innocence and admired their energy. The two boys were filled with so much life. The world had yet to scar either of them. "What a blessing," he thought to himself. A great blessing youth and naiveté could be sometimes. The sight of them made him think of Bria. She was just as innocent and beautiful. He had to find where she was. He needed her to know the truth about who he was to her. He wanted to shower her with love and affection. He hadn't given much thought to how complicated things could be between them once she returned. None of that mattered to him. He was willing to do whatever it would take to make things work with her. After losing Ariane, Bria was all he had left in the world to live for; that and revenge of course.

Sin took a deep breath, inhaling fresh air into his lungs then blowing out his stresses. He made his way down the steps towards Dom Brigandi. He had just reached the bottom of the stairs, when the youngest of his two nephews came running over to him and hugged him around the waist.

"Uncle Sin," the young man said as he ran into Sin's arms trying to avoid his brother.

"Whoa, be easy playboy," Sin said sticking out his hand, holding his older nephew back.

"He play too much. He gets on my nerves," the older nephew said with anger in his voice but still he stopped his pursuit out of respect from his uncle's request.

"I'm sorry about your girlfriend, Uncle Sin. She was real pretty," the younger nephew said innocently as he looked up at Sin with his big brown eyes and no front teeth in his smile.

"Thanks lil' man," Sin said rubbing him on the head affectionately. "You looking fresh in this suit. Let me get you right," he said as he fixed his nephew's jacket and tie.

"You got some money on you?" When the boy shook his head no, Sin reached in his pocket and pulled out a knot of money. "What I always tell you?"

"Always say what you mean and mean what you say," the young nephew said. "And look a man in his eye when you talk to him."

"Right," Sin laughed at how the little boy recited off those jewels. "But that's not what I was talkin' about. I told you to always keep some cash on you. You never know what you might need it for." He peeled a bill off the top and placed it inside his little nephew's hand. Then he peeled off another and handed it to his other nephew. Their screams of joy brought a much needed smile to his face as he watched them race off towards Cassie to show her how generous he had been to them. He put the money back in his pocket just as Dom Brigandi walked up on him.

"I hate having to come to these things," Dom said.

"Yeah and I don't have time to be going to anymore," Sin warned as the two men stood next to each other facing the street.

Dom understood exactly what Sin meant by his last statement. He looked over at him and smiled. "Trust me I don't either. So you stay safe out here too." Dom turned back towards the street, looking for his driver. He checked his watch. "Where the fuck is he at?" he asked aloud then paused as a black car pulled up to the curb. Dom took a step towards the car then paused again as the dead body of his driver fell out onto the side walk with a hole in his temple.

A man in a black mask leaped out the backseat onto the street. The car was the only thing between him and Dom. Quickly, he aimed the gun at his target, using the roof of the car to steady himself and fired twice. The first shot tore through Dom Brigandi's throat causing him to reach for his neck with both hands. The second shot hit him in the head making his body twist violently as he fell into Sin's arms and they both fell to the ground.

Beans threw Cassie and her sons to the ground, shielding them from harm by covering them with his body. Elijah hurled himself to the ground as well, paralyzed with fear and disbelief.

Another masked man leaped from the car onto the sidewalk, holding a much larger gun in his hand. He shouted something that no one could understood then fired a bunch of shots in rapid succession into the air, over the heads of the small group now huddled on the ground in front of the church. Then both men were back in the car and as fast as they had appeared, they were gone.

Beans leaped to his feet and sprinted down the steps towards Sin's stretched out body on the sidewalk. His tie blew in the wind like Clark Kent entering a phone booth as he made it to Sin in a split second. Cassie meanwhile was trying to calm the screams of her terrified sons as she frantically searched them to make sure they hadn't been hit. It was then that she saw Beans' face as he stood over Sin's motionless body.

Cassie's body went numb. Her heart was sinking fast like she was on a rollercoaster ride. "No!" she shouted, scrambling to her feet and down the steps. Cassie saw all the blood leaking on to the concrete as she stood over Sin's body with tears building in the wells of her eyes. Her knees seemed to collapse involuntarily as she kneeled next to her brother, touched him with her gentle hands and began to sob uncontrollably. The black hand of death seemed to be on her family and she couldn't take it anymore as she wept like there was no ending in sight.

Elijah was still shaking like a leaf in the wind as he rose to his feet. He had never experienced something so frightening. He looked towards his scared stepsons than down the steps at his wife. They each needed his comforting and protection but his feet felt rooted to the ground. Frozen in fear, he couldn't bring himself to move and for it, he felt like a coward. He did not know this was what he had signed up for when marrying Cassie.

"Help me get this muthafucka off me," Sin said.

Cassie gasped hearing her brother's voice. With all the blood, she was sure that he had been hit but was relieved to see he was fine.

Beans helped get Dom's dead body from on top of Sin,

then helped Sin to his feet. Both men looked down at the dead crime boss. His throat and the front of his head was gone. Sin looked over his shoulder at the terrified looks on the faces of Elijah and his nephews. "C'mon they don't need to see this," he said. "Let's get everybody out of here and somewhere safe," he told Beans then helped Cassie to her feet.

CHAPTER 6

CASSIE BUMPED INTO ELIJAH AS she rushed into the bathroom and he was walking out. “I’m sorry hun,” she said as she shimmied passed him.

Elijah paused for a second looking as if he wanted to say something to his wife but then kept walking into the bedroom.

Cassie noticed that he had become conspicuously reserved as of late, saying little and being distant. She had had enough and felt the need to say something. “What’s wrong with you?” she called out from the bathroom. “You’ve been acting different lately.”

“Cassie please, not now, I’m running late as it is,” Elijah said uninterested in where the conversation was headed.

"Don't do that," she pleaded with him.

"Do what?" he asked as if he didn't know what she meant.

"Be standoffish. I can tell something is bothering you. Now what is it?"

"You know I don't like being late. We can talk about this another time?" Elijah dodged her question again.

"No, we're gonna get to the bottom of this shit right now," Cassie demanded emerging from the bathroom in a black Sophia Kahn pencil dress that fit her body perfectly.

Elijah stared silently at his wife. She was the most beautiful woman he had ever met in his life. It was moments like this, when her beauty rendered him speechless that he understood why he fell head over heels in love with her.

"You've been acting strange since the thing at the church with Sin, is that it?" she asked while slipping on a pair of heels.

Elijah lowered his eyes from hers as she hit the nail on the head. "It's not just that. It's everything," he admitted. "The explosion at the cemetery. The shooting. The fact that somebody killed your father and is trying to kill your brother," his voice filled with emotion as the volume increased. "We could have been killed in front of that church. You, me and the boys," he barked.

"You think I don't know that," Cassie replied. "But luckily we weren't." She closed the distance between them and caressed the side of his face.

"What about next time," he said rubbing his hand over hers. "I don't want to live in fear that my family will be murdered."

"Everything will be ok," Cassie said.

"How can you be so sure? Don't you see what's happening all around you," his voice rose with a bit of anger and disgust. "You act so nonchalant about it. Treating it like it's normal or something."

"It is normal. To me," Cassie admitted truthfully.

"Not to me," he removed her hand from his face and turned his back to her. Elijah picked up his watch and placed it on his wrist. "Shit, not to anybody," he said turning back to face her. "This ain't what I—," he paused but it was already too late.

"This ain't what?" Cassie asked aggressively. "This ain't what you signed up for, marrying me, marrying into this family?"

"It's not what I thought it would be like. No," he admitted honestly though he tried to lessen the sting of his statement. "I love you, that's why I married you," he said.

"Through sickness and health," Cassie reminded him.

"But this is neither. This is war. I didn't know I was joining the fucking army," Elijah raised his voice.

Cassie smiled at his sarcasm, although she didn't find it funny one bit. "Power and prestige comes with a price. That is what you wanted, right Elijah? Well this is it," she replied.

"What are you talking about? You sound crazy," he tried dismissing her point.

"You're not dumb Elijah and neither am I. You knew what marrying me came with and you knew what it would get you. The political boost you wanted so bad," Cassie said looking at him with piercing eyes. "Now I've never questioned your love for me because I know you truly do love me. But don't insult my intelligence by pretending you didn't know the dangers or the benefits of marrying Marion Holloway's daughter," she said using her hands to form quotations as she spoke.

Elijah remained quiet. Truth was, he did know what he was getting into from the start but the reality of it was far greater than he imagined and it had him a little shaken. He walked over to his wife, wrapping his arms around her and kissing her on the nose. "I'm just worried about you. That's all. Can you blame me for that?" he asked. "I would lose my mind if anything was to happen to you. It's my job to worry about you, to want to protect you."

"I know," she said looking up into his big brown eyes. She loved Elijah but she could tell things were wearing on him. He had been strong for her after her father's death. Building her back up with love and now she would have to do that from him. "I'm sorry you have to deal with all my family's craziness. I promise you, things will get better."

Elijah sighed. “And I’m sorry for how I’ve been acting baby. I just been a little stressed, that’s all,” he confessed. His tone was lower and more relaxed.

“I have a little time before I have to meet Ashleigh, So I think I can help you with that,” Cassie said seductively, kissing him and licking his bottom lip. She slowly dropped to her knees, unbuttoning his slacks and pulling out his slightly erect manhood. Elijah’s head fell back in pleasure as she took him into her mouth.

* * *

The death of Marion Holloway caught the underworld by surprise. But what was more astonishing; strange even, was the lack of any long lasting turmoil after the death of such an important man, the streets had pretty much gone quiet. The media soon abandoned the story for more sensationalized news and the police had grown silent. It seemed like all the power and fame Marion had amassed over the years was for nothing as he was easily swept away like yesterday’s trash. Even his political friends and business partners had become distant, trying to disassociate themselves with him. Something about it all just didn’t sit right with FBI Special Agent Roe Mosley, so he decided to do some digging for himself. Today he was meeting with Mason Holloway and Agent Mosley knew he had to tread lightly. He understood the importance of not ruffling the feathers of the mayor elect.

Mason's secretary, a fresh-faced, green-eyed brunette in her early thirties, politely greeted the agent and led him into an oversized plush office inside the Manhattan headquarters. Agent Mosley had a seat and waited for Mason to join him. After a few minutes passed the door opened and in walked Mason Holloway. Agent Mosley stood as the two shook hands, to his surprise Mason was taller than he expected. Sharply dressed and handsome with a bright smile. Mosley could see why he had all the makings of a political star.

Once the men sat, Mosley didn't waste any time explaining why he was there, "I was the agent assigned with bringing your father to justice. Now I'm the one here seeking justice for him." Mosley couldn't refrain from chuckling at the irony of it. "I'm investigating your father's death, Mr. Mayor. Do you have any idea of who would have wanted to kill him?"

"No, I wouldn't," Mason said. "My father was a great business man. He was an even better man. This gangster that the newspapers have been portraying him to be, I never knew that man. That is not the man who raised me. If what they are saying is true," Mason paused. "Then my father did a great job keeping that away from all of us. We knew nothing of that business of his."

"I find that very hard to believe," Mosley said. "Unless you've been living under a rock. It's well documented that your father has been long thought of as the top black crime figure in this city, maybe the whole country. You think his wealth came purely from the cement business? Only months before his death, at one of your campaign events, I remind you. An attempt was made on his life," Mosley pointed out. "How many businessmen have people trying to assassinate them?" he asked.

"Plenty," Mason answered seriously. "My father had many business ventures, not just his cement plants. He's never been arrested for a crime, that's well documented too," he countered. "When you're as successful as he was, there is no telling how many enemies you may have. Jealousy and greed make people do strange things."

"So you think it was one of his "business" partners?" Mosley pressed for an answer while trying to read between the lines of Mason's statement.

"Like I said before, I really wouldn't know," Marion reiterated. "My father worked hard for everything he had like I have. He instilled that in all of his children. He sent us to the best schools, to get the best education, so we would never be mixed up in anything illegal. So I find it hard to believe that I'm even having this talk with you."

"All except your brother, Yasin," Agent Mosley said.

"You can't save them all," Mason replied with a hint of sarcasm and a laugh. "Yasin has a different mother than the rest of us. He was brought up much different. Four out of five ain't bad though," he said. "Whatever Sin is into, I assure you, it is not a direct reflection of my father or any of my mother's children," Mason said drawing a line in the sand and making it perfectly clear where he stood.

"Speaking of your brother. Have you seen him lately?" Mosley inquired.

"No, I haven't."

"And your mother," Mosley asked, "How is she taking the loss?"

"Not well," Mason said. "How would you be holding up if the person you spent more than half your life with suddenly was no longer there?" he asked rhetorically. "But we are all here to support her. Times like this is when family is most important."

"Indeed," Mosley replied. "Well thanks for your time," he said as he rose to his feet and turned to leave before stopping himself. "By the way, any word on your missing daughter?"

"You're the police. Shouldn't I be asking you that?" Mason said for the first time showing a bit of hostility.

"I guess so," Mosley admitted. He could see he had hit a sore spot and chose to back off. Reaching in his pocket, he pulled out a card and placed it on the desk. "Just in case you think of something and if you ever need anything," he said offering his friendship.

Mason picked up the card and looked it over. He stood

and shook the agent's hand once again. "Thank you," he said.

"No, thank you. I know you are a very busy man, I appreciate you making time Mr. Mayor sir," Mosley responded then exited the office.

* * *

Later on that same day, Agent Mosley found himself sitting in a spacious living room, in a stylish apartment overlooking Central Park. He could see how easy it was to feel like you were on top of the world being up this high and surrounded by so much luxury. Mosley had gotten lucky, receiving a call from Cassie, that he could interview her at her sister Ashleigh's apartment. He leaped at the opportunity knowing it would save him a great deal of time being able to speak with both daughters at the same time. Upon entering, he was taken aback by how gorgeous each of the Holloway daughters were in person. The pictures in their FBI files, had done them a great disservice and vastly understated their beauty.

Special Agent Mosley had received a completely different greeting from each of the Holloway daughters upon arriving. Cassie was her normally warm and friendly self, maybe not as much as her brother had been but Mosley chalked it up to Mason's political charm that had won him over.

Ashleigh was another story. She was snooty and unkind. Behaving like a spoiled rich brat, spending most of the time scrolling through her phone. "Special Agent huh? What's so special about you?" she rudely questioned one of the few times she spoke, looking him up and down then back at her phone. When Mosley asked if she knew of anyone who would want to harm their father, Ashleigh replied with a one-word answer. "No," then went back to ignoring him leaving Cassie to field the bulk of his questions.

"Are you sure you don't have any idea of who would want to kill your father?" Mosley asked.

"My father was a very important man. I'm sure he had plenty of enemies," Cassie said. "But they are a mystery to me. You would know better than I would," she said.

"Why is that?" Mosley questioned. He was starting to feel like the Holloway children were reading from a script. They all had the same things to say about their father. So they were either telling the truth or had been trained very well. He was leaning towards the latter at the moment.

"Because it's your job too," Cassie replied to him. "You and your fellow agents have been digging into my father's affairs for years. Never once finding anything. I would know since I'm the family accountant," she said. "But that never stopped you guys. Now you want my family to believe that you are concerned with finding his killer?" she laughed. "This has to be some sick joke the government is playing on my family. I bet you guys are getting a good laugh at us, aren't you?"

"I chased your father for many years and I was never able to get anything substantial enough to stick to him," Mosley admitted with a bit of frustration and defeat in his voice, which made Cassie smirk with pride. "He was a very smart man and as hard as it may be for you to believe, you gain a certain level of respect for a man after all those years. Maybe not for what it was that he did but how smart he was in doing it. So yes, I want to know who killed your father. I would've rather seen him in handcuffs than dead but someone denied me that pleasure. I want to know who it was," he said honestly. "But you don't seem that concerned with it yourself," he added.

"I'm very concerned with it," Cassie insisted all the sweetness quickly disappearing from her tone. "I loved my father, very much. That can never be questioned. No one wants to see anyone in their family hurt, let alone killed. But what would you have me do, Agent Mosley?" she asked. "I'm not a killer or a gangster. I'm just a grieving daughter. So I have no choice but to leave the crime fighting to guys like you."

"So you have no desire to seek revenge?" he asked.

"No," she quickly answered. "That's not in my nature."

"What about your brother?"

"Mason," she chuckled. "You can't be serious."

"No, Yasin. Is that in his nature?" Mosley quizzed.

And there it was. Like a light bulb going off in her head, Cassie now knew what Agent Mosley's true intentions were. His inquiries had nothing to do with her father's death. His investigation into her father hadn't stopped, it had only switched courses. The focus was now on Sin.

"You'd have to ask him that yourself," Cassie said.

"That's the thing, he's pretty hard to track down. Do you know how I can get in contact with him?" Mosley asked clearly underestimating Cassie.

"I wish I could help you," she said.

Mosley looked over at Ashleigh, hoping to get some help in locating Sin but she just shrugged her shoulders.

"If you don't have any more questions," Cassie said. "We really have to get going," she said letting Mosley know his time with them was up.

"Very well," he said standing to his feet. "Oh, one last thing," he said. "I noticed the beautiful ring on your finger. Congratulations. It's nice to know people can have a second chance at finding love. I wish I had been so lucky."

"Thank you," Cassie replied.

"The way your son's father suddenly disappeared years ago had to be hard on you," Mosley quipped.

Cassie didn't bat an eye at his attempt to rattle her. It was a poor choice of subject but she knew what he was getting at. "My sons' father got cold feet. He decided to run from his responsibility. Looking back on it, he did my sons and I a favor," Cassie said with a smile. "If I saw him today, I would thank him."

"Cold feet," Mosley repeated with a nod, a wag of his finger and a smirk. "Your good," he said. "You ladies have a good day," then he turned to leave.

Cassie stared at the door as it closed behind the agent. Her eyes lowered and filled with rage. Mosley had obviously done his homework on her. By picking at an old scab, he had tried to get a reaction out of her but Cassie didn't flinch. She was too clever for that.

CHAPTER 7

ASHLEIGH'S PASSIONATE MOANS SEEMED TO drown out the sound of the running water as she pressed her body against the steamy glass shower. Every nerve pulsated, and her mouth oohed in pleasure from the intense feeling coursing through her body. Each stroke brought her closer to the point when her soul would separate from her body for one heavenly moment.

"Ooh, oh my God," she gasped. The dick felt so good and was so thick, filling her wetness completely. Both her arms were pinned behind her back. She loved being dominated and her body being taking full control of. Every thrust was pure ecstasy leaving her wanting more. This was better than anything she had ever felt before. Her heartbeat began to increase. The air around them seemed to sizzle. The hot water raining down on them was both sensual and soothing. Ashleigh felt submerged in carnal pleasure.

"Oh fuck," she moaned, succumbing to the rapture as her body began to spasm. All her muscles tingled and she felt the strokes become more urgent, growing faster and more powerful. Her screams grew louder as she felt his manhood begin to throb. Ashleigh rubbed her breast, sucking on her own nipples as she called out lustfully.

"Fuck me. Give me that big dick daddy," she begged while caught up in the moment, digging her nails into his forearms. She felt the climax building as he pushed deep inside of her. His body spasmed, unleashing his seed. Ashleigh collapsed on to him, her back in his chest and before long they were bathing each other.

Still breathless, she stepped out the shower minutes later and grabbed a towel. Strutting over to the mirror and wiping the fog clear. "Damn, you trying to make me fall in love, huh?" she asked looking over her shoulder into the mirror. A wide smile was spread across her face.

Beans smiled back as he exited the shower wet and naked. "You don't want to be in love ma. Not with me at least. You like playin' these games."

Ashleigh sucked her teeth. "Whatever Beans. It's complicated."

"You make it complicated," he replied. "You supposed to reward loyalty with love and doubt with distance. It's not really that complicated," Beans said.

"So this is love now?" she asked.

"I ain't say all that, I'm just saying in general," he corrected himself.

"Whatever," Ashleigh said.

"Yeah, whatever," he replied. "But I tell you one thing, I'm glad we stopped playing hotel tag. You got me out here moving like a side chick or somethin'."

"You're such a likeable asshole," Ashleigh laughed while turning and tossing a towel at him.

It was something about Beans that she just couldn't get enough of. She loved his bravado. The vibe he gave off was so magnetic to her. He was sexier than he was handsome, although he wasn't bad looking at all. Ashleigh took pleasure in his nakedness, admiring his solid built frame as he dried off. His light caramel skin glistened and tattoos covered his arms and upper body. Her eyes slowly trailed down to his swinging manhood and a lustful grin creased her lips.

"By the way," he paused noticing her staring below his waist. "Who was that random ass nigga you brought to ya pops funeral. I told you about being more aware of how you move."

"Is that really what you're worried about?" she teased.

"Yeah," Beans smirked.

"Well that random nigga saved my brother's life," she embellished the facts a little.

"But who gonna save his?" Beans jokingly asked, although he was quite serious.

"Now you sound jealous," Ashleigh sassed.

"Don't play yourself," he said quickly putting her sassiness in check as he entered her personal space. "What's mine is mine, what ain't, ain't. So what's shit to be jealous about," Beans said looking her up and down.

They were now face to face, close enough that their lips could touch. Ashleigh's heart began to race with nervous energy as she looked at him. She stared at the scar on his face, she always wanted to know how he got it but was always too afraid to ask. She was sure Beans wouldn't tell her, he never told anybody. Beans made her feel like the young teenage girl who had the ultimate crush on him. His gangster was his sex appeal. It was why she couldn't leave him alone. Ashleigh knew she was playing with fire, going back and forth between Beans and Case. They were both dangerous men and her double dipping could eventually lead to bloodshed but her selfishness made her care less than she should. She wasn't thinking straight being so carefree but she was enjoying herself.

"So what's yours and what's not?" she snapped back. She was in her feelings a little. She liked to know that Beans cared.

"Anything I want is mine," he said scooping her off her feet, placing her on the sink and kissing her aggressively.

"Aah, Beans," she called out with an excited giggle as he lifted her off her feet. Ashleigh slipped her tongue into his mouth and wrapped her legs around his waist as they started another round.

* * *

"Oh my God," Ashleigh said lifting the cover and looking underneath it. "They should put that thing in the hall of fame," she said as they laid in the bed and she marveled at the size of his manhood.

Beans smirked as he played with Ashleigh's hair, the softness of it felt like silk in his fingers. The sun was slowly creeping through the curtains covering the room in a sheet of light as Beans put his arm around Ashleigh's waist and pulled her to him. He cuddled up in her hair then kissed her on the forehead.

Ashleigh laid quiet on his chest momentarily then after a few minutes she started up again. "I'm for real," she said smacking him on the chest and lifting the sheet again. "You should let me take a flick of it for the 'gram and post it. At least let me take a few to brag to my girlfriends with. They'll never believe me without it," she joked as she reached for her phone on the nightstand.

"Nah, stop playin'," Beans laughed grabbing her and

pulling her back on the bed. "We both know you ain't bout to tell nobody about us."

"Yeah, but I'd like to," she said with lust in her eyes, shaking her head and looking under the covers again.

Beans laughed then moved the hair from out her face so he could look directly into her eyes. There was something about them that looked different to him. Even in the midst of them enjoying one another, there was still something missing in her stare. He knew she had taken her father's death harder than the rest of her siblings. He felt for her, maybe more than he had been willing to admit to himself. "Who you think you fooling' ma? Not me," he said letting his true feeling spill out a little bit. "You like keeping secrets."

Ashleigh gave his statement some thought. "I guess," she said rolling her eyes. "Everybody don't need to know I'm fuckin' my brother's best friend."

"Why, what you worried about?" he asked.

Ashleigh turned her body and sat up, placing her weight onto her elbow. Her naked breast now exposed from underneath the sheets. She flipped her hair over her shoulder. "I'm not worried at all. I don't give a fuck what anybody thinks. I do what I want, with who I want. It's just none of anybody's business," she snapped. "Speaking of my brother, have you seen him lately?" she asked.

"Nah, not for a couple days," Beans said. "It's like the

nigga disappeared and shit. Why, what's up?"

"The FBI came by here, asking questions about my dad and Sin," she revealed.

Beans sat up in the bed instantly. "The Feds? By here? When?"

"The day before yesterday," she told him.

Beans brow wrinkled and his eyes lowered. "Questions like what?" he asked.

"Regular shit, like do I know who killed my father and do I think Sin is the type to seek revenge," she explained.

"Aaand?"

"And what?"

"And what you say?" he asked sternly tired of going back and forth with her.

"I am Marion Holloway's daughter. You know I don't talk to no police," she said trying to sound like a gangster.

"You always play the tough girl role in the movie, huh?" Beans said, pushing Ashleigh onto her back then hovered over her. Her face was bare of any make up, a sight almost no one else got to see. Her skin was soft and blemish free and her natural beauty was on full display. "You know I see right through that, right? I see the real you. That's who I like," he told her.

"Sure you do," she said smiling as she looked up at him. He leaned down and kissed her lips. Ashleigh could feel his length swell up against her. "No Beans," she said giggling.

"Not again. We can't."

"Why not?" he protested with a few more kisses, trailing down to her firm breast and erect nipples.

"Because that would be the third time this morning," she said. "I can't take it anymore," she confessed.

Beans ignored her, continuing to kiss on her breast.

Ashleigh burst into laughter at his refusal to obey her wishes. "Stop," she screamed while laughing and pressing her hand onto his chest, trying her best to keep him at bay. "I'm tapping out," she said sliding from under him. "You tryna beat it up and have me walking all funny and shit," she teased as she rolled off the bed and retrieved her panties off the floor. "Besides, it's getting late." She walked over and opened the curtains completely, letting all the morning light in.

Beans found humor in her statement. "Oh shit, you putting me out," He laughed while getting up off the bed. He picked up his pile of clothes from the bedside and started getting dressed.

"No, it's not that. "It's just," she paused trying to think of a good lie really quick. "Cassie is supposed to stop by in a few. We're going shopping."

"Cassie ain't coming over here," Beans said.

"She might," Ashleigh tried to sound innocent, knowing she had just been caught in a lie. She really had plans on meeting up with Case.

"It's all good ma. I'm just fuckin' wit you," he said putting her worries at ease. Beans stepped into his pants and slid his shirt over his head before grabbing his jacket. "I know what this is," he said.

"What's that supposed to mean?" she questioned following him out the bedroom, through the kitchen and to the front door. "What are you saying?"

"I'm saying we just having a good time. Nothing else. Leave ya feelings at the door," he said kissing her on the cheek.

"Really?" she twisted her neck.

"You had fun right?" he smiled ignoring her question.

"Yeah," she answered.

"Me too. 'Til next time then," he said smoothly, stepping out into the hallway. "I'll call you later."

Ashleigh didn't know how to feel. She forced a smile as she closed the door then pressed up against it, listening as the elevator doors opened and closed. "Leave ya feelings at the door," she said out loud, thinking about what Beans had said. It made her upset and it was at that moment Ashleigh had to ask herself was she in love with Beans. Although she didn't care what most people thought about her. How he viewed her was always important to her. The school girl crush she had on him always gave Beans a special spot in her heart. But now her crush was blossoming into something more, she would have to eventually accept it. The thing was she felt the same way about Case.

CHAPTER 8

BEANS STOOD IN THE MIDDLE of Sin's living room with his arms stretched out to his side and his palms facing the ceiling. "What is there to talk about? We should be moving on those pasta eating muthafuckas right now," he said blowing rings of weed smoke into the air.

"I understand how you feel Beans but we can't be reckless," Cassie said taking the weed out his hand and inhaling a few puffs. "Not with the Feds watching and trying to build a case against you guys," she said trying to be the voice of reason.

"We look like sitting ducks out here. What the fuck is

going on? We have to retaliate," Beans insisted.

"And we will. We just have to be smart about it," Sin replied.

"Fuck that. You always trying to be strategic and shit," Beans barked. "We need to pull up with the shooters, ever where we know they're at and get busy. What's the point of having power, if we ain't gonna use it?"

"We ain't on the block no more. We fighting for more than just a street corner. So we can't use street corner logic," Sin expressed.

"We used to be on some, whoever shooting the longest that's who's shooting to win shit. Let me find out all those suits making you soft and shit," Beans said taking the weed back from Cassie and inhaling another toke.

Sin rose from his seat and quickly was in Beans' face. He was close enough that Beans could feel his breath on his skin as he spoke. He had so much anger, so much hate built up inside of him it was threatening to spill over. "Nigga you know how I play. Don't ever question my gangster. The Commission is dead. All of them. And there's nothing anyone can do to stop that from happening. They took something from me that I could never get back. If you think I'ma let that ride, you outcha muthafuckin' mind," Sin said.

"That's what I'm talking 'bout. There goes my nigga," Beans smirked seeing the fire in Sin's eyes.

"Y'all not thinking clear. Let's stay focused," Cassie told

them stepping between them.

"What is there to think about?" Beans replied exhaling a cloud of smoke and searching for an ashtray to flick his ashes.

"The bigger picture," Cassie replied. "Why are they still coming after y'all?"

"Because they fear us. But obviously they don't fear us enough," Beans ranted.

"True but that is the obvious reason. There is something much bigger going on. Something we're not seeing," she expressed. "Y'all got rid of Mike Di Toro. That benefitted them all. That should have ended all of this."

Sin put his hands in his pockets and walked towards his bar. "You're right," he told her. Sin understood the ferocious way he had gotten rid of Mike Di Toro would send shock waves through the underworld and put him on everybody's radar. It also sent a crystal clear message that he was far less mild-mannered than his predecessor. He was a man that if necessary would go to the extreme to get the job done. Any man with that type of mentality had to be not only respected but feared. Everybody knew, the person who controlled the fear, controlled the streets.

"All warfare is based on deception. It's the art of war. Whoever is pulling the strings behind the scenes is smarter than we're giving them credit for. We gotta be smarter too." The mental game of chess wasn't foreign to him.

Beans hot temper wouldn't allow him to sit idle and do nothing. All he saw was red. "I got a team of shooters ready to go. All we gotta do is rundown on them grease ball muthafuckas right now."

"And then what?" Sin asked.

"And then they'll be dead. Very fuckin' dead."

"I ain't gonna stop you from doing what you wanna do. I would like for us to move as a cohesive unit but we all bosses here. I'm just moving a certain way on this one. If that don't work for you, I understand," Sin told him.

Beans took a long pull of the weed then blew smoke out his mouth. He trusted Sin with his life that wasn't about to change now. Even if he didn't see eye to eye with him at the moment. He would always remain loyal. "So what's your plan my nigga?" Beans asked.

"To win," Sin said simply followed by a grin, not willing to reveal much more than that. With everyone on his team's loyalty in question at the moment, he felt the need to play everything close to the vest. His mind was a concealed weapon and he was keeping his plan to himself for now.

"Have you spoken with daddy's friend Catanzano?" Cassie inquired.

"Briefly but he is pretty much out the loop. Since the war with Di Toro, there has been so much change inside all the families. He doesn't have any insight into the thinking of the new bosses," Sin explained.

"I don't trust none of them. Catanzano, The Commission, none of them. They are at war with each other one minute then united the next," Beans declared.

"Nothing brings people together like a common enemy," Cassie joked.

"We gotta switch up how we been moving. With the Feds on us and The Commission out for the kill. We don't have the manpower to go to war wit' all of 'em. Only way to beat em' is to outsmart 'em. In the meantime, let's start hitting their pockets. I want to shut down each one of their most lucrative operations. Can't go to war with thin pockets and starving soldiers breed disloyalty." Sin knew the strongest cards he had was the ones he hadn't played yet.

"That's smart," Cassie admitted to him. "Now that brings me to one more thing," she said.

"What's that?" Sin asked.

"You promised to feed me and since I don't smell anything cooking in here," she inhaled deeply through her nose. "I guess that means you're treating?"

Sin laughed. "Of course."

* * *

Sin nodded his appreciation to the doorman holding the door open allowing them to exit the building into the brisk breeze on a frigid night. A light fog floated through the block as steam rose from the manholes in the street like smoke. Sin's senses were on high alert and he immediately felt something wasn't right. He looked back over his shoulder and realized the doorman's face didn't register with him. He had made it his business to know the names and faces of every staff member in the building and he had never seen the man before. He didn't like new faces, they made him uncomfortable. Sin looked up the block then back down when a black Navigator floating up the street caught his attention. The window lowered on the truck and Sin reached for the gun in his waistline, only to watch as a cigarette come flying out of the window as the vehicle passed by them without incident. Still Sin remained focused on the truck, call it a gut feeling but something felt off.

"What about Jewlz?" Cassie said to him then repeated herself when he didn't answer. "Sin," she called to him. "I said what about Jewlz?"

"What about him?" Sin asked breaking from his trance and rejoining the conversation.

Cassie sighed in frustration, realizing he hadn't been paying her any attention. "He's graduating in a few weeks and the job at the casino was promised to him in more peaceful times. That's no longer an option. He needs to remain close. Somewhere we can keep a close eye on him" Cassie said.

"Nobody is dumb enough to go after Jewlz. That lil' nigga a square," Beans interjected as he circled his car to the driver side and tipped the valet holding the door open for him.

"Gotta keep the squares close my nigga, cause them circles a roll off on you sometimes," Sin replied as he thought about the snitch in his crew. He hadn't made anyone aware of the problem yet and didn't plan to until he could figure out exactly who it was. Even Beans wasn't above suspicion.

"Even though Jewlz is not involved in the business. It's better to be safe than sorry. Our new enemies may not play by the same rules as the old ones. You said it yourself no one has insight to how they are thinking," Cassie reminded them.

Beans nodded his head. Cassie had soaked up all the knowledge her father had given her over the years and as the family's accountant, she had proven herself to be a vital part of the business. But no one really knew how involved she truly was and that was the way they all preferred it. Cassie had managed to create the perfect dichotomy between worlds and was one of Sin's most valuable assets. She was the closest thing he had to a consigliere.

The valet pulled Sin's blue Jaguar XF up just as Beans pulled off.

"I think we should have Jewlz run Holloway Cement and Construction," Cassie suggested. "He's a fast learner. We could teach him the ins and outs of the business in no time.

Let him learn about the building contracts we have with the city. It's legit. He's clean. It works."

Sin remained quiet momentarily but by the look on his face Cassie could see that he was giving her suggestion some thought. "Let me think on it and I'll get back to you," he said as they got in the car and pulled into traffic.

"Another thing, what's with all the friction with you and Beans? That's not like you. Is everything alright?" Cassie asked as they merged onto the highway, taking advantage of their time alone. She was concerned about her brother and felt the need to check on him. Cassie knew Sin buried his emotions deep inside. Getting him to share his feelings was like pulling teeth. He was most like their father in that way. Sin had rarely even mentioned Ariane's name since her death but Cassie knew him better than most. His even temperament always allowed him to mask whatever he was dealing from everybody else except her.

Sin shrugged his shoulders. "It nothing."

"Gotdamn Sin. Don't do that," she responded quickly.

"Do what?" he pretended not to already know what she meant.

"You with the not letting anybody in shit. It's not nothing, you're not good and I know it. You can pull the wool over everyone else's eyes but not mine. You get that shit from daddy. I've never seen two people bury their feelings so deep inside and not be willing to share them with anybody," she said in frustration.

"I'm good. I promise you."

"Bullshit," she snapped. "Everybody needs to vent sometimes Sin," Cassie expressed.

"Not me," he replied looking over at her, the muscle in his jaw flexing. He wasn't interested in the discussion she was trying to have at the moment and sought to put an end to it. "That's not how I'm built sis. Everybody got things they're dealing with. Family shit. Business shit. Street shit. That's life. I'm not looking for sympathy."

"That not what I'm trying to do and you know it," she challenged him.

"What you wanna hear Cassie huh? That I'm hurt. That I'm fucked up in the head. That I haven't slept in weeks because every time I close my eyes all I see is her face," Sin couldn't bring himself to look at his sister, feeling the tears beginning to form in his eyes. "I never knew I could feel the way I felt when I was around her. Then as fast as she came, she was gone. I feel like I was robbed. How am I supposed to deal with that emptiness?" He was so broken inside, he felt different. His soul had been damaged beyond repair. Life just didn't have the same joy for him anymore. He was fueled only by thoughts of revenge and rage. It made him angrier, more unpleasant to be around. His heart was scarred and blackened. He didn't want to do it anymore. "I be feeling like none of this is worth fighting for. It won't bring her back to me," his jaw clenched as he spoke.

Finally, he looked over at Cassie with big tears dripping down his face. She could see the pain pouring from his soul through his eyes. She felt the burden of grief he had been carrying around. The guilt he was dealing with. The weight of responsibility he felt to make things right for everyone. "Sin watch that truck in front us!" Cassie suddenly shouted as she looked back towards the highway.

Sin slammed on his brakes causing the car to come to an abrupt stop. An old worn out U-Haul truck in front of them had stalled in the middle of the highway with its hazard lights blinking. Sin pounded on his horn, "What is this muthafucka doing? They gonna cause an accident. They need to move that piece of shit to the side of the road," he said quickly wiping the tears from his face. The near wreck forced him to gather himself and focus on his surroundings. Sin glanced to the right, a black Yukon with darkly tinted windows pulled to a stop right next to his car. Sin looked in his rearview mirror as another Yukon boxed him in from the rear. Then suddenly the back door of the U-Haul lifted up and two men holding automatic weapons began raining bullets down on Sin and Cassie.

"Get down!" Sin shouted while pushing Cassie's head down. With nowhere to go Sin threw his car into reverse and pressed down on the gas, sending the car backwards. The sound of squealing tires rang out as he slammed into the truck behind him.

"Oh my God!" Cassie shouted.

"Just keep your head down!" Sin ordered as he shifted into drive and mashed down on the gas again, propelling the Jaguar forward.

He maneuvered around the U-Haul and raced up the highway at high speed, swerving through traffic trying to put distance between him and the would be assassins. The two Yukon trucks gave chase firing at the Sin's car. The bullets pinging off the car sounded like it was raining steel outside. Then one of the shots penetrated the cabin, crashing through the back window, shattering the glass and hitting the headrest, right where Cassie's head should have been had she not been crouched down. Suddenly there was a loud boom that rocked the car. A bullet blew out one of the tires causing Sin to swerve wildly, losing control of the car. He veered to the right, side swiping a car in the next lane then bouncing back into another vehicle as he tried unsuccessfully to regain control. The impact caused the Jaguar to spin out of control, sending it barreling through the guardrail and into oncoming traffic. The badly damaged Jaguar finally skidded to a stop in the middle of the opposite side of the highway.

"You ok?" Sin shouted to Cassie just as the blinding lights of an eighteen wheeler shined into the car and the blaring of its horn filled the air, followed by the squealing of its tires as it tried to stop.

The sound of exploding glass and crumpling steel filled the inside of the car, only to be followed by the sound of the airbags. Sparks flashed everywhere as the eighteen wheeler plowed into them and pushed the mangled Jaguar across the pavement. Sin felt like a ragdoll being tossed around inside of twisted metal as the car began to roll several times, coming to a rest on its hood, in a muddy ditch.

The world was spinning and Sin felt woozy, barely able to keep his eyes open. Feeling like he was floating in and out. Still, he was able to call for his sister. "Cassie," he grunted out but received no answer before he finally lost consciousness.

CHAPTER 9

ROLLING OVER IN HIS HOSPITAL bed, Sin found himself alone in a room empty. Miraculously, he had only suffered minor injuries, mainly bumps and bruises. But as he sat up in the bed, there was only one thing on his mind. He rose to his feet, ignoring the pain and exited the room.

The hallway of the hospital was filled with imposing men in dark suits, who stood stoic in their positions against the wall like they were there to guard the president. Sin didn't recognize any of them and immediately knew they weren't his men but he wasn't alarmed due to the fact that Beans stood in the midst of them seemingly unfazed. When Beans spotted Sin, he made his way over to him.

"What's with all the new faces?" Sin asked.

"Courtesy of our friend from Miami," Beans told him.

"What?" Sin said shocked to find out the men belonged to his connect.

"The connect is here too." Beans revealed.

"Here? At the hospital?" Sin asked.

"Yeah. In the chapel," Beans replied.

"What the fuck is going on," Sin thought to himself looking around at the men but that was a matter for another time. At the moment he only had one concern. "How's Cassie?" he asked causing Beans to look away from him and he instantly felt a crushing feeling in his soul. "Beans, where's Cassie?" this time he asked more sternly grabbing him but still received no answer, growing his frustration.

Hearing Sin's angry voice, Ashleigh rounded the hallway corner and could see the look of confusion on his face. "Ashleigh, why won't anybody answer me? Where is Cassie?" he asked. She took his hand into hers but didn't look at him, the odd melancholy stirring his instincts once again. He snatched his hand away from her. "Somebody better answer me, right now" he demanded.

"Sin, Cassie was—" was all Ashleigh could manage before tears made it impossible for her to continue.

"What is it," Sin barked.

"Cassie was hurt really bad tonight," Beans told him. "She's in a medical induced coma. There was a lot of trauma to her spinal cord and the doctor's feel she might not walk again," he explained.

Sin's heart skipped a beat and he sighed deeply putting both hands on his head. Not again, he thought to himself. How much more loss could he endure before it broke him completely. "Where is she?"

"She's in Intensive Care, on the eighth floor but—."

Before Beans could finish his sentence, Sin was headed for the elevator with two of the hulking bodyguards on his heels.

The elevator doors opened on to the eighth floor's ICU and Sin quickly rounded the corner, right into the unwelcoming glare of Emma Holloway. The domineering matriarch of the family stood at Elijah's side while he spoke with the doctor. Mason rose from his seat in the waiting area as soon as he spotted Sin. He strolled out into the hallway accompanied by Agent Mosley whom he had been speaking with.

"Good to see you again Yasin," Agent Mosley spoke. "It's good to see that you are ok. I would like to ask you a few questions about tonight's events—."

"Since when the feds handle traffic accidents?" Sin asked.

"This seems like more than just a traffic accident. To me it looks like some pretty determined people want to see you dead," Agent Mosley replied.

"I wouldn't know anything about that. So you wasting ya time," Sin said then walked away from him but not before give Mason an icy stared.

"Like it or not, Mr. Kennedy, you will eventually have to speak to me," Mosley called out to him. He offered his condolences once again then Mason escorted him to the elevator.

Sin walked up behind his brother-in-law and placed a hand on his shoulder. "Elijah, are you ok?"

When Elijah turned and made eye contact with Sin, he immediately broke down. "Oh my God," he wept like a child falling into the arms of his brother-in-law.

"I'm so sorry man," Sin said embracing Elijah and patting him on the back. The guilt he felt multiplying by the second.

"What happened?" Elijah begged to know.

"The tire blew, I lost control of the car and we got into an accident," Sin chose to keep the details to himself for the time being. He didn't want to arouse Elijah's fears more than needed. He had enough to worry about with his wife fighting for her life in the hospital room. "I'm sorry bro. I hope you can find it in your heart to forgive me."

"That's between you and God," Emma interjected. Her voice was haughty and cruel and she spoke in the dismissive tone that always infuriated Sin.

Sin took a deep breath before speaking. "You think I

wanted something like this to happen?" Sin seethed and his lip curled in anger. "Won't you go spread your evil somewhere else."

"Seems like anybody that gets too close to you gets hurt...or killed," Emma replied, pouring salt in an open wound, in a way only she could.

"I know you would never do anything intentionally to hurt Cassie," Elijah acknowledged. 'I just don't know what to do with myself. I can't even fathom the thought of losing her and the boys," Elijah broke down sobbing again.

"Oh shit, the boys," Sin asked looking around searching for them. "Where are they? Has anybody told them about their mother?"

"No. We haven't told them yet. I wanted to be the one to tell them. I just really don't know how I'm going to," Elijah confessed.

"I'll do it," Sin volunteered. "This is all my fault. I should be the one to tell them." In Sin's mind it was the honorable thing to do.

Elijah quickly agreed and Emma sighed loudly. She couldn't decide what annoyed her more Sin's show of strength or Elijah's weakness. Both sickened her equally. "I'm gonna go sit in the waiting area, Elijah this is a serious family matter the boys should hear it from you if not anyone of us" she said excluding Sin and implying his unworthy relationship to his nephews. Sin ignored Emma's remarks.

"I need to see her," Sin pleaded.

Elijah didn't object. He just pointed to Cassie's hospital room.

The room felt cold and dull when Sin entered. He walked to the side of Cassie's bed and reached for her hand, moving the hair out her face and kissed her on the forehead. The sight of Cassie lying motionless in the bed made the hairs on the back of his neck stand up. She appeared so weak and didn't look like herself. Cassie had a vibrant spirit and was so full of life but now she was anything but that. She looked like her soul was being held hostage by an empty shell. There were tubes sticking out of her mouth allowing her to breath and the machine that kept beeping was the only indication that there was still life left inside of her. Cassie had a large bandage wrapped around her head to close up a nasty gash she had received in the crash. There was a halo brace keeping her neck and spine from moving and another large brace around her neck that seemed to be holding her fragile body together.

There was a deathly stillness in the room. Sin felt like he was losing it all. His mind, his friends and loved ones. He looked up towards the sky, suddenly feeling the rare urge to pray. But his prayer wasn't for himself, it was for those close to him. He pleaded with God to heal his sister, save her life and allow her to walk again. He asked for God to protect those around him. He knew the war with The Commission was something that had to happen just like the sun rising in the sky. He knew there would be death, he just hoped there would be more on their side than his.

He took a seat next to her bed. "I remember when Pops first brought me to the house and told y'all who I was. Nobody said anything to me. Everybody just stared at me like an animal in the zoo. Your mother had that look on her face, she always gets when she sees me till this day. Mason looked dumb in the face but you," Sin shook his head and continued. "Without any hesitation, you walked over to me and gave me the biggest hug I've ever had in my life. From then on, me and you have been like this," he said twisting his fingers together. He took a deep breath and like that he had snapped back. "I'm gonna take care of this. I promise you." He said then rose to his feet and leaned over her. "I'm gonna kill anybody who had anything to do with harming you," he whispered to her then kissed her cheek before turning and exiting the room. He marched passed the waiting area, giving Emma and Mason a look that could kill, then got on the elevator.

Sin strolled confidently off the elevator and rounded the corridor with Beans just behind him. They bent another corner then walked through the doors of the small hospital chapel. The chapel was thick with dark suited bodyguards but was silent. His connect was in town and he needed to know why. Sin marched down the aisle with Beans stepping stride for stride, only to be stopped dead in their tracks by two hulking bodyguards.

Near the front of the chapel, Sin watched as another bodyguard approached a woman seated alone in a pew and whispered in her ear before stepping away. He then nodded to the men blocking Sin and Beans' path and they stepped aside but only allowed Sin to pass.

Sin approached the woman, who slid over so he could join her. "Yasin," she said. His name rolling off her lips seductively.

In the testosterone-saturated drug world, Reina was the stuff legends were made of, a woman with access to the highest levels of cartel life. She was narco royalty. A queen pin who lived, operated and loved inside the upper echelons of the drug world. A fashionista as powerful as she was beautiful. Her sun kissed skin looked naturally tanned and soft. She was slim but shapely with ample breast, and had long jet black hair, with thick lips.

"What are you doing here Reina and what's with all the suits," Sin questioned as he sat down.

"I came to offer my condolences for the recent loss of your father and for what happened to your sister tonight," she said.

"You could've did that with a phone call," Sin replied giving her a suspicious look.

She moved closer to him. "A phone call felt a little too

impersonal for our longstanding friendship," she confessed while rubbing his leg gently.

"It would've done the job," he said.

"You seem so uptight," she said moving her hand up his leg. "Besides it's always good to see you. I thought you would be happy to see me."

He removed her hand. "With you, it's never that simple. So cut the bullshit and tell me the real reason you're here?"

She smiled than removed the designer shades from her face, revealing her deep brown eyes, thick eyelashes and high cheek bones. She was flawlessly beautiful. "I came to offer you my help," she explained.

"That's awful nice of you but I don't need any help."

"Oh but you do," she shook her head back and forth. "The Commission has flown in a small army of men, just to wipe you and your organization out."

"How do you know?"

"I hear things," she said as she placed the end of her glasses in her mouth. "They're pulling out all stops. You're gonna lose this war," she proclaimed.

"I'll find a way. Trust me, I always do," he said confidently.

"But at what cost?" Reina asked. She admired his strength. He was a man of impeccable character but he was too stubborn for his own good. "Your father is dead and your sister is upstairs clinging to her life. You're outmanned.

It is obvious to everybody but you that you can't win. Why won't you take my help, you don't trust me?"

"I'm a little thin on trust right now," he said truthfully. "Why do you want to help me so bad? If I win, you win and our business continues to run smooth. If I lose, there will always be someone for you to do business with. So you still win."

"Do you really need me to answer that?" she asked.

"At this very moment. Yes. I told you I'm having trust issues."

Reina paused and stared off into the distance. After a few seconds passed, she turned back to him and said, "Yes, it's true, I can do business with anybody I choose. I have the power to make men very wealthy, that is something that isn't easily turned down. But everybody isn't you. I enjoy doing business with you. We've made a lot of money together. And nobody fucks me like you do," she admitted. "That's also good for business." Her honesty didn't amuse him. "Now let me help," she demanded. "With one phone call, I can put a hundred soldiers in New York to help you in this war. Within a month, that number would grow to five hundred. All you have to do is say the word," she offered.

"And these men, they would be under my control?" he questioned considering the offer.

"Yes."

"They will answer to my voice and my voice only?"

"Yes. For as long as you need them," she explained.

Sin sat quietly for a moment in deep thought. He wanted to make sure he was making the right choice. Whichever way he chose, he wanted to be absolute in his decision. He stood to his feet. "Make it happen," he replied then began to walk up the aisle of the chapel.

"Yasin," she called out to him causing him to stop and look back. "Aren't you gonna light a candle and say a prayer?" Reina asked pointing towards the votive candle rack near the altar.

"Never waste a prayer for peace in a war zone," Sin replied before disappearing through the doors of the chapel. And like that he had swung the balance of the war back into his favor.

CHAPTER 10

ASHLEIGH SAT INDIAN STYLE ON the bed, looking up at Case as he stood in front of the bed. His gaze was fixed on her, searching her eyes as if he could see straight to her soul, and deep down inside of her to the ugly unhealed wounds and pain she hid beneath what people saw on the beautiful surface.

"Why you staring at me like that?" she asked him.

"Because you're so beautiful," Case replied then smiled charmingly at her.

Ashleigh returned the gesture, forcing a smile. She didn't feel pretty at the moment, she felt weak and hopeless. She lifted the small mirror off her lap and stared at her reflection. She was trying to see what everybody found so beautiful when they looked at her. But all she recognized was the same pain in her weary eyes that she always saw. Ashleigh missed her father, without him she felt hollow. Thinking of him gave her instant heartache. Ashleigh sniffled once then wiped her nose. She pushed her thoughts to the back of her mind then picked up the rolled up dollar bill and sniffed a line of coke off the mirror. Ashleigh leaned her head back, eager for the drug to take effect. She enjoyed the numbing relaxation the drug gave her. It took her thoughts to a place where there was no pain, no heartbreak. It took her mind off of losing her father, off of Cassie's accident. It allowed her to slip away into another world. The more she sniffed the further away those thoughts seemed to go. Coke was the crutch she had been searching for, a coping mechanism like none other and Case had turned her on to the drug. Ashleigh loved how it felt as it flowed through her system. She leaned in and snorted another line.

"Damn ma, be easy with that shit. You gonna burn your nose up," Case explained pretending to care. "I can't have my chick walking around with the drippy nose and shit. That's where you heading, the way you using your nose like a vacuum."

"Please nigga, that'll never be me," Ashleigh replied as she did another line. Ashleigh felt like she was floating on a cloud. The higher she got, the more liberated, sexy and carefree she felt.

Case enjoyed watching as her fondness for the drug grew. He knew by the look in Ashleigh's eyes that she was hooked. Even if she didn't know it yet. He planned to use it to gain her unquestioned trust and loyalty. It was their little secret.

Ashleigh loved that she could trust Case. It allowed her to let her guard down and made her speak more freely to him. She had always admired street niggas, now she had her very own thoroughbred. Someone who wasn't connected to her father organization in anyway or to her brother the way Beans was. That was what appealed to her about Case. In her mind, he was his own man. Not to mention that he was a fly, sexy Harlem nigga. Case moved, dressed and talked different than the men she was used to. The way he had bossed up at the cemetery, coming to Sin's aid, Ashleigh knew he had all the makings of a street king. She had been raised as royalty, a king's daughter, and she couldn't wait from her chance to ascend to the queen's seat. She had studied her mother over the years, thinking that she was the most beautiful woman she had ever seen. Ashleigh watched as Emma played her role so elegantly and now she wanted that for herself. Beans was a gangster's gangster but when it came to being a boss, Ashleigh would always see him in Sin's shadow. She had strong feelings for him but she had stronger aspirations to be on the arm of a boss.

Case admired her as she got up off the bed. “Hurry up back ma, you got a nigga dick all hard and shit. Switching that fat ass around,” he said smacking her on the ass as she passed him on the way to the bathroom. Ashleigh sucked her teeth. “I got something you could suck," Case quipped while grabbing his manhood.

"You know you can’t handle these lethal lips nigga. Turn that ass into a minute man," she boasted before disappearing into the bathroom.

Ashleigh turned on the faucet and splashed water on her face. Her mouth tasted like medicine from the cocaine she had snorted. She held her hand under the water and drank some, hoping to rinse the taste out of her mouth. She still hadn’t gotten use to the bitterness of the drip in her throat that came after sniffing coke. Ashleigh turned off the water.

‘Ayo,” she heard Case call out to her from the other room. “How your brother handling all this beef that’s been coming his way?” he inquired.

"I don’t know,” Ashleigh replied. “It’s been so much going on. Now with Cassie in the hospital. It’s just crazy. I don’t want to think about that shit right now. It’s blowing my high.”

"I ain’t trying to do that ma,” Case said. “I’m just saying if it was me, I'd be in them streets pulling up on niggas, ya dig?” He knew exactly what to say to play on her feelings,

"Somebody would have to pay for even thinking about touching one of mines, feel me?"

"I know that's right," she spoke with pride. "But Sin is going to make them Italian fucks pay for that shit, trust me. My brother doesn't play about family. He taking over the family business from my dad and he was the same way."

"Oh yeah?" Case inquired. "Sin the head of the family now?"

"Yeah," she admitted. "My mom doesn't like it. She be buggin' the fuck out. But who she thinks is gonna take over? Mason? Psss," she sighed. "He not built like that. Not for that life." Ashleigh was talking faster than usual, rambling on. The coke had control of her tongue. She was giving Case everything he wanted out of the conversation. He just kept quiet while she provided all the information he needed. "But my brother Sin," she continued blabbing, "Now that nigga is bout that life. He a G for real," Ashleigh bragged.

"So I'm saying, ya brother's man, what's his name?"

"Who you talking 'bout Beans?" she asked while pulling her hair into a ponytail. Ashleigh stepped out of her panties and took off her bra then headed back in the room. Fully nude, she switched her hips as she walked passed him and plopped down on the bed.

"Yeah, that nigga," Case said. "He holding him down right?"

"Of course. Beans is the realest nigga on my brother's

team." She tried her best to hide it but her face brightened as she spoke about Beans. Maybe if she wasn't so high she would have been able to conceal it better. She was satisfying a longtime itch every time they had sex and Beans never disappointed. Just the thought of him made her pussy tingle.

It sickened Case to his stomach seeing her light up at the mention of Beans' name. He flared his nose but tried hard to hide his displeasure. He was more successful than she had been with his deceit. "Ok cool. You know my main concern is you," he reassured her. "So if niggas is after your family like that. I'll do whatever I can do to help. Cause all that shit trickles down, ya dig what I'm saying? I'll kill a nigga over you, ma."

Ashleigh lit up. "I know. You as solid as they come in my eyes baby. My brother needs somebody like you on his team. Someone that's gonna hold him down." Ashleigh got up on her knees and waved her finger for him to come to her. "Like how you hold me down."

Case walked over to her. "No doubt ma. All I'm saying is, I'm here for whatever, nah mean? I don't know what I'd do if something was to happen to you," he said as Ashleigh laid her head on his chest.

"I'm gonna let my brother know, he need a nigga like you—"

"Nah," Case said lifting her chin so she looked him in his eyes. "I ain't no groupie ma. I ain't looking for no handouts or no put on. Let him come to you. Let him mention it first," Case said smoothly.

"Ok," she quickly answered not even questioning why.

"When the time is right, me and him gonna talk," Case said knowing Ashleigh had no idea about his true intentions. "Now why was you looking all sad earlier?" he asked running his fingers through her hair.

"I was thinking about my father," she admitted.

"You don't have to stress about that ma, let me be your daddy," he said kissing her lips.

Ashleigh kissed him back slipping her tongue into his mouth. She run both hands up his up his chest and removed the wife beater he wore. She trailed kissed down to his waist then pulled down his basketball shorts. Ashleigh gripped his naked, muscular butt and pulled him towards her, taking his erection into her mouth. She began to rock her head back and forth, sucking him in aggressively like she was trying to make him cum in seconds. After a few minutes Case pulled back from her, unable to take the pleasure she was giving.

"I told you, you couldn't handle it," Ashleigh smirked seductively at him.

"Turn around," Case commanded her and she quickly did as he said.

Case grabbed a fistful of Ashleigh's hair and she arched her back, biting down on her lip as he dove deep inside her from behind. Ashleigh panted with every stroke as sweat dripped down her back. Case slapped her ass aggressively.

“Oh yes, daddy,” she moaned as Case gave her long meticulous strokes bringing the freak out of her. "Fuck me. Fuck me harder" she called out. The cocaine flowing through her system had her senses heightened, enhancing the pleasure she was receiving. The drug always made the sex between them more intense.

"You want this dick don’t you," Case taunted, spreading open her ass cheeks and sticking his thumb in her butt. "Tell me you want this dick.”

“I want it daddy, please," she gladly submitted to his request. “Please daddy, give me all that dick.” The feeling was euphoric.

Adrenaline pumped through Case’s body and he began to pound Ashleigh harder from behind as her ass cheeks rippled to his movement. He got off on seeing her so submissive in his hands. He had her body, no doubt, but Case was seeking more. He wanted complete control of her mind, to manipulate and do with whatever he pleased. So he had introduced cocaine to her through sex as a way to make the feeling more explosive. Ashleigh loved the high. As her dependency grew, her guard shrunk and after a while they had disappeared completely. Now every conversation about her family and her brother’s movements were spoken with less reservation. Case was reeling Ashleigh deeper into his clutches and he planned on using her for everything she was worth.

"Is it good to you?" Ashleigh asked in the midst of switching positions.

“Sshh,” he instructed as he flipped her onto her back. Case pressed his forehead against hers, staring passionately into her eyes as he reentered her wetness. She was a beautiful pawn in his sadistic game of revenge but he couldn’t deny that the pussy was the best he had ever had. Ashleigh was built like a video vixen and with the coke fueling her sex drive, she was nastier than a porn star. Case was going to kill her but he was enjoying her in the meantime. So much that he hated to share her. Images of Ashleigh fucking Beans in the car began to flash in Case’s mind, enraging him. His thrust became more powerful. His stroke more forceful, pounding her as hard as he could. Ashleigh absorbed every blow like a champ, unaware that he was taking his anger out on her. Suddenly, she began to smack him in the face as he stroked her.

“Harder,” he commanded.

Ashleigh fought with all her might, slapping him across the face. Instead of angering him, it excited Case. He wrapped his hand around her throat, applying just enough pressure. He really wanted to squeeze every breath out of her lungs with his bare hands, until her body laid lifeless on his bed. But he knew now wasn’t the time. Everyone in her brother’s organization had an expiration date as far as he was concerned. Sin was at the top of his list but Ashleigh wasn't that far behind. Case dreamed of blowing Beans' brains all over Ashleigh than smothering her to death.

Case had originally under estimated how powerful Sin was and now he had to move wiser. By coming to his aid at the funeral, he was sure it had gained him some respect in Sin's eyes. He planned on using it to his advantage in order to get close to him.

"Ahhh," Case moaned. "Take this shit," he said through clenched teeth as his nut built up and his thrust became more precise. Case pulled out and Ashleigh quickly flipped around to taste him.

"Mmm," Ashleigh smiled, her face filled with joy as she swallowed his seed. "Oh, you taste so good baby," she fed his ego while rubbing his manhood on her lips as he kneeled overtop of her.

Case looked down at her and thought to himself, "What a waste of a good piece of ass." It was a shame that he had to get rid of her.

CHAPTER 11

MASON HOLLOWAY SAT ALONE BEHIND the oversized desk that once sat in his late father's home office, now it sat in his. The house was quiet. His wife and son were asleep, leaving him alone to work. Mason was frantically going over his speech for the upcoming inauguration. He was normally a great speaker but was feeling a bit of added pressure due to his desire to make a great impression on the people of New York. It was times like this that he missed his father the most. He wished he could just make a call and hear his voice. One brief talk was all it always took to get Mason going. Instead, he had hoped his father's old furniture would provide him the inspiration he needed. Still he was struggling to come up with the right words. His frustration was mounting as each minute passed. Finally, he tossed the pen down, sighing deeply feeling a sense of defeat.

"Maybe if you worked as hard to find our daughter as you do at everything else, she would already be home."

Startled, Mason's eyes rose to the sound that was coming from the door. His wife, Khari stood in the doorway trying her best to drown her grief with the oversized glass of wine she held in her hand. Khari wore a scowl on her face as she watched her husband work.

He met her glare with one of his own indicating he wasn't in the mood for her in a drunken state or any state for that matter. Mason had long adopted the practice of neglecting his emotional responsibility to his wife. Choosing instead to throw himself fully into his work. Tonight wouldn't be any different as he quickly turned his attention back to his speech.

Khari sucked her teeth. "Just like I thought," she said disgusted by him.

"I thought you were sleep," he said wishing she was.

Khari swigged her wine then pitched the glass at him like a fastball. The glass shattered on the desk in front of him, spilling wine all over his paperwork.

Mason jumped up from the desk, trying to salvage the

papers. "What the hell is wrong with you. You're fucking psychotic I'm working on my speech. Damn!"

His coarse language angered her further. "Do I look sleep to you?" she asked. "Oh no Mason, I'm wide awake and I'm tired of your shit. I bet I got your attention now motherfucker. That's all you care about is being the mayor. What about being who you are to this family?" Khari seethed as she looked around the room for something else to throw at him. Normally she wouldn't dare talk to him that way, in fear of a physical confrontation but she had enough of Mason's recent behavior. She was fed up with how he was handling Bria's kidnapping and tired of the way he treated her. His attitude towards her had went from neglect to downright cruelty. She had long been aware of his unfaithfulness, but he no longer attempted to hide it. He came and went as he pleased and she was supposed to just smile for the cameras and play the happy wife for all the watching eyes. But she was anything but happy. "I'm on to your shit," she warned.

"What is that supposed to mean?" he asked. "I'm doing everything I can."

"You know exactly what it means," she snapped back, tears building in her eyes. "Our daughter is out there somewhere and you're too busy fucking around to do anything about it."

"What are you complaining about now?"

"You're fucking that green-eyed bitch from your office. How could you continue to disrespect me, with our baby missing."

Mason laughed to himself. "You're crazy."

"And you're selfish. You don't care about anybody but yourself. Not even Bria," Khari said.

The truth was, Mason had grown to love his accomplishments more than he did his role as a husband. He remembered a time when their marriage made him happy but it no longer did. Khari was once vibrant and extremely intelligent, giving her physical appeal a regality that beauty sometimes does not have. It was no surprise that he had fell in love with her. Most of his colleagues envied him for having such a smart and beautiful wife. Secretly Mason always feared losing her. He was smart enough to recognize she was destined for greater things than just being some politician's trophy wife. That made him insecure, jealous even and he quietly celebrated when she decided to give up on her dreams of becoming an actress. He was sure that she would have been successful, award winning probably and couldn't bear the thought of having to live in her shadow. Now she lived in the shadow he casted. A position that suited him more but clearly had taken a toll on her. She drank more excessively and she had begun to depend on the pills the doctors had prescribed, a little too much. Where he once saw elegance and grace, he now saw a broken woman.

Still, Mason couldn't find it within himself to care enough.

"I'm doing everything in my power to find Bria," he said firmly looking directly into her eyes. He was trying his hardest to ease her mind and appear strong and convincing as possible. "But that doesn't change the fact that I am going to be mayor of this city very soon. I don't have the luxury to sit around on my ass doing nothing, like you. I have a job to do. I have a responsibility to the people."

"Got dammit Mason. You just don't get it," Khari shouted as tears rolled down her face. "What about your responsibility to Bria, to MJ, to me," she pleaded. "Fuck the people, I'm your wife."

Khari said the words but deep inside she knew her marriage was nothing more than a charade. She was just in over her head and didn't know how to escape. Mason had once threatened her life when she brought up the idea of a divorce. He knew it would hurt his image and kill any campaigns he would have moving forward. She had been a part of the Holloway family long enough to know those weren't idle threats. That was partly the reason for the tears, she truly felt trapped.

Khari had considered trying to rekindle their love but she had such a strong aversion for Mason, that she couldn't stomach the thought of him touching her in a sexual manner. She couldn't turn to her parents for help. She had long alienated them, leaving them in the projects for her new life, never to return or visit. She had no close friends to confide in, Mason made sure of that. And she couldn't expect the authorities to help her, the Holloways had so many of them in pocket, which was sure to get worse now that Mason was to be mayor.

"Lower your voice in my house before you wake up my son," Mason demanded. He circled the desk, leaning up against it, his body arrogantly at ease with a smug grin on his face. "You got some nerve. Some wife you are. Look at you. You're either drunk or a zombie on pills every minute of the day. Not knowing if you're coming or going. You ought to be ashamed of yourself. Hell, I'm ashamed for you," he began to chuckle while shaking his head back and forth. "Shit, on second thought, I'm ashamed of you really."

Khari walked towards him until they stood face to face. He smirked, taking pride in slinging insults at her. The look of self-importance on his face enraged her. Khari let the detest build in her mouth, then she spat it like venom. "Fuck you," she shouted as the saliva hit his face. She cocked back to slap him but he caught her hand by the wrist in midflight.

The simmering hatred he had for her instantly bubbled over. Mason swung his open hand swiftly, slapping her across the face with enough force that it sent her to the floor. "Crazy bitch," he barked before wiping his face and instantly cocking his closed fist back ready to deliver another blow.

"Is that how you get your shit off now, Mason?" she asked looking up at him with blood leaking from the side of her mouth. "Cause Lord knows you don't fuck me anymore." Khari had no fear in her eyes, only tears. She didn't even feel the sting from the cut on her lip.

Mason noticed her steel look and lowered his fist to his side. "Get your ass up and get out of here before I hurt you for real this time," he threatened while pushing her with his foot.

"What you gonna do Mason?" she taunted. "You gonna kill me, you gonna make me disappear? Or are you saving that trick for your next election?" Khari spoke in a contemptuous tone as she rose to her feet.

Mason laughed nervously. "Now I'm convinced you're crazy. Won't you go do what you do best, self-medicate like usual. I got work to do." Mason turned, walked back around the desk and sat down.

There was a long silence in the room. Khari shook her head, "What happened to the man I married?"

There was another long pause as Khari stood in front of his desk hoping for an answer. Finally, Mason looked up from his notepad and said, "You happened. Now close the door on you way out."

Khari turned and hastily walked out the room, crying hysterically.

When Mason heard the door slam shut he put the pen down on the desk. He leaned back in the chair and exhaled a deep breath. Reaching in his pocket, Mason removed the card he had received from Agent Mosley. He held it in his hand, studying it, thinking hard about the conversation they had shared. Mainly the part where the agent told him if he ever needed him for anything, not to hesitate to call. This felt like one of those times. Mason needed his daughter back home. It was the only way to stunt Khari's growing suspicion. Everything he had worked and schemed for was in jeopardy of falling apart if she ever managed to figure things out.

CHAPTER 12

THE MEETING PLACE WAS A rather unnoticeable eatery in Brooklyn. Years ago, when Sin was just a young hustler on the come up, it was one of his favorite spots to grab a bite to eat while soaking up knowledge from some of the old timers. He hadn't stepped foot inside the place in more than a few years. But as he walked through the door flanked by two bodyguards, the familiar smell of hot wings and jumbo shrimp filled his nostrils, bringing back nothing but good memories.

The place was thin of customers when he entered, a typical crowd for the early afternoon. Another reason why he had chosen it as the meeting place. Sin knew the type of people that frequented the spot tended to mind their own business. They wouldn't even bat an eye at him or the person he was meeting with. Sin entered the front door and easily spotted Khari sitting alone near the back, at a table by an old jukebox that they had shared many times before as young lovers.

Khari noticed Sin as soon as he walked in. It was hard not to, there was something about him that demanded attention. It was more than just his smooth bronze skin, mesmerizing brown eyes and good looks. It was a vibe, Sin exuded power and the command of a boss, even without the bodyguards. Khari studied him as he strolled up, her heartbeat began to quicken in her chest. They were once young lovebirds but she had admired from a distance as Sin evolved into a man. His baggy jeans and Timberlands maturing into tailor made suits and expensive shoes. As he reached the table, she gazed up at him. Sin was the sexiest man Khari had ever seen and the aura of self-confidence that surrounded him, only amplified his physical appeal. She started to get up to greet him, hoping for a hug but that thought was quickly cut short.

"You ain't gotta get up," Sin said abruptly as he took a seat and the hulking men guarding him sat at a nearby table. He was clearly still upset with her.

"How have you been?" Khari asked touching his hand gently, showing her concern for all he had been through but her question was met with an awkward silence. Sin had barely made eye contact with her since sitting down. "Well, thank you for coming," she continued. "I know things between us didn't end on a good note last time we spoke and our situation hasn't exactly been ideal but—"

"Look Khari, I didn't come here for a trip down memory lane," he interrupted her before the conversation went somewhere he wasn't interested in it going. "The only thing I care about is bringing Bria home, safely. No more, no less."

"C'mon Sin, don't act like that with me," Khari pleaded. "I know what I did to you was wrong and I'm sorry. I don't know what else to say."

"There's nothing you can say to me," he replied before getting quiet as the waitress came over to take their order.

Khari spoke first as the waitress disappeared a few minutes later. "We once shared something so special Sin. You mean to tell me you never think about us and how we were? That never crosses your mind?" her voice cracked as tears built in her eyes

"Nah. That all ended for me when you married my brother," Sin responded showing no emotion.

"I deserve that," Khari acknowledged as she shook her head. "Well I've thought about it every day for the past eight years. Every time I look at Bria I'm reminded of what we had. I've never felt a love like yours, before you or after you.

She's my piece of you to love. And I need her back." Tears began to flow from Khari's eyes and race down her face. "I made a selfish choice by marrying your brother. I was young Sin. I wanted the prestigious lifestyle, the security."

"I'm glad to see you got everything you wanted," he said.

"And more," she replied sarcastically. "But trust me, I'm paying the price for that life," she said turning her face slightly allowing Sin to catch a glimpse of the bruise on the side of her cheek.

Sin reached across the table, grabbing her by the chin and turning her face to get a better look. "That nigga did that?" Sin asked already knowing the answer. Although he didn't show Khari, he suddenly felt compelled to do something, even if he didn't know why. "Who was she to him?" he thought to himself at that moment. Was she his brother's wife? Or was she the mother of his child? She was both, causing Sin conflicting thoughts.

"Yeah," she said lowering her eyes from his in shame.

"How long has that been going on?" he asked.

"Long enough," she answered wiping her tears with a napkin as the waitress returned with their drinks and the table got silent again.

Sin stared into her eyes. The light that once shined so bright had been dulled and her pupils were dilated. She had been taking something to cope with the suffering in her life and from the looks of it, it was getting the better of her.

"Why haven't you left him?" Sin questioned.

"My life is already a living hell," she confessed. "Between your brother and his evil bitch of a mother. If I left, it would only get worse. That's why you're my only hope, Sin. I need you. I just have this feeling, in my gut, that Mason is not telling me the whole truth," she said.

"You think he had something to do with Bria getting kidnapped?"

"I don't know," her voice raising an octave. "Why no ransom calls. No demands. Something about this whole thing just isn't right. Call it a mother's intuition."

Sin picked up his drink and downed it in one big gulp. "Mason is a sucka of the highest level but even I can't see him having his own..." Sin quickly caught himself. "I mean; I can't see him having Bria kidnapped."

"Not even to win the election?" Khari questioned. "I wouldn't put anything passed that man and his mother."

Before Sin could respond his phone started ringing. "Hold that thought," he said to Khari. "Hello," he said picking up the phone on the second ring.

An elderly woman's voice greeted him on the other end. She was frantic with worry and spoke in short frenetic spurts. Sin recognized the voice immediately, "Ok, Ms. Yvonne. Just calm down," he spoke in a composed tone trying to ease her concerns. "Yes, ma'am, I'm on my way."

"Ms. Yvonne. Ms. Yvonne?" Khari questioned with a raised eyebrow as Sin hung up the phone. "I haven't heard that name in years."

"Yeah," he said quickly dismissing her inquiry. "I gotta go but I'ma look into what you said," he told Khari before turning to walk away.

"Sin, wait," she grabbed him by the arm stopping him. Khari stood to her feet. The look in her eyes told him what was coming next. "You think, when this is all over...maybe me and you can try again." She caressed the side of his face.

Sin pulled his head back rejecting her affection. "Let me make this real clear for you Khari. There will never be anything between me and you again...ever. You made your bed and laid in it comfortably when all was right in your house. So continue to do that or don't, either way I don't give a fuck. Not about you, not about Mason. My only concern is Bria and bringing her home safely. And once she's home, the first thing I'm gonna do is tell my brother the truth, to his face." Sin snatched his arm away from Khari. "I gotta go. I'll call you when I know something."

Khari stood frozen as a crushing pain seared through her chest. She quickly lost the battle with the tears swelling in her eyes. She had never felt more hopeless then she did watching Sin walk out the bar. There was no one left for her to turn to.

* * *

The group of young men gathered in front of the building in a circle with a visible cloud of smoke surrounding them, suddenly fell silent as the Lincoln Navigator pulled up to the curve. Sin exited the backseat almost simultaneously and stalked straight towards the group of young men before his bodyguards could react. The group noticed Sin immediately as he approached. They knew who he was and knew who he was there for. None of them wanted an issue with him. They feared him and quickly began clearing out as he marched towards them. Most weren't brave enough to look him in the eyes or speak as he passed. They just spread out allowing him to enter the circle.

Without saying a word to any of them, Sin walked over and extended his hand to Lil' Smoke who was laying on the ground in a fetal position, covering his head. He had been punched and kicked repeatedly.

"Get up Lil' Smoke," Sin commanded as he extended his causing the young man to peek from his guard. "What the hell is going on? Your grandmother just called me stressing. She said you trying to join a gang," Sin spazzed as he looked around at the group of young men. "Didn't I tell your ass not to let me catch you out here no more?" he said pulling Lil' Smoke up to his feet.

Lil' Smoke remained quiet, looking down at his shoes,

avoiding eye contact while Sin barked on him. There was blood on his lip and a mouse under his eye.

"You hear me talking to you?" Sin tapped the back of his hand on Lil Smoke's chest.

"Yeah," Lil' Smoke finally spoke. He was mad and embarrassed that Sin had intervened in his initiation. He could hear the snickering from the rest of the gang over his shoulders.

"What the fuck you think you doing out here, playboy? This shit ain't for you," Sin told him.

"Who said?" Lil' Smoke challenged with bass in his voice.

"I said!" Sin replied. "You got your grandmother scared. She doesn't wanna have to bury you no time soon. That's all this gonna lead to."

Lil' Smoke sighed. "Man, a nigga gotta eat. I'm trying to get money."

"Oh you hustling' now, lil nigga?" Sin began to aggressively pat him down and go in his pockets. He found a food saver bag filled with crack and tossed it on the ground.

"Yo, what you doing?" Lil Smoke objected.

"You don't need to be doing that. You know if you need anything, you can come get it from me."

Lil Smoke sucked his teeth. "Who wanna live like that. I ain't tryna depend on the next man. I'm tryna to stand on my own two," he explained.

Sin couldn't help but respect where he was coming from but he didn't agree with the young man's way of going about it. "I ain't telling you what I think. I'm telling you what I know. This ain't the path you wanna take. Check this out, you really wanna earn your keep?" Sin asked.

"Hell yeah," Lil' Smoke said sticking his chest out.

"Aight, come work for me," Sin told him.

The young man's face lit up with excitement. Hyped by the opportunity. He had heard all the stories from people in the streets, about how his father, Sin and Beans had the projects on lock back in the day. He was itching to carve his name out in the streets and reach the status of those three.

"Don't get too excited playboy. It ain't what you thinking. I got a job for you at my dealership, washing cars."

Lil Smoke's nostrils began to flare. "Fuck that," he protested. "I ain't washing no cars."

"Who the fuck you talking to," Sin raised his voice. "Check this out," he said through clenched teeth as he pulled the young man closer. "You banned from out here, you understand me?" Y'all hear that," he raised his voice turning to all the young men standing around. "He ain't welcomed over here no more. If I hear y'all letting him bang. I'ma starve this whole block. Now c'mon," Sin said nudging Lil' Smoke toward the car.

"Yo my nigga, what the fuck you doing?" a grimy looking, light skinned man said as he stepped out the front door of the project building. He appeared to be a few years older than the rest of the group of young men. "Lil' Smoke, you alright? I heard you took that fade like a G," he called out to him.

"Yeah. I'm good," Lil Smoke quickly answered not wanting to anger Sin any more than he already was.

"Yeah he good. This family business," Sin said turning over his shoulder looking back at the man.

"Fuck you mean? Lil' Smoke is family. So he is my business," the man stated boldly. "Plus that work in his pocket belong to me, the money does too. This my block homie. Lil Smoke work for me. Anything that gots to do with him, gots to do with me. Nah'mean?"

"Oh, so you Gunna?" Sin asked as he turned around and approached the man. "Just the man I wanted to see."

"Yeah, nigga I'm Gunna," the hustler bragged proudly while grabbing the crotch of his sagging sweatpants. "Who the fuck is you, old bitch ass suit wearing nigga. What the fuck you wanna see me about," he chuckled at himself. "You must've made a wrong turn or somethin'," he boasted flipping open his fleece hoodie so Sin could see the 9mm on his waist.

Sin laughed. "You must be new around here."

"Yo Gunna, I don't think you wanna play it like that," one of the young hustlers whispered trying to give him the heads up that Sin was the plug. Gunna would be best served to try and do business with him instead of beefing. "That's Sin. He the—"

Gunna quickly dismissed the youngster, ignoring the advice. "Nah. He don't want to play it like that wit' me. I don't give a fuck who dis nigga suppose to—"

At that moment Sin swung on him, connecting solidly, blooding Gunna's mouth. Sin reached in Gunna's waist, removed his gun and before anybody knew what happened he had it jammed under Gunna's chin. The two bodyguards seemed to appear out of nowhere with guns drawn on the rest of the group, dying for someone to move.

Sin began to smashed Gunna's face with the gun, pounding him relentlessly to the ground in broad daylight in the middle of the projects. Finally, he put his foot on Gunna's chest and stood over him pointing the gun at his head.

"Should've listen to ya man," Sin told him. "Don't let this suit shit fool you. I'll blow ya fuckin' head off and all these niggas'll look the other way. Now if I hear about you or any of your niggas coming around my nephew again, my face gonna be the last one you ever see," Sin said as he took his foot off Gunna's chest and left him there leaking on the ground.

Sin walked a few feet behind Lil' Smoke on their way back to the truck. Lil' Smoke looked back over his shoulder at him.

"What!?" Sin barked at him.

"Nothing," Lil' Smoke answered nervously and turned back around. He had never seen Sin like that and now understood why his name was so respected in the street.

"Get ya ass in the car man. I'm taking you home," Sin shaking his head in frustration.

* * *

Sin instructed his bodyguards to stay in the hallway then pushed open the door as he heard Ms. Yvonne's aged voice invite them to come in. Making his way through the small but nicely decorated kitchen, he found the elderly woman sitting on the couch in the living room. Her apartment was perfectly clean. The way Sin always remembered it to be since he was young. Ms. Yvonne was a longtime friend of his deceased mother. As kids, her son Smoke, Beans and Sin were as thick as thieves.

"Look who I found," Sin said standing next to Lil' Smoke with his hand on his shoulder. The woman had tears in her eyes as she rocked back and forth, clutching a bible close to her heart with both hands. She just looked at her grandson, shaking her head, unable to find the word suitable to say to him at the moment.

"Go in your room for a sec, playboy. Let me holla at your grams," Sin told Lil' Smoke. Once the young man had disappeared to the back of the apartment Sin took a seat next to Ms. Yvonne and kissed her on the cheek.

"I don't know what to do with that boy anymore," she said. "He don't respect my rules. He don't come home like he supposed to," Ms. Yvonne said in her southern accent. Although she had lived in Brooklyn most of her adult life, Ms. Yvonne still spoke with a bit of a country twang. "I'm really doing the best I can with him, Sin. I promise you but I'm getting' old and he barely listens to me anymore," she shook her head in frustration as tears trickled down her face. "I lost my only child to those streets." Her voice lowered and she pointed towards the window. The way she spoke, it was like her heart was bleeding as she relived her son's death all over again. "I can't lose my grandson to them too. You know they will swallow him whole. He scares me cause he acts just like his father." She pulled a picture from inside the bible and handed it to Sin.

"I've kept that picture inside this bible ever since it was taken. I prayed for you boys every night back then. Still do. Even though my son is gone, I prays for you and Sean all the time," she explained. "Sean never stops by anymore though. But I still prays for him."

"That's just the way Beans, I mean Sean is," Sin told her. "Some people handle grief differently. He don't mean anything by it though, Ms. Yvonne."

The picture was of her son Smoke with Sin and Beans as young kids on the playground in the projects. The trio had big smiles on their faces and it reminded Sin of his youthful innocence. They had grown up, ran the streets and got money together, the three of them had been as close as brothers. Sin sat quietly for a moment studying the picture. He remembered it like it was yesterday. The image took him back to a fun and simple time in his life. That all changed with the death of his friend. The streets had claimed Sin's innocence and he never saw things the same again. After Smoke was murdered, Sin took on the responsibility of taking care of the family he left behind. Sin sent Ms. Yvonne money faithfully, purchased groceries when she needed and refurnished her whole apartment. But more importantly Sin pledged to always look after Smoke's son, who was small at the time of his father's death. That's why Sin was the first person Ms. Yvonne called during times of trouble.

"Everything is gonna be ok," Sin promised as he passed the photo back to her. "Don't worry yourself to death. I'ma take care of it. He's gonna come work for me at the car dealership from now on."

"Thank you, Yasin. Thank you so much. He could really learn a lot from you," she said patting him on the leg.

Sin nodded and smiled. His charming grin was like sunshine to rain as it quickly dried Ms. Yvonne's tears. "No problem. Whatever I can do to help," he said as he stood up and closed the buttons on his suit jacket. "While I'm here is there anything else you need?" he asked scanning around the apartment.

"No, no, no. You've done more than enough," she insisted rising to her feet.

"You sure?"

"Positive," she assured him. "Oh, that reminds me," she snapped her fingers and walked towards the kitchen with a feeble, unsteady gait. "I made a pot of gumbo the other day. I remembered how much you just loooooved my gumbo. I'm gonna put some in a Tupperware for you to take."

Sin waited until she disappeared into the kitchen before going in his pocket, peeling off five hundreds and dropping them onto the coffee table. "That sounds great. I'm starving," he said as he rubbed his hands together then followed her into the kitchen.

CHAPTER 13

SIN STOOD WITH HIS BACK to the workers in the warehouse behind him. With the ongoing war against the Commission, Sin knew he had to stay on top of business to make sure he continued to make money. War was costly. "Yeah, everything is smooth," he spoke confidently into the phone.

"Ok. We'll speak again real soon," Reina's sultry voice replied then hung up the phone on her end.

"Let's move. Hurry it up!" Sin waved his hands, barking out orders as he turned and directed the cars being off-loaded from the trailer. It appeared on the surface as a routine delivery of luxury vehicles to the dealership but it was actually the monthly drug shipment arriving. Select cars had been lined with kilos of cocaine and they would be stripped, relieved of all the product and readied for the showroom floor. It was an all-night process. When the last car rolled off the truck into the warehouse, Sin lowered the door and shouted, “Let’s work. Start breaking these shits down. Time is money.”

The operation ran like clockwork and more importantly it had remained undetected. Every month the kilos were delivered to the dealership the same way. They were then picked up and transported to another spot for distribution. Five hours in, Sin was still walking back and forth overseeing the controlled chaos. He was keeping a close eye on his money, making sure no bricks were unaccounted for.

Outside on the street as the sun began to come up, Gunna blew the smoke from his nostrils then passed the blunt to Lotti. Gunna’s face was battered and bruised, black and blue and his eyes was still swollen from his encounter with Sin. He was fuming with thoughts of homicide on his mind and his eyes were glued to the service door of Manhattan Motors. He was waiting for Sin to emerge. They heard he routinely took out the trash around early in the morning and was always alone when he did it. Lotti’s sister had gotten them the inside scoop from a friend that used to work at the dealership. Gunna figured they shouldn’t have any problems getting the drop on Sin and laying him to rest.

Then what was his would be theirs. Just the thought of becoming king made Gunna's dick hard.

Lotti leaned back in his seat and took a long pull off the blunt. He immediately began coughing nonstop.

"Take it easy boy, you know you got baby lungs. Here, take this," Gunna said passing him a bottle of Hennessey.

"Man, what time dis nigga supposed to come out this spot?" Lotti asked then turned the bottle up to his lips. "Shit, it don't seem like nobody even here this early."

"Look alive young boy. This might be what we been waiting on," Gunna said full of excitement as he noticed a garbage truck approaching in his rearview. He waited until it passed. "C'mon," he said then cocked a round into the chamber of his gun. Lotti did the same then hopped out the Chevy Impala and fell in line with Gunna.

Ali pulled the garbage truck into the alley. He and Barkim were seated in the cab of the truck dressed like sanitation workers. Beans and Kyrie were dressed the same as they hung off the back of the truck.

Beans gave the alley a quick survey then unclipped the walkie-talkie from his hip. "Yo, we here," he said then waited for the service door to open.

Sin stepped out into the alley carrying two large industrial trash bags with X's on them and tossed them into the back of the garbage truck. Kyrie leaped off the truck and helped him do the same with seven more bags with the same white mark.

"Everything on point," Beans asked clinging to the back of the truck.

"Like always," Sin replied. "Yo, tell the nigga Ali to drive smooth. Be quick but don't hurry," Sin said with a slight nod.

"C'mon nigga. I got this," Beans said giving Sin a pound as Kyrie leaped back on to the truck.

"No doubt. I'm a see y'all in a minute," Sin said.

"Ok Bet. Go!" Beans shouted banging on the side of the truck. The garbage truck eased off down the alley and disappeared around the corner.

"Ayo."

Suddenly, Sin stopped in his tracks at the sound of the voice. For a moment, he thought it was a homeless man in the alley until he felt the cold steel of a gun smashed against the side of his face. He collapsed to the ground, spitting out blood.

Gunna grabbed Lotti's hand stopping him from striking Sin again. He wanted to take his time to send a message. He wanted Sin to know that he wasn't the one to fuck with. "Look at me muthafucka. I want you to see my face. I'm the last face you gonna see before you die," Gunna whispered as he knelt down beside him.

Sin stared up at the man standing over him and immediately recognized him. "Gunna," he uttered under his breath.

"Yeah. Who's not to be fucked with now? Huh, muthafucka," Gunna bragged then struck Sin in the mouth again.

Sin wiped the blood from his mouth then began to laugh out loud. This only seemed to anger the two robbers even further.

"What the fuck is so funny nigga," Lotti asked.

"Y'all two clown ass niggas. With all the cameras around this muthafucka, you don't think somebody seen you by now?" Sin asked.

Gunna didn't get a chance for another word to escape his lips, before he felt the gun pressed to the back of his skull.

"Not here Beans," Sin instructed as he rose from the ground. "Take these niggas inside."

Gunna looked over his shoulder. Barkim, Ali and Kyrie, all had Lotti on the ground at gun point.

The men entered the dealership and headed straight for a solid steel door that led to the warehouse basement. When Sin reached the bottom of the steps, he found his crew hard at work putting the cars back together. Things suddenly became silent as every eye in the room landed on him and the men behind him. There was a look of confusion on the workers faces. He slowly began to walk around the room. His strong presence spreading all through the space as he moved. The entire room felt it and Sin could feel their eyes following him. All the members of his organization were present, "Perfect," he thought to himself. "There's a traitor amongst us," he announced. "Somebody on the team is working with the Feds," he said with a calm fury catching everyone off guard. His voice was steady and his manner was measured. You could hear a pin drop in the room as he stared in the eyes of his men. The smell of fear was strong in the air. There was a snake amongst them. The thing he despised most and he needed to weed it out of his circle immediately. "A disloyal nigga in the family is like having cancer. If the shit ain't dealt with, it'll spread."

Barkim's heart was pounding in his chest. His palms quickly grew moist. The guilt made him feel like Sin's comments were aimed directly at him. He felt like a sinner standing at the pearly gates of heaven. He had betrayed every man in the room. If he could have slithered out of the room through one of the cracks in the floor, he would. There was a knot forming in his stomach and a lump in his throat. He wanted to be anywhere but there. When his eyes met Sin's, Barkim's heart dropped into his ass. Sin's piercing eyes seemed to be staring right through him, right into his soul. Choked by fear, Barkim held his breath, staring steely-eyed at Sin but on the inside he was waiting for a bullet to rip through his head. As seconds passed, no bullet came and he let out a silent sigh as he watched Sin's eyes shift from his and stop in the middle of the room.

"Just like cancer the only way to get rid of disloyalty, is to cut it out at the root," Sin said looking down at Gunna and Lotti. They were on their knees in the middle of the circle that had been formed. The fear resonating from their eyes spoke volumes, even if they didn't. Sin had to restore order within his organization and the two men presented the perfect opportunity to set an example for all in attendance. "These niggas came here to kill me but I still got more respect for them than I do the rat amongst us," Sin said pulling the .45 from his waist.

"C'mon fam. We were just gonna rob you. You ain't gotta do all this," Lotti begged nervously.

"Don't call me fam, nigga," Sin spoke sternly. The way he looked at Lotti sent a chill up his spine. "Y'all came here to rob me with no mask? Don't play me," Sin threatened. "I know how the game go."

Lotti knew he was a dead man but still he tried pleading for his life. "Please my nigga, that's the tru—"

Sin pressed the gun against Lotti's forehead. He closed his eyes as Sin squeezed the trigger. The .45 slug entered between Lotti's eyes and exited the back of his head. Lotti's body flew backwards so hard his knees sounded like snapping tree branches and a reddish mist filled the air.

BOOM! BOOM! BOOM!

Sin dumped more bullets into his body causing it to

flop around like a fish out of water. Before circling around to Gunna, who remained firm, seemingly unbothered by the blood splatter on his face or having just witnessing his man's death. Gunna was going to be a gangster to the end and he refused to beg for his life. He wasn't built like that plus he knew his pleas would fall on deaf ears. He and Sin both knew that the next time they met, one of them had to die. Unfortunately, it was him. Gunna accepted his fate. He had been on the other side of the gun enough times to understand how it went. He took a deep breath and waited for death to come.

A bullet would have been merciful and done the job but Sin had another plan. He tucked the gun in his waist and pulled a garbage bag from his back pocket, slipping it over Gunna's head. Gunna began to squirm and scream as Barkim and Ali restrained him. Sin extended his hand towards Beans, who handed him a heavy duty pipe wrench. Sin took it and without hesitating, swung it as hard as he could. A loud cracking sound echoed throughout the room and Gunna's body crumbled to the floor. Sin swung the wrench, over and over again until a bloody pulp began to ooze from the trash bag. Some of the men standing around began to turn their heads, no longer able to stomach the brutality.

Barkim fought back vomit, watching Gunna's head be reduced to slush, thinking of what would happen to him if Sin found out about his betrayal.

Sin stopped swinging and the room fell silent once again. There were stunned looks on all the faces in the room. They had just witnessed Sin commit a vicious set of murders and he never once raised his voice, lost his cool or showed an ounce of emotion. Sin wiped the sweat from his brow. "Ok let's get back to work," he said addressing the room before turning and walking out. He knew there was a rodent hiding in his crew that needed to be dealt with and when he found out who it was their punishment would be just as severe.

* * *

Barkim rested his head on the side of the toilet and wiped the drool from his mouth with the back of his hand. He had long ejected all the contents in his stomach, now it was just dry heaves and thick spit. The muscles in his stomach were aching from the cramps in them and he felt fatigue as he leaned against the toilet. He couldn't shake Sin's word from his thoughts or the vision of the two men he killed. He knew he was next, it was only a matter of time. He picked up his phone off the floor next to him and quickly dialed a number from memory. He listened impatiently, his frustration growing as it rang and rang with no answer on the other end. "I need to speak with you right away. Call me back," he spoke in a nervous whisper as he left a message on Agent Mosley's voicemail for the third time. He had called him multiple times over the past hour and still hadn't been able to reach him. Sin's threats had Barkim spooked and he was just ready for it to all be over. Whatever he needed to do to make that happen, he was willing to do, now more than ever because Sin was out for blood. A knock at the door made Barkim jump and he instinctively pointed his gun at the door.

"Are you okay in there?" a woman called out from the other side of the door. Her accent was exotic and complemented her sexy, sultry voice.

Barkim nerves were a wreck and his hand trembled as he gripped his weapon. "Yeah, I'll be out in a minute ma," he answered but never lowering his weapon.

"I get paid by the hour," she reminded him.

"I ain't one of these broke niggas out here ma. Money ain't a thing," he said. Barkim lowered his gun as he heard her walk away from the door. He slammed the toilet down and pulled himself up off the floor then walked over to the sink. Taking out a small bag of heroin from his pocket, Barkim emptied some onto the back of his hand and snorted it. Heroin had always been his drug of choice but he found himself indulging more frequently as of late. It helped slow him down, calm his nerves. When finished, he looked at himself in the mirror, making sure to wipe any residue from his nose before heading back into the room of the hotel.

The thick Puerto Rican woman in the room greeted

him with a smile as he made his way over to the bed.

"What's all that shit you was talking when I was in the bathroom?" Barkim asked rhetorically. He put his gun on the nightstand and removed a knot of money from his pocket. He peeled and tossed hundred dollar bills at her one at a time, "This how it feels when you fucking wit' a boss ma," he bragged confidently. A polar opposite of himself from mere moments ago. By now he was accustomed to playing a role and he put on a face well plus the drugs was coursing through his system now.

"Ay Papi," the woman purred seductively, crawling across the bed like a sex kitten. The way he spoke to her made her pulse quicken and she instantly became moist.

Barkim laid back on the bed, allowing her to loosen his belt. She reached in his jeans, releasing his erection. Her beautiful face lit up and her eyes twinkled as she stroked him. With a flick of her tongue, she let a trail of spit leak from her mouth to the mushroom head of his dick. Then began twisting both hands in opposite directions on his shaft like she was grinding pepper before taking him fully into her mouth. Barkim sighed in pleasure as he felt the warm, wetness of the back of her throat. She was like an oral magician, making his manhood disappear and reappear in her mouth. The short, tight fitting dress she wore began to rise up and her fat ass peeked out. She began jiggling her ass cheeks, moaning as she smacked his rock hard dick against her face. Barkim grabbed the back of her head, thrusting his hips as he fucked her mouth. He threw his head back, pumping harder, feeling his climax nearing. "Drink this dick ma," he commanded her as he erupted from the pleasure, releasing some much needed tension and stress.

"Still under five minutes," she bragged with a smile, wiping her mouth.

"I can't front ma, you the best," he said. Barkim and the woman weren't strangers at all. The Puerto Rican bombshell was one of the many women in his stable but she was definitely his favorite. She knew how to please him like none other in the bedroom. Her body was unmatched and she enjoyed role playing.

"Somebody still wants to play," she said rubbing on his still erect manhood with one hand and her throbbing clit with the other.

"You already know," Barkim replied. That was one of the effects of the heroin. Barkim would stay hard for the rest of the night and the thick Rican mami would reap the benefits as she climbed on top of him.

CHAPTER 14

SUNDAY DINNER WAS A TRADITION at the Holloway Estate for as long as anyone could remember. It was a once every week event but over the years, as all the children began to leave the nest, it went from every Sunday gathering to a once a month way for the family to get together under one roof and catch up. Today's meal was a little more special than the others because it was Cassie's first since coming home from the hospital.

Jewlz was running late and as usual he was driving at a high speed when he turned on to the street his parent's house sat on. His date's jaw dropped when he drove through the gate and his parent's home came into full view.

"Oh my God," the young lady gasped. "This is where

you live?" she asked in astonishment.

"Yeah," Jewlz laughed as he parked in front of the beautiful Mediterranean-style home. He pulled the gun he had recently started carrying from under his seat and reached across her, placing it in the glove compartment. His date didn't bat an eye she was still stuck on how pretty the house was. The gun only added to the bad boy image she had of him. All the girls on campus looked at him that way. It enhanced his sex appeal. Jewlz exited the car and looked around as if he was waiting for paparazzi to start snapping pictures. When no flashes came he circled the vehicle and helped his still stunned date out the car.

"I've never seen a house this beautiful before," she said. "It's so big."

"You say that a lot huh?" he joked causing her to hit him playfully. "It's just a house ma. Same as any other. Living room. Bedrooms. Bathrooms. Kitchen. Walls. Floors," he said smoothly.

"I get it, I get it," she laughed. "So you lived here your whole life?" she asked him.

"Yeah, since I was born," he replied.

"And what do your parents do for a living?" she inquired.

"Get on my nerves," he tried to avoid her question with a joke.

"Stop playing," she said. "Tell me I wanna know."

Jewlz sighed. "Before my pops died, he did a lot of work with the city and he owned construction and cement companies," Jewlz explained.

"He must have sold a lot of cement to afford a house like this," she said.

"Yeah, something like that." he told her. "Most of the high rises and streets in the city were built with my father's cement and by my father's company," he stated grabbing her by the hand and leading the way. Jewlz could feel the moisture in her palms. "You nervous?" he asked as they walked towards the front door.

"A little. This is kinda intimidating" she admitted. She truly had no idea what she was about to walk into.

"You don't have anything to worry about. My family is regular, just like anybody else's," he smirked.

Jewlz led her into the house, where he was immediately met by Etilda, his parent's housekeeper. A smile spread across the woman's face when she spotted him.

"Jewlzy!" Etilda shouted with excitement. She hugged and kissed him on the cheek over and over. "How are you my handsome prince?"

"I'm good Tilda," he said squeezing her tight. "How about you?" he asked.

"Never better. And who is this?" she asked seeing the young lady at his side. "Que linda," Etilda complimented her looks.

"This is a friend of mine from school—."

But before he could properly introduce his date, his mother's voice could be heard calling out to Etilda from across the house.

Etilda sighed causing Jewlz to chuckle. "I have to go. Cassie is with Elijah in the den," she told him knowing he would be excited to see her.

"Who else is here?"

"Mason's in the dining room with Khari and your mother is in the kitchen."

"Why?" he asked.

"I don't know," Etilda laughed. It was no secret that Emma couldn't and didn't cook.

"Where's Ash?" Jewlz asked surprised she hadn't been mentioned.

Etilda shrugged her shoulders. "Ms. Ashleigh Holloway has yet to arrive," she spoke in a proper tone fitting for his bourgeois sister then hurried off towards the kitchen.

"That's Tilda," Jewlz said turning to his date. "She's been our housekeeper for years. She helped raise me. She's practically family," he explained then escorted his date across the marble floor of the foyer and guided her into the remarkably decorated home until they entered the den.

The room abruptly fell silent when Jewlz and his date entered. Jewlz froze mid-step at the sight of Cassie confined to a wheelchair. Her appearance had drastically changed. She was rail thin and looked like she was made out of fragile glass. Her legs appeared weak and delicate, like she couldn't stand if she wanted to. She didn't resemble anything close to her normal self. She looked pale and sick. Her glow had been dimmed even if only temporarily. It crushed Jewlz heart to see Cassie in such a feeble state, still he forced a smile as her gaze fell upon him.

Even through her pain, Cassie's heart danced with the joy of a proud big sister as she looked at her baby brother. Jewlz stood tall and handsome, a perfect blend of both his parent's good looks and Cassie truly adored him. He was the baby of the family and she like all his siblings wanted nothing but the best for him. Only a few weeks away from graduation, he was maturing into a man right in front of her eyes.

"Good to see you Jewlz," Elijah said walking over and extending his hand to shake.

Jewlz shook it and pulled him in for a half hug, "How is she?" he whispered in Elijah's ear.

"I'm not deaf. I can hear you," Cassie announced as she attempted to wheel herself over to him. "And I'm fine," she proclaimed.

"Hold on big sis," Jewlz said as he rushed over to her. He could see it took all her strength just to move. He didn't want her to strain herself.

"I'm fine boy," she said knocking his hand away. "I don't

need a nurse. I got one of those. I need a hug."

Jewlz smiled. He could see despite her condition her tough spirit hadn't been broken. He leaned over and hugged her gently.

Cassie could feel his tentativeness. "I'm ok Jewlz. You not gonna hurt me if you hug me," she reassured him as the two of them embraced lovingly.

"Where my nephews?" he asked.

"They running around her somewhere," she said.

"I know they're glad to have you home. We all are," Jewlz said sincerely looking over at Elijah as well.

"Definitely," Elijah said staring at his lovely wife while nodding his head. "It's been a tough few weeks for everybody but we gonna get through it like we get through everything, as a family." He placed his hands on his wife's shoulder and smiled at her. Cassie rubbed his hand and returned the gesture.

"Hey everybody!" Ashleigh burst through the door loudly, commanding the attention, with big designer shades on her face and a Céline handbag hanging from her wrist. "Hey Elijah. Hey Jewlz. Hey whoever you are," she said to his date, quickly by passing them and heading straight for Cassie. "Oh my God," Ashleigh paused and gazed down at her with a somber expression. She covered her mouth as tears formed in her eyes.

"It's not as bad as it looks," Cassie tried reassuring her

but to no avail, Ashleigh was already bawling as they embraced. Cassie rubbed Ashleigh's back. Somehow she had found herself offering comfort instead of the other way around.

"How's everybody doing?"

Everybody turned toward the doorway, where the unfamiliar voice had come from. Case stood in the door holding a large bouquet of white lilies and roses. Ashleigh released Cassie from her embrace and wiped the tears from her face before speaking. "Hey y'all remember Case right?"

"Yeah," Jewlz said with a hint of apprehension.

"Nice seeing you my man," Elijah said.

Case nodded to everyone then turned his attention and charm towards Cassie. "Your sister told me what happened to you. I'm sorry. I brought you these. I know they won't make you feel better but I thought they'd be nice to look at, while you get better," he said then smiled brightly.

"That's so nice of you. Thank you," Cassie said then looked up at Ashleigh. "I need to speak with you, in private," saying the last part under her breath.

"Oh my God, these are so beautiful. Thank you," Emma said as she walked in on the conversation and took the flowers out of Case's hand to everyone's surprise.

Case looked around the room and noticed nobody said anything so he played along as well. "No problem ma'am," he said.

"Aren't you a sweetheart and handsome too," she replied. "Tilda can you put these in some water immediately," she called out.

Emma instantly noticed the unfamiliar face standing at Jewlz side and quickly gave the girl the once over. "Cute but not cute enough," she thought to herself, at least not for her baby boy. She decided in that moment that she didn't like the young lady and was determined to make sure she didn't stay around long. Emma knew she could be intimidating to some of the most powerful men in the world. The young lady didn't stand a chance. "And who are you, might I ask?"

It was then that Jewlz realized he hadn't introduced his date. "I'm sorry everybody this is—."

"I was speaking to the young lady Josiah," Emma interrupted. "She does know her own name doesn't she?"

"Yes ma'am," the young lady spoke up nervously. "Hi I'm Kelsey."

"Mm Hmm," Emma said in an unpleasant and dismissive tone. "Well then dinner's ready everyone."

* * *

Khari hadn't said much and she had eaten even less, avoiding the table conversation by drinking away her sorrows. She felt anchored down. Drowning in her own pain with no way to come up for air and no one to save her. The man who should've been able to, hated her and she hated him more.

As Khari scanned the table, she felt alone. In a room full of family, she truly had no one to turn to. So she poured herself another glass of wine and disappeared in plain sight amongst all the chatter. Between the drinking and the pills, Khari was coming apart at the seams. Her life was a mess and no one even noticed. They hadn't noticed the weight loss from the stress. No one noticed as she slipped deeper into the darkness of depression nor the bruises on her skin from the abuse. "Or maybe they just don't care," she thought to herself.

Her mind instantly shifted to Sin. He was her only hope but he had been so standoffish with her. She could still feel his silence and see the way he looked at her with such disgust. His words were harsh and stung like salt into an open wound. That wound was her heart and it now yearned for what could have been. Sin was everything a woman wanted and everything Mason wasn't and she had blown it. He was her first love but she was his first heartbreak. That was something not easily forgiven, probably never now that he knew the truth about Bria. She couldn't blame him for hating her, she had earned it. But Khari missed the days of being young and in love with him. Things were far less complicated then. Sin treated her like a queen, always tending to her needs, in ways Mason had never been able to measure up to. She smiled remembering what it felt like to be touched by him and instantly became aroused.

"What you smiling about?" The sound of Mason's voice startled Khari from her daydream.

"Huh. Oh nothing," she replied not realizing she had been grinning so hard. Then before he could pose another question, she got up, without saying another word, grabbed her glass and headed straight for the bathroom. Her head was pounding suddenly. She placed her fingers on her temples and could feel them thumping. A mixture of stress, lack of food and alcohol had brought on a migraine. This headache would surely last all night if she didn't take something fast. Khari reached the bathroom but as she turned the knob she found the door locked.

Startled by the twisting of the doorknob, Ashleigh jumped to her feet, dropping the small bag of coke in her hand, spilling it out onto the bathroom floor. "Who is it?" she said nervously as she dropped to her knees trying to salvage as much as she could.

"Girl you alright," Khari asked hearing the noise coming from behind the door.

"Khari?" Ashleigh replied, looking up at the door, somewhat relieved that it was only her sister in law. She knew Khari was so spaced out most of the time, she would be easy to fool.

"Yeah, it's me. You sure everything is alright?" she asked.

"Umm...yeah" Ashleigh said as she made a frantic

attempt to clean up the mess. Finally, she slid the bathroom rug over the spilled coke, stood to her feet and flushed the toilet. She looked in the mirror, checking her appearance and making sure there were no traces of coke on her nose. She ran the water briefly before cutting it off and opening the door.

"Girl, what you hiding?" Khari questioned as soon as Ashleigh cracked the door.

Ashleigh quickly got on the defense. Her heart was beating so fast in her chest, she thought she would go into cardiac arrest. "What you mean?" Why you say that?"

"Your frequent trips to the bathroom all night," Khari's eyes were filled with suspicion. She stared Ashleigh up and down, something about her was different. Then it hit her. "Girl, you pregnant?" she blurted out in a half whisper.

"Pss. Girl hell no. Just the wine running through me. That's all," Ashleigh laughed as she stepped around Khari.

"Oh ok," Khari said as she entered the bathroom, closing the door behind her and quickly found a bottle of aspirin in the medicine cabinet. She shook out two aspirin into her hand, popped them into her mouth and chased them with wine. She stared at herself in the mirror. She hated the way she looked, she always had. Everyone always praised her beauty but she never saw what they did. All she could see were her flaws staring back at her. Her skin was too dark, her lips, hips and thighs not small enough. Her butt too big. She had her nose done but now that wasn't even good enough anymore, she hated it. She slammed the medicine cabinet shut and headed to the kitchen for a refill.

As she strolled pass the dining room, Khari could hear her husband's laughter. The sound of his voice made her cringe. Everything about him sickened her. "I hate him," she mumbled to herself once she entered the kitchen and began searching for a bottle of wine.

At that moment, Emma came strolling in the kitchen carrying an empty dish and placed it next to the sink. The two women's eyes met and Khari offered a forged smile. Emma didn't even bother to return the gesture. If there was anyone Khari hated more than Mason, it was the evil woman now standing across the room from her.

"I noticed you barely touched your food. Was it not to your liking?" Emma quizzed striking up conversation.

"Not much of an appetite," Khari admitted.

"It didn't affect how you felt about the wine though I see." Emma had been paying attention to Khari's behavior at the table and took the opportunity to mention it. "I'm a sucker for red wine myself," she said pretending she hadn't just insulted Khari. She walked right pass Khari and pulled a bottle from the wine chiller. "This particular one is my favorite. Chateau Lafite Rothschild," she said placing the bottle underneath the built in corkscrew on the counter. "It's to die for. Would you like a taste?" she asked trying to ease the tension a bit.

Khari knew that innocent, twinkle eyed look on Emma's face was disingenuous but she played along. "Sure," she said.

Emma filled Khari's glass then grabbed a glass and poured herself one. She eyed Khari closely, watching as she took her first sip. "It's so good right?" she spoke in a soft, friendly tone. But as usual, Emma's intentions weren't pure and she suddenly changed the tone of the conversation.

"So, did you enjoy your little lunch date with Yasin the other day?"

Khari froze with the glass to her lips as she watched the wickedness return to Emma's eyes. She felt like prey being swooped in on and Emma's fangs and claws were out.

"How long have the two of you been having these little rendezvous?" Emma asked with a smirk.

Khari was a deer in Emma's headlights. "I don't know what you are talking about," she said caught off-guard.

"Let's not play this little game honey. We both know you've never been a good liar," Emma taunted placing her glass down on the counter.

Khari was in utter shock. "You had me followed? How dare you. I am not one of your subordinates. I'm refuse to be under your thumb."

Emma's villainous laugh sent a chill through Khari. She took great pleasure in watching her squirm. "How many times must I prove to you, that I'm in total control of everything and everyone around me."

"What do you want? You want to have me around here running scared because you think you know something? I bet you can't wait to tell your little Mason all about it, huh. You know what, I don't even care anymore. Yes, I met with Sin. I asked for his help with finding my daughter. Since that doesn't seem to be of great importance to anyone else around here these days. So go ahead, tell Mason that." Khari placed her glass on the counter and began to walk away. She was tired of Emma and all her games. She was no longer willing to play along.

Emma began clapping her hands slowly in a condescending manner. "Finally, you've decided to get a little stand up for yourself. I like it," Emma nodded her head. "But here's the thing Khari, I know everything. I know the things that keep you awake at night. Your dirtiest secrets. Like the one about Sin being Bria's father."

Khari froze in her tracks. Her world had just came crushing down all in one moment. She couldn't feel her heart beating and a lump formed in her throat. She became cotton-mouthed as a jolt of fear surged though her body.

"Are you okay darling? You look a little pale," Emma teased noticing the look on Khari's face. The power had shifted back to her. "I overheard the two of you talking, the night Bria went missing. I told you that nothing and I do mean nothing gets by me. I always win," she insisted.

"So you've finally got what you wanted. A way to get rid of me. Why haven't you told him?" Khari asked. "Oh I know. You're just waiting for the right time to embarrass me in front of Mason. In front of the family."

"Now before you go having a nervous breakdown on me, I need you to relax and pay close attention to what I'm about to say to you. This little piece of information could either work for you or work against you," Emma said putting her fingertip to her lip. Khari could see the evil brewing in her monster-in-law's mind. "I want you to continue meeting with Yasin. Get close to him. Get him to trust you again. Hell sleep with him if you have to. I know that's not beneath you," Emma couldn't resist slinging an insult. "However, you will report back to me his every move. I want to know it all. Who he's with and what he's doing. If he takes a shit, I want to know the brand of tissue he uses. You got it? You give me what I want... and you get to keep on living your lie without having your day of atonement."

Khari felt trapped. She wanted to die. The hollowness inside of her was growing with each passing second. "Emma...Please, don't do this. I'll—."

"Oh stop it with the begging. Just when I thought you were getting a backbone," Emma shook her head, disappointed. "Just do as your told Khari, that's all." She closed the gap between them and grabbed Khari face, squeezing it tightly. "And if you even think about trying to fuck me over, I'll make your life more of a living hell then it already is," she threatened then released her face. "Oh, and try to smile a little more would you. My poor Mason doesn't need all your negativity around him right now, I mean his "daughter" is missing for crying out loud." Emma said lifting Khari's chin and smiling.

Khari pulled her head away and cringed at the amusement on Emma's face. She knew Emma was taking great pleasure in her torment. Rage burned in Khari's soul. "You're a sick bitch."

"No my dear, you're the one that's sick. You are the one who can barely make it out of bed without popping a pill to make it through the day. You think I don't know about your little magic candy that you've been over indulging in. You're the one who has my son thinking Bria is his child. When in fact she's not." Emma began to laugh again. "How convenient, a bastard father with a bastard child. Listen, you're nothing more than dead weight that my Mason has been carrying, don't ever think otherwise or get beside yourself. Now make yourself useful before I decide to rid this family of you altogether."

"You're the devil in the flesh," Khari said through tears.

"And you're weak. Lucky for Mason, he has me. What did you think, you were going to come into my family and disrupt it with your depression and questionable loyalty? I knew from day one you were a mistake and you weren't to be trusted."

"How dare you speak about trust, you conniving bitch," Khari seethed.

Emma moved closer to Khari's face. Their noses touched. "If I were you, I'd tread lightly around these parts, it would be wise to remain on my good side," Emma warned. "Just this time, I'll let your slick tongue slide."

Khari hated the ground Emma walked on, but what options did she really have. She knew the depth of evil the woman was capable of. Emma could and would do anything to destroy her. Which meant her threats weren't to be taken lightly. Khari had no other choice but to make a deal with the devil.

Emma began to walk away leaving Khari in her thoughts but turned around before exiting. "By the way, long sleeves will be appropriate from now on, I don't know why you insist on displaying those horrific looking bruises on your arms. Have some class about yourself," she said before disappearing into the dining room.

* * *

Mason sat alone in the corner of the room, watching the entire family share laughs and tell stories. The sound of his son giggling as he played with his nephews, suddenly caught his attention and for a moment he found himself staring. What normally would've been a joyous moment for him was anything but. He felt a tremendous sadness. The family wasn't whole. The sight of innocent children enjoying themselves made him long to see his daughter's face once again. He missed her and the guilt he felt weighed on his conscious. The father in him would no longer allow him to remain idle. Despite what Emma felt, it was time for Bria to come home. She was his daughter, which gave him the ultimate say so in the matter. His mother would just have to understand. He had lived most of his life obeying her commands and letting her guide his every step but not this time. He felt less of a man allowing her to dictate to him now. He was the mayor in waiting. He would soon hold the most powerful office in the city. He was done taking orders or directions from anybody. Mason rose from his seat and walked through the house until he came to his father's old office. He entered and locked the door behind him. The room was empty besides a few file cabinets against the wall. He walked over to the window and pulled his wallet out his back pocket. He removed the card he had gotten from Agent Mosley and dialed his number. Mason's heartbeat quickened upon hearing the first ring. He took a deep breath trying to calm his nerves. He wasn't quite sure if he was making the right decision. He could be opening a can of worms but he was desperate.

"Hello," Agent Mosley said as he answered the phone.

"Hello Agent Mosley, this is Mason Holloway."

"Mason? I didn't expect to hear from you," the agent replied somewhat surprised.

"Yeah. I hoped I wouldn't have to make this call," Mason admitted. "But I'm running out of options."

"I'm listening." Agent Mosley said intrigued.

"I need my daughter back home where she belongs," Mason explained. "I don't know if you have any children or are able to understand how difficult this has been on me and my wife. But I need my baby girl home. As soon as possible."

"I have children of my own," Agent Mosley admitted. "So I understand exactly how you feel. I would do anything to protect my children and keep them out of harm's way. But I'm still not sure the meaning of this phone call."

"If you can help me find my daughter and return her home safely. I would owe you, big time. As the soon to be mayor. A favor to me can go a long way," Mason said.

"What kind of favor, Mr. Holloway?" the agent asked.

"Anything. Just name it," Mason replied.

"Sin." Agent Mosley named his price. "I want Sin." Just the mere thought of it had Agent Mosley salivating.

"You get my daughter back agent, and he's yours. I'll give you everything you need to bury him under the jail. I promise you." Mason meant every word he said, trading Sin for Bria was a no brainer. He could tell the agent was interested but didn't give him a chance to answer. "That's the deal Agent. I look forward to hearing from you soon,"

Mason said then hung up the phone. His confidence was through the roof. There was no doubt in his mind that Agent Mosley would accept the offer. Soon he would have everything he wanted. Bria would be back in his arms and Sin would forever be out of his way.

CHAPTER 15

SIN FLOWED INTO THE lobby of the Mandarin Oriental in Manhattan. He had been summoned to the upscale hotel for an impromptu meeting with Reina. He had no idea she was back in town, so the call to meet came as a surprise. Sin wasn't too fond of surprises. Although she had refused to provide him with any details, Sin could tell by Reina's tone on the phone that whatever she needed to speak with him about was of urgent importance. He stepped onto the elevator and pressed the button for the penthouse. As the elevator doors opened onto the top floor, Sin stepped off and was immediately stopped by a large, muscular built bodyguard. He spread his arms out wide, allowing the man to frisk him. Finding him clean, the bodyguard opened the door to the penthouse suite and motioned for him to enter.

The Oriental suite was appropriate for a woman of Reina's powerful stature. Everything about it screamed five-star luxury. From the fine art and expensive furnishings to the large floor to ceiling windows that offered a beautiful bird's eye view of Manhattan.

Sin heard the sliding door of the terrace open. Then the clicking of Reina's high heels as she sauntered across the marble floor and into his view. She wore a black silk robe, that stopped just above her thighs and hugged her body. Her hair was up in a messy bun but somehow it still looked flawless. The diamonds in her ears and around her wrist were of the highest quality, reserved for an empress and spoke to her wealth. But the chrome .45 she held at her side told another story. She was the perfect contrast of beauty and power, elegance and danger.

"You son of a bitch," she screamed, her fiery temper on full display. "You have a chivato working for you. Which means he's working for me. Your shitty judgment has put me, my men and my business all at risk. I should kill you right now," she seethed.

Sin ran his hand over his face, exhaling as he shifted in his stance. "I have it under control. It's something I am taking care of," he said calmly.

"Taking care of?" she repeated. "You know how I take

care of these things, Yasin?" Suddenly her voice lowered to a threatening whisper as her eyes grew wide with excitement. "I put a bullet in the head of any man who talks to the police. I cut out his tongue and then I kill his whole family, uno a uno."

"Calm down," Sin demanded. "I said I have it under control. These things take time."

"Time you don't have," she warned as she lifted the gun and aimed it at him. "Give me a name," she commanded as she moved closer to him. "Give me a name Yasin. Right now or else," she shouted growing increasingly impatient.

The crazed look in her eyes didn't rattle Sin. He was well aware of her deadly reputation but still he remained firm and unshaken, feeling no fear. "I don't have a name to give you. But if I did, you know they would be dead already," Sin stated.

Reina knew he was telling the truth. Sin was a man of impeccable honor, that was something she admired about him. If he knew the identity of the informant within his organization, he certainly would have handled it by now.

"No name," she said shaking her head back and forth. "This does not please me to hear such a thing. But lucky for you Yasin, I have a name."

Sin sighed deeply as he prepared to hear the name of the person who had betrayed him. His heart pounded in anticipation No matter the name, he knew it was going to be someone he least expected. Someone close to him. Close enough that it would hurt to hear it. Maybe close enough that doing what was necessary would tug at his heartstrings but he wouldn't hesitate when the time came. "Who is it?" he asked.

"Ah. Ah. Ah," Reina smirked then traced the gun over Sin's chest.

He quickly smacked it away then grabbed her around the neck with both hands, staring in her eyes. "What is this some type of game to you? I'm not playing. Tell me who it is," he demanded in a low raspy tone.

Reina stared up at him and felt tingles run up and down her spine. Sin's aggressiveness was turning her on. She put her hand on his chest, softly caressed him as she moved them up to his neck. "How about I tell you everything in the morning," she said seductively then kissed him, exploring his mouth with her tongue and his body with her hands.

Sin stopped her suddenly and pulled his head back as he pushed her away. His heart and mind still belonged to a ghost. He hadn't been with a woman since Ariane and hadn't felt the urge to. "Can't mix business with pleasure ma," he said rejecting her advance.

"Never stopped us before," she retorted, stepping back and dropping the gun on the floor. "I wanna feel you inside of me," she purred then untied her robe, exposing her naked body to him. Her body felt like it was on fire as her hands made their way down between her legs. She rubbed on her clit then entered her two fingers inside her wet vagina.

Sin watched as she teased him. He was trying to fight against becoming aroused but the more he stared, the more the sexual tension in the room built. He could hear her juices dripping as she fingered herself. Reina spread apart her pussy lips, giving Sin a full view of her pinkness causing a bulge to grow inside his pants. Reina moved closer to him, pressing her body against his while sucking on his bottom lip. Once again Sin turned his head away.

"Why resist what we both know you want. You need to release all that built up tension," she said seductively. She could feel his rock hard manhood poking through his slacks. "You want the name or not," she dangled the carrot then kissed him.

He kissed her back, first hesitantly then more forcefully as she tugged at his belt, releasing his long and thick manhood from his pants. Sin pulled his shirt over his head. He could no longer resist his primal instincts or the natural attraction he felt towards her. He gripped her neck, kissing her aggressively as he tore her robe from her body. Her breast filled his hands as he licked and squeezed them with one hand while palming her ass with the other. Sin lifted her up, the two of them kissing wildly as he carried her into the bedroom. He laid her on the bed and she put her legs in the air and spread them wide open like a peace sign. A pulsating sensation shot through Reina's as Sin entered her and she began to moan loudly.

"¡Dios mío!" she cried out in pleasure as he stroked in and out of her. She knew speaking Spanish during sex excited him.

Sin's bronze, tattooed covered body glistened with sweat and his muscles flexed as he dove deep inside of her. The sound of their bodies slamming together rhythmically echoed through the room. He had so much sexual frustration built up, it made the sex between them more intense. Sin grabbed her hips, pulling them towards him, pounding her as he felt her body tense up.

Reina's toes curled and her body began to quiver as the orgasmic rush filled her body. "Te necesito Sin. Cógeme," she moaned and called his name loudly as she begged him to take her, Sin continued to stroke.

Suddenly he pulled out of her and flipped her onto her side. He laid down next to her and eased into her from behind. He rocked in and out of her as she rotated her hips in a circle, taking him deeper inside her. Sin closed his eyes and imagined he was making love to Ariane, he palmed her breast as his pace quickened. He could feel his climax building. Reina could feel it too and gyrated harder on his pole, throwing it back. She felt his body get tense, then one last power stroke before he pulled out. Sin let out a loud grunt as he exploded on her ass cheeks and Reina moaned as he rubbed it in.

They laid there for a moment until she caught her breath and he regained his strength. Then they picked up where they left off at and continued until the early hours of the morning.

* * *

The cool air of the morning greeted Sin as he joined Reina out on the terrace. She was staring out at the view of the Hudson River then turned to face him. They had fucked all night and Reina wore nothing but a smile and a white sheet as she puffed on a joint. Sin was in the process of getting dressed but currently only had on his slacks and a wife beater. Reina stared lustfully at him, wishing for one last romp in the sheets before he left her presence.

Sin noticed the look on her face but chose to ignore it. His mind was on one thing and it wasn't between her legs. "Before I go, I'ma need that name," he insisted.

"Are you sure you don't want to stay a little while longer?" she flirted.

"Nah. Back to business ma," he said as he put on his shirt and placed his watch on his wrist. The lustfulness was out his system. It was nothing more than a brief moment of weakness but the feeling had passed. "Now do you have a name or not," he asked seriously, growing tired of the games.

Reina felt tingles through her body. Sin was the only

man that wasn't afraid of her. She liked when he talked to her that way. His strength and aggression turned her own. The way he put her in her place made her feel like a delicate woman. Something no other man did for her. They all feared her power and dreaded the consequence of what might happen to them.

"How can I say no to such a beautiful man," she beamed then her face grew serious. "The name of the person in your crew that has been working with the Feds is Barkim." The name came rolling off her tongue with an accent.

Sin closed his eyes as he heard the name. It was like a punch to the gut. He sighed deeply before rubbing his hand across the top of his head. The revelation that Barkim was the Judas amongst them made his blood boil. "How do you know? How am I supposed to know what you're saying is the truth?" he asked needing assurance. He had inherited his father's sense of deliberateness. He wouldn't just kill his close friend on the word of his connect. He wanted to be sure. He needed proof.

"I have my sources in the bureau and they have never been wrong. Not once," she insisted. "If they say he's a confidential informant, then he is and has been for some time now."

Sin shifted in his stance but still had a suspicious look on his face.

"Since when has my word not been good enough?" she

asked seeing his facial expression. Reina exhaled a cloud of smoke then disappeared inside the hotel room only to return moments later holding a big yellow envelope. "Barkim was arrested a year ago by FBI and DEA agents after he sold two kilos of cocaine to an undercover agent in New Jersey."

"Barkim never was arrested," Sin said.

"As far as you know," she explained. "He agreed to help the feds and was immediately put back on the streets. They have been using him as an informant to gather information not only on you but on other major dealers as well. It's all in the paperwork," she said looking over at Sin as he went through the papers. She could she the look on his face changed as he read through them and realized that what she was saying was true.

The feeling was deeper than betrayal, it felt like defeat had washed over Sin. He was furious. He couldn't believe he hadn't picked up on Barkim's deceptive vibes earlier. The fake smiles, handshakes and hugs. With so much on his brain lately, from Ariane's death, Cassie's health to Bria's kidnapping, he had let a snake slither through the cracks in his organization. And now that oversight was gonna cost him everything. "This nigga Barkim is working with the Feds," he said to himself, still not able to believe it. Sin could only imagine the type of information Barkim had been feeding them. "What has he told them? What do they know?" he asked.

"Lucky for you not a lot," Reina told him. "He is either the biggest fuck up in the history or he is having second thoughts because he has yet to provide them with enough evidence for them to arrest you. But he has gotten some major players in other states taken down."

"A rat with a conscious," Sin said shaking his head. Everything about how he did business had to change, Barkim knew too much. In Sin's eyes, Barkim was a weak, disloyal coward and he had to be dealt with immediately. His only conflict was what to do about Ali. Sin had always thought of Ali as A-1. He was low key and handled his business discreetly, be it drug transactions or murder. But none of that mattered. "Did he know his brother was working with the Feds? How could he not know? Shit, I didn't know," Sin thought to himself. Either way he couldn't take the chance. They both had to go.

"I want you to kill that chivato, before he can put the both of us in jail," Reina said although it was no need to. Sin planned on doing that anyway. "I'm flying back to Miami tonight. I expect him dead by then," she expressed to which Sin just nodded in agreeance.

CHAPTER 16

A LIGHT DRIZZLE HAD BEGUN to fall as Barkim's car came to a stop in back of the barbershop. He exited his vehicle, scanning his surroundings out of habit. He had become extremely paranoid and jumpy as of late. He had begun to switch up the way he moved. Barkim never wanted to be caught slipping if Sin was to become aware of what he had been up to. Working with the feds was weighing heavy on him but he was in too deep to go back now. Barkim understood that once you were in bed with the federal government it was forever. He would always be under their command. Even after helping to bring down Sin and the rest of his crew, he would still probably have to do their dirty work. He might as well have been a government employee now. Agent Mosley really couldn't be trusted but he was Barkim's best chance of making it out of all this alive. But with the feds it was all about getting a conviction and they would use whoever they felt they had to, just to make it happen. Barkim could feel the sands in the hourglass, it was only a matter of time before Sin found out the truth. It was like his whole world had been turned upside down. He felt a way about crossing his longtime friend but it was all about survival at this point. He wasn't interested in doing the type of jail time the feds were handing out. "Better him than me," he told himself daily.

Barkim circled the car, his big Cuban link swinging as he moved. He paused for a homeless man in the alley, holding a cup in his outstretched hand. Barkim reached in his pocket and stuffed a few bills inside his cup then kept it moving into the backdoor of the barbershop. It was late at night, most of the lights in the shop were off and it was empty, except for his barber who had been waiting on him to arrive. Barkim had become so nervous he didn't like other patrons in the shop when he got his haircut. So he started paying his barber to stay late just for him.

"What up Black?" the barber greeted him by the name he was called around the way because of his dark chocolate complexion.

"I can't call it," Barkim replied. "How you?" he asked

with a pound then sat in the chair.

"Same ol', same ol'. Where's it at tonight my nigga. I know you know," the barber inquired.

"Shit," Barkim said leaning back in the chair. "I'on know. This bitch I been tryna fuck, just hit a nigga phone tho. I'm definitely about to go see about that." Barkim bragged pulling out his phone. "Look at the ass on this bitch," he said showing the barber a picture of the woman.

"Damn, she thicker than a muthafucka," the barber said than cut on his clippers.

The chime of the bell over the door echoed caught Barkim by surprise as Kyrie and the twins, Cairo and Egypt, walked into the barber shop. Barkim was in the middle of telling a story and his barber was listening without saying a word. He suddenly stopped speaking, his words seemingly stuck in his throat momentarily as he spotted the trio. An electric bolt of panic shot through him. The front door was supposed to be locked. The fact that it wasn't let Barkim know he had been set up. He knew they were there to kill him. His mind began racing trying to figure out how it would happen.

"What up B?" Kyrie said taking a seat in a chair directly in front of Barkim.

Cairo and Egypt sat down in empty barber chairs on both sides of Barkim. There was a brief moment of silence, the only sound was the buzzing of the clippers. Barkim's palms became sweaty as a nervous jolt of energy surged through his body.

"You tell me playboy," Barkim replied taking the temperature of the room while trying to appear calm on the outside, although his heart was pounding in his chest.

"Sin wants to holla at all of us. Something about the beef with the Italians. He wanna make a move on them later on tonight," Kyrie said.

"Why he sent you? Why he ain't call me himself?" Barkim questioned.

"He ain't really fucking with the phones right now," Kyrie explained without trying to say too much. "You know how he get," Kyrie said laughing.

"So he got you out here running around like an Uber driver, picking niggas up and shit."

Kyrie shrugged his shoulders, "Fucked up right? He could've at least gave a nigga some gas money," Kyrie joked.

Barkim laughed but he wasn't buying it. His paranoia had heightened his senses and he could feel something in the air. Although Kyrie appeared his normal self, the twins' facial expressions hadn't changed since they walked in. They hadn't even spoke and stared at Barkim with hooded eyes, seemingly ready to strike like twin cobras at any moment. Barkim gripped the gun on his lap, underneath the apron. He knew Sin had sent the youngster thinking it wouldn't alarm him. Had Beans walked through that door it would have been a dead giveaway. Still, Barkim made up his mind he wasn't going anywhere with them and he would shoot his way out of there if necessary. He thought about the forty thousand dollars in cash he had stashed at his crib. All he had to do was make it back home and he was skipping town tonight with just the clothes on his back. As for his younger brother Ali, he would get word to him as soon as possible to do the same thing. The hard part would be having to explain to him why he needed to.

Barkim remained calm, trying to disarm any suspicion that he was aware of what was happening. "Aight, as soon as I'm finished we can roll." Barkim continued to study the room. His heart pounded in his chest. He felt like the eyes of the grim reaper was on him. He could feel the heat coming off the twins as they stared at him.

"Nah. We gotta go right now," Kyrie insisted.

The barber turned the chair, almost as if to hinder Bakim's sight line. But through the mirror, Barkim could see Kyrie over his shoulder and caught him and one of the twins exchanging a look. Barkim instantly rose up out the chair, grabbing the barber around the neck then firing at Kyrie.

The bullets barley missed, instead going through the wall behind Kyrie. From there, shots rained in the shop as the twins pulled their guns and let off shattering all the mirrors in the shop. Barkim fired back as he moved towards the backdoor using the barber as a shield. Kyrie fired hitting the barber in the head, then in the chest. Blood splattered on Barkim's face. He released the barber from his clutches, letting his body fall lifelessly to the floor. Barkim fired twice more as he backed out the door, turning and racing for his car. He could hear the bullets hitting the door behind him as he ran. It wasn't until he made it to the car that he felt a burning sensation in his side. Looking down, Barkim saw the blood stain growing on the side of his shirt. He sped out the alley in reverse just as Kyrie and the twins came spilling out of the barber shop sending shots at him.

"Oh shit," he said nervously as a bullet came through the window right into the headrest of on the passenger side. Barkim drove into the night until the sound of gun fire became further and further in the distance. His heart was pounding, his mind was racing and he was bleeding. He knew he had to get out of the city immediately. "Fuck," he shouted as he banged on the steering wheel. "I should've been got the fuck outta here. This nigga Mosley not answering my calls and shit. He left me out here to die," he steamed. Barkim lifted his shirt to examine how bad his wound was and breathed a sigh of relief seeing he had only been grazed. "Fuck this shit," he said then pressed down on the gas, accelerating the car towards the expressway.

* * *

Sin leaned against the window with his hands in his pockets, staring out at the Brooklyn Navy Yard. Most of the buildings were empty or under construction and through Holloway Cement & Construction, Sin had access to most of them. He stepped back from the window, looking over at the two dead bodies of Barkim's men. They laid slumped against a few old, rusted oil drums. Sin's shirt was covered in blood. In the middle of the filthy warehouse, over Sin's shoulder, Ali tried to speak, but all Sin heard was a gravelly indistinct mumble. Ali had been beaten relentlessly and was tied to a chair, hunched over like an athlete after a crushing overtime loss. His lips moved but nothing he said was audible.

Sin heard footsteps coming from across the abandoned warehouse. When he turned around, Beans came bopping through the door carrying a brown paper bag.

"This nigga say something yet?" he asked pulling a breakfast sandwich out of the paper bag and offering it to Sin. When Sin shook his head, Beans shrugged his shoulder, tore at the wrapping and took a bite.

Sin looked down at his watch. It was six thirty in the morning. "Do the nigga look like he can say anything?"

"I didn't mean to break his jaw," Beans said with a mouthful of food.

Ali's face was bloody and swollen with his jaw hanging limply toward his chest. Sin and Beans had pulled him out of his apartment at four in the morning and Ali still had on the clothes he had worn from the night before. Only now they were covered in blood and torn. Beans walked over and knelt next to him, lifting him slightly, positioning his head so that he could place the little tube of smelling salt to his nose. Ali jerked back in the chair and began coughing, sending a spattering of blood down his chest. He squinted through swollen eyes and began to mumble once again. His words were impossible to make out, neither Sin or Beans would have understood them if he hadn't been repeating them throughout the brutal beating they had given him.

"I can't. He's my brother."

"Yeah, we know." Beans said then turned and looked at Sin. "This nigga won't break." In some twisted way he was proud of Ali.

Sin moved closer, now standing beside his battered victim. "Listen Ali, I'm gonna find him anyway. You just making it hard on yourself. Do yourself a favor and just tell me where he hiding at." He turned Ali's face to look at him. "Barkim is a dead man. There's nothing you can do to stop that. You understand me?" Ali slowly nodded his head. "Aight then, tell me where that snitching ass nigga is hiding and we could get this over with. He went against the crew, he didn't give a fuck about me, you, nobody. He didn't even give you a heads up. Why you protecting this nigga."

Ali tried to move his right arm, which felt broken, and groaned at the pain.

Beans yelled, “Tell us where he is, Ali! What the fuck is wrong with you!”

Ali tried to open his swollen eyes, as if straining to see who was yelling at him. “Fuck y’all. He’s my brother.”

Beans sighed deeply, throwing his hands in the air in frustration. Sin pulled the gun from his waist as Ali looked up at him, pleading for mercy through his swollen eyes. Sin stared back emotionless. He watched Ali begin to tremble and listened to his strained breathing. Sin raised the gun, his hand was calm and steady. He pressed the barrel against Ali’s forehead. Ali didn’t move or blink, feeling the cold steel. He didn’t even shake anymore. It was like he was prepared for what was to come next. He took one last deep breath then Sin fired once. The shot sounded like a hammer striking wood. Ali’s head flew backwards. The smell of Ali’s blood mixed with the foul odor of his shit suddenly filled the air.

“Damn” Beans shouted covering his nose.

Sin stared at Ali for a moment. He couldn’t help but feel a bit of sadness. “Damn Ali,” he thought to himself then calmly walked over and lifting his jacket off an oil drum. “Make sure they disappear,” he said to a pair of bodyguards pointing to the bodies of Barkim’s men.

“What about him?” Beans asked standing next to Ali.

“Put ‘em where he’ll be found. I want word to get back to Barkim, that I ain’t playin,” Sin told him.

Beans stopped as the two of them exited. A smile

creased his lips.

"Nigga what you smiling about?" Sin asked.

"Yo, he wouldn't betray his brother. You gotta respect the nigga for that."

"Yeah, I just wish Barkim was as solid as brother Ali," Sin retorted.

CHAPTER 17

BARKIM'S HEART REVVED WHEN HE heard the knock on the door. He picked the gun up off the night stand and crept over to the window. He peeked through the curtains and saw just a single person standing out on the balcony of the motel. It was the person Barkim was expecting. He walked over to the door, quickly unlocking it. He stuck the gun out the door into the face of his visitor.

"You came by yourself," he questioned aggressively.

"Yeah."

Barkim swung the door wide open, snatching the visitor into the room and locking the door. "Sit down," Barkim ordered aiming his gun. "How I know you ain't tell nobody you were coming to meet me?"

"You don't," Lil Smoke said as he sat on the bed and scanned the room. "Man, you called me and said you had some information about my pops. So here I am. Now what's up?"

Barkim took a seat in a chair across from Lil' Smoke, while still keeping his gun on him. He was about to disappear for good but he had one last play to put together. Sin wanted him dead and after the shootout in the barbershop the feeling was mutual. He could never show his face again. So getting close enough to kill Sin himself was impossible. But Lil' Smoke was a move Sin would never see coming.

Lil' Smoke face was set in a grimace. He didn't feel right meeting up with Barkim. He heard the rumors in the street that Barkim was a snitch but the allure of learning more about his father was too strong for the teenager to ignore.

"Whatchu know about what happened to your father?" Barkim quizzed the young man.

Lil' Smoke jogged his memory for a second before speaking. "I know he was murdered by some niggas from Uptown or some Jamaicans. Some shit like that. Nobody really knows for sure," he said.

"What if I told you I know who killed him?" Barkim notice Lil' Smoke's icy glare soften some. The young man sat straight up, unable to contain his interest. "What if I told you, his two best friends killed him?" Barkim said.

"My uncle Sin. And Beans?" Lil Smoke uttered slowly. "Nah," he stood up preparing to walk out the door.

"I'm telling you the truth," Barkim insisted. "Your pops was the man in the hood. He used to put that real work in. That's how he got his name, Gunsmoke. He was getting money before all of us. He put us all on. Sin and Beans never liked being under him. You know how Sin is," he gestured towards Lil' Smoke. "He always got to be in charge."

Lil' Smoke shook his head in disbelief, not willing to except that what Barkim was saying was the truth. "I heard my pops, Sin and Beans all started together."

"Who told you that, Sin?" Barkim said with a raised eyebrow then shook his head. "Why you think Beans keep his distance from you and your grandmother. Sin only look out for y'all out of guilt," Barkim stressed.

"Man, you trippin'. How I know you ain't just saying all this shit to get in my head? Word on the street is you snitching."

"You got any paperwork to back that up. Niggas just hating. And when the hate don't work they start telling lies. If you don't believe me about your pops, cool. I just thought you should know the truth about people you think is your family." Barkim could see the look of confusion on Lil' Smoke face. He had definitely planted the seed. He unzipped the backpack pulled out a stack and handed it to Lil' Smoke. "Good looking shorty."

Lil' Smoke looked at the money in his hand then back at Barkim. "I got something you might want to know too," he said. "They found your brother Ali's body in Brooklyn last night. Somebody did him real dirty," he expressed.

Barkim's heart dropped into his stomach. "You see how Sin do family right," Barkim stated. There was no doubt in his mind who had killed his brother.

"You got any advice of what I should do?" Lil Smoke said as he made it to the door with Barkim following close behind.

Barkim reached in the small of his back and pulled out a .38 revolver. "Take this. You might need it," Barkim handed him the gun then closed the door behind Lil' Smoke.

Barkim felt sick as he raced over to his cell phone and quickly dialed his brother's number. The phone just rang and rang and rang. He took the phone away from his ear and slammed his fist into the table repeatedly. "No! No! Nooo!" he shouted. The news that his younger brother, Ali's body had been found was too much for him to take. He threw his phone across the hotel room and began swinging his fist wildly at the air as tears swelled in the wells of his eyes. He put his back against the wall, sliding down until he reached the floor and began crying like a baby. He wept like he never had before in his life. Although Sin had pulled the trigger,

Barkim knew he was just as responsible for what happened to Ali. Barkim knew it wouldn't be long before other members of his family turned up dead or went missing. Just the thought made him eject everything from his stomach. He thought by making a deal with the feds, he could somehow escape the inevitable consequences of the game. The terrible cost of those decisions didn't fully register with him at the time, only now did he see the peril of the situation. The deal he had made with Agent Mosley couldn't save him. He would have to pay the ultimate price with his own blood. Barkim sighed deeply. He was mentally exhausted and physically drained.

"How'd I let that muthafucka play me," he said to himself as he thought about Agent Mosley. "I let him use his bag of tricks on me."

The burden of his own betrayal was overwhelming but his hatred for what Sin had done to his brother made his disloyalty feel somewhat justified if only briefly. Still he knew he couldn't outrun his choices, he could no longer be a puppet for the feds and Sin would never stop hunting him until he was dead. He knew first-hand how ruthless and calculated he could be when he was angry. This shit is never going stop. There's only one way to put an end to all this shit, he thought to himself. In that very moment Barkim had decided to take his fate into his own hands. He pulled his gun from his waist and slowly ran his finger along the barrel as tears continued to fall from his eyes. After a few seconds had passed, he opened his mouth and rested the gun on his tongue. Barkim's heart knocked rapidly against his rib cage as he tasted the cool steel of the gun. He had used it plenty of times, taking other men's lives without so much as a second thought. Now here he was on the floor of the rundown motel room, isolated from the rest of the world and at the mercy of his own weapon. The irony of it made him smirk a bit. "The Feds. The Italians. Agent Mosley. Sin, especially Sin. Fuck em' all," was the final thought that ran through his mind just before the bullet did.

CHAPTER 18

SIN STOOD IN A CIRCLE of his bodyguards giving out orders when Beans tapped him on the shoulder. "Here comes your sisters," he pointed.

Sin looked up and saw Ashleigh pushing Cassie in her wheelchair. They were coming towards the group of men, along with Case at their side.

"Your sister really sporting this nigga," Beans chuckled.

"I'm glad he came. I been wanting to talk to him anyway," Sin said.

Beans face twisted into a snarl. "About what!"

"I want to feel him out," Sin spoke smoothly. "I'm thinking about keeping' the nigga close. We could use a few more soldiers on the team. He seems like a thorough nigga. Shit, we already saw he don't hesitate to let it fly plus, we getting a lil' thin around here," Sin said looking around. Beside him and Beans, Kyrie and the twins were all that was left of the main crew. The war with the Italians had cost Sin a lot of familiar faces. Most of the men under his command belonged to Reina. He definitely needed to start recruiting and building his army up again.

"Fuck that nigga," Beans instantly dismissed the idea. He wasn't feeling it or Case, at all. "We don't need no random niggas on the squad," he leaned in while talking low.

"I'm just trying to get a read on 'em. If Ashleigh gonna keep bringing him around. We gotta know more about this nigga," Sin explained

"I know enough to know I don't feel 'em. Something about him I don't like."

"It wouldn't happen to be that he fucking with Ash. Would it?" Sin joked.

Beans smirked. "I'm 'bout to head up the block with Kyrie and them before this parade shit start. I'm not about to be around a nigga I don't fuck with. But let me know when you ready for a bullet to be put in his head," he said walking off just as the group made it to where Sin was standing.

Sin laughed at Beans' comment then turned to greet his sisters as they walked up on him. "Looking good," he said to

Cassie then leaned over and kissed her on the cheek.

"Thank you. The doctor's said I'm healing slow but steady," she replied.

Sin looked at Ashleigh and caught her staring up the block in the direction Beans had walked. "What's up with you Ash? How you been?" Sin couldn't put his finger on it but it was something different about her.

"I've been fine and you?" she answered.

"You know me," he said.

"You remember Case, right? From daddy's funeral," she said.

"Yeah what's up?" Sin said giving him a pound. "I been wanting to holla at you."

"No better time than the present," Case replied.

"We gonna go meet up with the rest of the family and get ready for this parade to start," Cassie said wanting to give the two men the privacy.

Ashleigh didn't immediately move looking towards Case to see if everything was cool. He nodded at her and she kissed him on the lips before wheeling Cassie away.

"I appreciate what you did for me at the cemetery that day," Sin acknowledged. "That was some real shit."

"It's all good. I just did what came natural," Case said playing it cool.

"What came natural," Sin repeated nodding his head. "Ok, I like that." He rubbed his hand over his chin. "What my sister been telling you about me?" Sin asked

"Nothing really but I ain't blind, deaf or dumb," Case admitted. "Your name ring bells in the street."

Sin knew Case was probably lying about Ashleigh. She ran her mouth like a sportscaster and it had to be worst when she was pillow talking. Sin admired how Case didn't throw her under the bus. If she had told him something, Case was keeping it to himself.

* * *

Lil Smoke emerged from the subway station and pushed his way through the horde of people. Parade watchers were lined up two and three deep along the curb, leaving barely enough room on the sidewalk for foot traffic. Lil' Smoke managed to squeeze his way out to the street just in time to see the new mayor waving to the crowd from atop a slow-moving float as he passed.

Mason Holloway was surrounded by his entire family. Khari stood next to him holding their young son in her arms as he stared at the large crowd with big wide eyes. A mob of police surrounded them and their contingent as the parade moved towards City Hall. Behind the mayor's float, two cops on horseback rode closely followed by a local high school's marching band, beating drums, clashing cymbals and blaring horns.

Lil' Smoke quickly moved along the street in the

opposite direction of the parade, searching for Sin. Once the marching band passed, all that remained were clusters of people walking down the center of the street. At that moment, Lil' Smoke spotted Beans on the other side of the street. He reached into the front of his hoodie, gripping the taped handle of the .38 special he was carrying. Lil' Smoke's heart was racing and his breaths quickened. He felt as though he had just been running. He stood still trying to gain the courage to pull the gun from his hoodie. Just as he went to cross the street Kyrie stepped in front of him, cutting him off. Lil' Smoke backed up, startled then he saw the look of recognition appear in Kyrie's eyes.

"Yo, you Sin's lil' man right?" he asked.

"Ye—Yeah," Lil' Smoke hesitantly answered.

"You good?" Kyrie asked.

"Uh Huh."

Despite his words, Kyrie saw the conflicting emotions on his face. He glanced at the street then back at Lil' Smoke. "You sure?" he asked him.

Lil' Smoke remained silent. He looked across the street then back at Kyrie. "I'm just looking for my uncle Sin. You seen 'em?"

"He a couple blocks up," Kyrie pointed up the street.

"I ain't see him," Lil Smoke said, scanning the street again.

"He staying close to the family. Making sure nothing

happens. You want me to take you to him?" Kyrie asked.

"Nah," Lil' Smoke said. He spotted two more of Sin's guys blending in with the crowd. "Damn, y'all deep out here, huh?" He was growing more nervous by the minute. He really hadn't thought his plan through. He truly didn't know why he had come there.

"Yeah," Kyrie admitted.

"Why y'all out here protecting them anyway. I thought Sin don't rock wit' his brother like that. Ain't the Holloways on some uppity, bourgeois type shit."

"Nah, they ain't all like that," Kyrie laughed, and then he seemed to rethink the question. "Well, yeah, a little, I guess," he said. "C'mon, I'll let Beans know you here. You stay close to him until you see Sin."

"Nah I'm gonna fall back," Lil' Smoke said as he took a step back from Kyrie. "This ain't my type of crowd anyway." Lil' Smoke looked up and down the street one more time. All he saw were people watching a parade, and Sin's men watching the people. "I'm just gonna dip."

"You want me to tell Sin I saw you," Kyrie asked and stuck out his hand out.

"Nah, it wasn't that important," Lil' Smoke lied then gave him a pound before heading back towards the subway. When he made it to the steps, he stopped short at the sight of a black four-door parked at the curb midway down the block. Something about the men inside caught his attention.

They didn't appear to be watching the parade like everyone else. "Maybe their undercovers," he immediately thought to himself but for some reason he couldn't turn away. Lil' Smoke watched the car from the subway entrance until the men stepped out onto the street. Each man had one arm tucked inside their trench coats. He knew then that the men weren't cops, they were mafia henchmen. Probably there to do what he had come to do. All Lil' Smoke had to do was look the other way, walk down the stairs and let the hitmen do their job. He started to do just that but he was still having an internal struggle. One part of him wanted to kill Sin but another part of him still had love and respect for him. "Fuck it let nature take its course," he uttered to himself then started to jog down the steps before stopping abruptly. "Man what if this nigga Barkim was lying. It'll be fucked up to let them kill Sin over a lie," Lil' Smoke said. He shook his head then turned around, waiting until the henchmen rounded the corner before breaking into a full out sprint. A few blocks later, Lil Smoke looked at a big monitor that showed the stage. Mason stood between his wife and his son and he could see the rest of the family near the rear of the stage but couldn't spot Sin. He scanned the street once more finally spotting Sin and Case. They were talking with each other as if oblivious to everything going on around them.

When Lil' Smoke saw them, he ran out into the street

trying to get Sin's attention but didn't make it more than a few steps before running right into Beans.

"What you doing out here?" Beans said with a suspicious look as their eyes met. Before Lil' Smoke could reply, Beans eyes grew wide as he looked towards the sidewalk. He saw one of the henchmen leaping the barricade like a hurdler with a gun the size of a small cannon in his hand. The man's face told his murderous intention and as his feet hit the ground, he began spraying wildly.

As chaos ensued all around, people began to scatter like roaches with the lights on. Women grabbed their children, running and screaming. On stage, Mason was sprawled over his wife, who held their son in her arms, clutching him tightly. Their security detail quickly whisked them off the stage and out of harm's way, along with the rest of the family.

Sin pulled his gun from under his jacket when he heard the shots and Case did the same but neither were sure exactly where the shots were coming from. All they could see were people scrambling around.

Beans pushed Lil' Smoke to the floor and started firing with guns in both hands at the first henchmen, hitting him in the chest and dropping him. But Beans' gun work was no match for the other three henchmen who began firing nonstop. Their bullets hitting Beans multiple times, airing him out in the middle of the street. Shots ripped through his stomach, leg and chest. Beans' whole body twisted around. He took a few stumbled steps then collapsed. His head slamming into the concrete. His body jerked violently then went still.

Lil' Smoke was in shock seeing Beans body drop. He turned back to see one of the henchmen coming towards him. The man was locked in. Smoke reached into his hoodie but fumbled the gun as he pulled it out and it was kicked out of his reach by a passerby.

When the first bullet hit the man in the chest, it stopped his progress towards Lil' Smoke. He looked up surprised then the next bullet hit him in the head and he crumpled to the ground. Lil' Smoke was still in the middle of the street. He looked up and saw Sin holding a gun, after that it started raining bullets. It was like a sudden downpour of gunfire and hysterical cries. Bodies hit the ground like raindrops in the storm of movement and noise. People ran in every direction, some of them slithering across the ground like snakes looking for the safety of a doorway or storefront.

Lil' Smoke wanted to run for cover as well, shook by the sound of gunshots going off everywhere. Sin crouched over him with his head up like a turtle. He held Lil' Smoke down by the back of the neck with one hand and fired his gun with his free hand.

Case scanned the sidewalk in the direction Sin was firing. He saw a few more henchmen pop up with a gun in each hand. He fired in their direction, they fired back. Their weapons jerked with each shot. One of Sin's bodyguards joined in. He only managed to get off a few shots before a bullet struck him in the head. He fell face first onto the street, his gun coming to rest at his side as he laid dead at Case's feet.

Suddenly it went quiet. The gunfire seemed to go silent and there was only the sound of screams and people's feet pitter patting across the ground as they ran. Kyrie appeared in the middle of the street with a gun in his hand and the twins, Cairo and Egypt at his side. At that moment the silence ended and the shooting began again. Sin looked in the direction of the gunfire and saw a group of men charging up the sidewalk and another group in the middle of the street. They all moved in a crouched down position behind a hail of bullets.

Two of the bullets hit Cairo in her chest and she let out a squeal. Kyrie caught her in his arms as she went down. "Cairo!" he shouted as he held her. Her empty eyes stared off into space. There were two big holes the size of a small plates in her chest and her breaths were faint, if even at all. Blood leaked from the side of her mouth as her head slumped over to the right and her body went limp.

Egypt gasped, unable to contain her loud howling cry. Tears ran down her face. The sight of her twin's lifeless body sent a searing pain through her chest. Filled with rage, she squeezed off rapidly, sending shot after shot, dropping a few of the men. Kyrie picked up Cairo's gun and stood over her firing wildly.

"Stay down," Sin instructed Lil' Smoke as he rose to his feet and continued shooting, dropping bodies.

Suddenly a truck skidded to a stop in the middle of the shootout separating Sin's crew from the other henchmen and shielding them from the gunfire. The door flew open and one of Sin's bodyguards called out to him. "Sin c'mon!"

At the same time an army of cop cars swooped down on the scene with sirens screaming appearing out of the side streets. The cops jumped out, guns in hand, shouting from behind the protection of their cars. It seemed that the shooting wouldn't last much longer, not with sirens blaring and more police cars arriving by the second.

Sin raced over to Beans, calling his name. "Oh shit, c'mon get up my nigga, please." Beans laid face down in the street with streams of blood running from his body. Sin rolled him over, there was blood gushing from the wounds in his stomach and chest. Beans groaned then let out a painful shriek like a wounded animal. He was doing bad, bleeding everywhere but he wasn't dead yet.

"Yo, somebody help me!" Sin screamed at the top of his lungs but nobody could hear him over the gunfire. "Help!" he shouted again as he tried to left Beans off the ground. This time Case raced over to him. "Help me get him to the truck," he pleaded.

Case hesitated momentarily. The scene reminded him of how he tried to save Dre. He looked around contemplating putting a bullet in both Sin and Beans but he knew he wouldn't make it five steps before he was killed himself. He decided to help get Beans up and to the car, placing him into the backseat. He was now covered in blood himself.

"C'mon, hop in. I gotta get him to Doc, ASAP!" Sin shouted to Case.

Hearing the name Doc made Case freeze. He knew exactly who Sin was referring to. He couldn't go to Doc's with Sin. The Doc would surely recognize him from the night Ashleigh brought him there with a dying Dre. Sin would have too many questions. If he put two and two together, he would know that Case was the one robbing his spots out in Brooklyn a few months back. He didn't need anything spoiling his plans right now. "Nah. Go ahead. I'm gonna stay here and hold it down," he told Sin then closed the door as the truck pulled off.

Lil' Smoke felt vulnerable on the ground, in the middle of the street, in the open, amid the gunfire. Deep within him something powerful was urging him to run and hide but he didn't know which way to go. It was now a three-way shootout between Sin's crew, the mafia hitmen and the police.

"We gotta get out of here," Case shouted to Kyrie and

Egypt. "Let the cops shoot it out with them muthafuckas."

Egypt looked down at her twin sister's body. She dropped to her knees next to her in the middle of the street with no concern for her own life. She began crying uncontrollably, tears and snot ruining down her pretty face.

"C'mon let's go," Kyrie yanked her by the arm.

She pulled away refusing to move. She didn't want to leave her sister there. Their bond was like none other, unbreakable. Born together, Egypt felt they would always go out together. And now she felt cheated in death. She rose to her feet and began shooting again but at no one in particular. She only wished for a bullet in return. One to hit her in the heart, maybe that would stop all the pain she felt. She wanted to go out in a blaze of glory and die on the street right next to her sister. But Kyrie wasn't about to let that happen.

"What the fuck are you doing? Let's go!" he grabbed her forcefully by the arm, this time refusing to let her out his grip as he dragged her away from the scene and they blended in with the crowd.

When Lil' Smoke realized all Sin's crew were escaping, he followed suit. He darted from the street to the sidewalk into one of the doorways and pressed his body against the brick wall. The cops and the henchmen were still shooting. Lil' Smoke's only thoughts were to make it out of there alive then he wanted an explanation from Sin. He needed him to explain what happened between him and his father.

On the street everyone seemed to realize at once that the gunfire had suddenly ceased. Lil Smoke peeked his head out from where he had been taking cover and saw the mafia henchmen all dead on the street. A sense of calm descended on him followed by a bit of sadness as he spotted Cairo's body laid out. Lil' Smoke scanned over the street, he saw that there were more bodies, innocent ones, people who came to see the parade and watch the mayor's inauguration. Amongst the bodies, he spotted a lady clutching a small child in her arms, it looked like she had died trying to shield the child from the gunfire. Everyone's attention seemed to fall on the lady and child at the same instant. To Lil' Smoke, it appeared that everyone was looking for some signs of life and felt relief when the little child rose to her feet. She was covered in her mother's blood and started crying at the top of her lungs.

There was still much commotion and shouting, now mostly from the cops, who were swarming everywhere, but it seemed to Lil' Smoke that the street had suddenly gone silent. He stood in the doorway and looked behind him into what appeared to be a cigar shop. A dozen people who had been curled up in corners and hidden behind doors and counters were standing and moving toward him and the shattered window, wanting to get a glimpse at the mayhem out on the street. When Lil' Smoke turned back to the street he found waves of cops in uniform shouting orders and arresting everyone in sight. When another pair of uniforms started for the storefront, Lil' Smoke slipped into the crowd, and then into the back of the store, where he found an exit to an alley. For a while he hid behind a dumpster. When the noise on the streets began to die down, he headed back towards the subway and the train that would take him home.

CHAPTER 19

THIS WAS BAD AND SIN knew it as he paced the room, grinding his fingers together. He was covered in blood and with every step he took, his anxiety increased. He felt helpless with his best friend in the next room fighting for his life. It had been over an hour since Beans was brought to The Doc and still no word on his status. The wait was driving him crazy. The Doc was the best at what he did but he would need a miracle to save Beans. He had lost so much blood on the way there. Sin feared the worst while hoping for the best. He felt like he was fighting a war that he couldn't win. People he cared about were being slaughtered left and right. That was different for The Commission. It didn't matter how many mafia men he killed they kept coming in waves like off an assembly line. There was no love, no emotions on their side. That was his Achilles' heel and he no longer felt like he was giving as good as he got. A united Commission seemed impossible to defeat. They were too strong.

The reports about the shootout at the inauguration seemed to be on loop, on every news channel. Lucky for him, they were blaming everything on the mafia henchmen that laid dead in the street. He couldn't even enjoy the smallest of victories. He was at the mercy of the clock on the wall. All he could do was wait. He wasn't really a praying man, but he found himself doing more and more of it lately. Now he was coming to the Lord for Beans. He prayed for the Doc to save him. Sin knew he nor Beans deserved God's mercy. The life they lived didn't deem them worth. In reality Beans death would be just due. So would his own, it was the fitting end result. But Beans was more than a friend to Sin. He was his brother, his right arm. When the thought of shooting crossed Sins mind, Beans had already let of two shots for him. That's how they always rocked. One hand washed the other. He was truly the only other family Sin had besides his mom for a very long time. Before there were any Holloways in his life, Sin and Beans had held each other down, grew into men with one another with no one to groom them but themselves. Truly self- made men, and they both took pride in that.

* * *

2006

"This better not be no bullshit," Sin said looking up as he placed the brick back into the duffle bag and zipped it up. "If this shit goes wrong, It's back to them corners, grinding it out. My pops don't give a fuck, son or no son. He about his business. One fuck up, no more bricks. You feel me."

"Chill. I'm telling you, these niggas is one hunnit," Smoke said as they sat in the car. He rubbed his hand over his dark chocolate skin. "Now that you plugged in, we can really start eating out this muthafucka. Fuck all that lil' shit, we gonna be getting it like big dawgs. I can't wait to start shittin' on these niggas fa real."

Sin cracked a smile then nodded towards the window. "There go Beans right there," he said watching him cross the street to the car.

Beans jumped into the backseat and Sin tossed the bag on his lap. Beans unzipped it and saw eight bricks stacked up looking back at him. "Damn my nigga, you wasn't lying. Ya pops is heavy," he said in amazement. "Now who these niggas we going to meet up with it again?" he asked zipping the bag back up.

"Some niggas Smoke know from Brownsville," Sin replied.

"Yeah, they my niggas. Cool ass Jamaicans. I used to cop

trees from them all the time," Smoke assured them. "Shit'll be real smooth. They ain't even on no rah-rah shit. Straight money getting playa types."

"They getting money like you say, then they ain't all playa. Gotta be some type of gangsters to fuck with this kind of weight," Beans said sitting the bag next to him as they drove through the city.

They pulled up in front of a corner store. It was late and everything was quiet on the block.

"Yo, you sure this the spot? This shit look closed," Sin said peering out the window.

"Yeah this is it," Smoke said. "Pull around the corner," he instructed.

Sin did as he said then pulled to the curb and parked. He pulled his gun from the middle console and made sure it was off safety.

"Yo, I told you it ain't even like that fam. Everything smooth. In and out. These my peoples." Smoke told him.

"These ya peoples not mine," Sin reminded him then tucked his gun in his waist. "Yo, Beans you strapped?"

"Always," Beans answered from the backseat, cocking his gun.

They hopped out the car and walked to the side door of the store. Smoke knocked on the door in a rapid rhythm and it immediately opened. A slim brown skinned dread head kid answered the door with a blunt hanging from his lips and a gun in his hand. He wore a pair of sweatpants with one leg rolled up and a Bob Marley t-shirt and Jamaican flag wrist band on.

"What's good Dread?" Smoke greeted him.

"Wah gwan?" he said dapping Smoke up, letting him pass then immediately stopping Sin and Beans. He attempted to pat Sin down but Sin knocked his hand away. "Easy star," the dread said. "Be cool, every mon ah get check."

Sin eyed Smoke suspiciously. "Everything'll be smooth. No rah-rah shit right?" he reminded him of what he had said in the car. Smoke shrugged his shoulders. Sin lifted his shirt showing the dread his weapon. "If I can't bring this in, this don't come in either," he said lifting the duffle bag in his hand.

Smoke quickly interjected before the situation escalated. "They good dread. I promise They my breadren," he said.

"Me deal wit you. Smoke, me nah deal wit ya bruddas. Me can get the link fa you, but me nah know ya breadren dem," the Jamaican said.

"We don't know you either," Beans said instantly not feeling the situation.

"Everybody be cool," Smoke said.

"We came to do business," Sin said. "Now you wanna do business or not," he asked the dread kid.

"Yo where Donovan at?" Smoke asked.

"Every ting cris," Donovan's voice could be heard before he

emerged from the backroom. "Let di mon en em tru," he instructed then waved them forward.

The trio entered in the backroom where Donovan sat eating a plate of Oxtails, surrounded by a group of men. He wore a Rasta turban head wrap, a pair of dark shades and sported an unkempt beard tate had specks of gray in it. "no problems. the yout dem get a lil' over irate sometime, every ting cris" he told them.

There was a sense of uneasiness in the room that could be felt by all. Sin was thoroughly inspecting his surroundings, he had already noticed the guns poking out from the men's waist and had mapped out an exit plan in his mind if things went wrong. He didn't have a good feeling about these cats. The look on Beans' face said the same thing.

"every ting cool now" Donovan said noticing the stoic look on Sin's face. "Wah gwan, you must be the boy Sin dem? Ya breadren Smoke speaks real highly of you," he acknowledged to which Sin just nodded.

"I told you, these my peoples," Smoke turned to Sin with a smile on his face, trying to get him to relax a bit.

"I appreciate all the pleasantries but I'd prefer to get right to business, so we can be on our way. I'm sure a businessman like you can understand that," Sin said.

"Yeah, yeah. All that's cool but before we do that. I need to take a piss right quick," Smoke announced. "I know you got a bathroom in this muthafucka Donovan," he asked looking

around.

"Right tru that door," Donovan pointed.

"Hurry the fuck up nigga," Sin said through a clenched jaw, clearly upset with Smoke. "I ain't trying to be here no longer than I have to."

Smoke nodded then disappeared through a door that separated the front of the store from the back.

The room fell silent and after a few minutes passed, it began to feel awkward. Beans eyes continued to shift, scooping the whole scene. He was watching Donovan's men and they were watching him. Something about the whole play wasn't right. He knew Sin felt it to. "Where the fuck is this nigga Smoke? What's taking him so long?" he uttered to Sin.

"Him soon come," Donovan said with a smirk on his face.

"It's all good," Sin spoke up. "I got the bricks right here. If you got the money, we can handle this little business while we wait."

Donovan sat his plate to the side and wiped his hands on his pants. "Let me see tha tings now," he asked and nodded to one of his men. The man walked over and Sin handed him the bag then he handed it off to Donovan. He unzipped it and his eyes lit up seeing the white bricks inside. He picked one up then lifted what could only be described as a baby machete, used for cutting mangos or sugarcane, and poked a hole into the brick. He dipped his finger in it and rubbed the coke along his gums, they instantly became numb.

"Bombaclot," Donovan said showing his satisfaction.

"Yo, where the fuck is Smoke," Sin now questioned aloud, his head on a swivel.

"No worries," Donovan said calmly. "Smoke had to go on fah a minute," Donovan laughed then nodded to one of the men in his group. "Pay di mon," he said.

Then all hell broke loose. A burst of bright white flames lit up the backroom as the shooters let off a hail of bullets, spraying everything in sight. Sin dove head first behind a stack of wooden pallets. Beans took cover behind some wood crates. It was then that both men realized they had been set up by Smoke. He had left them to die.

"Sin behind you!" Beans shouted.

Sin spun around with his gun in hand. The benchman was a split second too late. Sin fired first, airing him out, sending him crashing through a bunch of boxes.

Beans crawled across the floor over to Sin then popped up firing, laying down a few more men. Sin let his gun bark, the bullet catching a dread kid in the neck. The dread's weapon fell from his hands as he reached for his neck. Sin let off two more shots that tore through his head, killing him.

Donovan snatched the duffle bag and darted through the door that Smoke had disappeared through.

"Let's get the fuck outta here," Beans shouted to Sin now that all Donovan's men laid dead.

"Nah, I ain't leaving without out those bricks," Sin said as

he bolted through the door after Donovan with Beans on his heels.

Now on the street Sin and Beans ducked for cover, squat walking from car to car as Donovan's bullets rained down on them. Sin popped up and fired, hitting Donovan in the arm. He dropped his gun as he fell to the ground. Beans raced up the block towards where Donovan had fell between cars but when he got there the Jamaican was nowhere to be found.

"Fuck," Beans said aloud disappointed that he had gotten away but as he turned back towards the street Donovan popped up with the machete and swung it. Beans wasn't quick enough to get completely out the way as the blade slashed the side of his face, opening up a nasty wound.

"Pussy ya dead!" Donovan shouted as Beans grabbed for his face feeling the burning sensation.

Donovan lifted the blade again but didn't get a chance to use it.

Boom! Boom! Boom! Boom!

All four shots from Sin's gun hit Donovan square in the chest throwing him back against the SUV behind him. Sin fired once more then his body fell slumped to the ground. Sin walked over to check on Beans. "You ok?"

Bean nodded his head no. "It feels like my face is split in two," he said holding his face as blood leaked through his fingers.

Sin removed his shirt and wrapped it around Beans' face making him resemble a dog with a protective scratch collar. He picked the duffle bag up off the ground then grabbed Beans by the arm. "C'mon we gotta get outta here."

* * *

Smoke moved at a frantic pace inside the stash spot as he stuffed the bricks into a duffle bag. He felt little remorse for lining his two best friends up. It's a dirty game and I'm playing to win, he told himself. He really didn't care to justify his actions. The money he planned on making from the bricks Sin had left behind would comfort him enough when the whispers of what he had done started in the streets. He had a son to feed, neither Sin nor Beans knew that type of stress, pressure or responsibility he felt at such a young age. But now he had bricks to do it with. Regardless of how the streets reacted to what he had done, they were still gonna cop that work. That's how it went and Smoke knew that.

He stuffed the last few bricks into the bag, zipped it up and draped it over his broad shoulders. As he turned for the door his heart sunk into his stomach and his face wore the shock he felt.

"Going somewhere playboy?" Sin asked as he pointed his gun at his one-time friend.

"Damn, the Jamaicans fucked up," Smoke thought to himself staring at his two friends who should have been dead. "Yo

my niggas. Y'all made it," he said in a cheerful tone, pretending to be happy to see them. "Shit got crazy in there, nah'mean? I got out the best way I could. The Gunsmoke way," he spoke in his signature raspy voice.

"You a faggot ass nigga son. You set us up. Served us to them Jamaicans like jerk chicken," Sin said.

"C'mon my niggas, this Smoke... Gunsmoke. We go back," he banged on his chest. "I would never do no shit like that."

"You a bitch," Beans barked as he stepped towards Smoke with his gun drawn. The shirt around his head was soaked with blood and his face looked gruesome. His finger twitched, prepared to squeeze the trigger. The Jamaicans they had killed earlier in the night were both he and Sin's first bodies. It gave Beans a rush and he enjoyed the feeling. Now as he stared at Smoke he couldn't wait to experience the euphoria again.

"So eight bricks," Sin stated calmly then tossed the duffle bag he retrieved from Donovan at Smoke's feet. "That's how much it cost you to have us killed. That dread must've jumped at that chance. They get the eight keys. You get the twenty-two out the stash house, everything good" There was fury in Sin's eyes as he spoke. The game had taught him a lesson tonight. Money and power were the greatest temptations known to man. "Damn, you wanted to move me and Beans out the way this whole time huh. That 40, 30, 30 split wasn't working for your greedy ass. You had to

have it all."

Smoke looked them both in the eyes and confessed. "It was for my son. I gotta get him out this hood. I don't want him to come up like we did. I don't have a pops with unlimited bricks at his fingertips. I saw a chance so I took. Fuck it."

"Fuck your son! You lucky I don't slide pass your mother's house, kill her and that lil' nigga," Beans expressed. The pain he felt from the cut in his face, left no room for sympathy at the moment.

"C'mon Sin. You gotta feel me. At least understand my reason," Smoke pleaded his case, knowing Sin was always the thinker in the crew and the most level headed.

"Nah my nigga. I could never understand sucka shit. I ain't cut like that," Sin replied rejecting Smoke. "We came up from the mud, splitting slices of pizza in threes. Me, you and Beans. You switched sides on your crew, now you gotta stay there. Ain't no u-turns or forgiveness on this side," he expressed coldly. "But the best way to deal with a fake nigga is to be real with him. So for that reason alone, I'm gonna always make sure ya momma and Lil' Smoke straight. So you can die knowing that," Sin stated with such finality, Smoke closed his eyes, knowing what was to follow.

Sin and Beans aired Smoke out, hitting him with every bullet from their clips. His body absorbed every shot, keeping him upright as each one entered his flesh. Smoke was dead before he hit the ground and Sin and Beans' brotherhood had been established in bloodshed.

* * *

Only the tramp of the Doc's shoes was heard as he entered the room causing Sin to look up. A lump formed in his throat as he rose to his feet to meet the Doc, exhaling deeply, bracing himself for the news. The Doc's face was filled with worry lines, he looked emotionally and physically exhausted. All things that read bad to Sin.

"How is he doing, Doc?"

The Doc sighed wiping his brow. "I, um,"

Involuntarily Sin reached out and grabbed the Doc by the collar of his shirt. Pulling him close he demanded answers, "What the fuck is going on in there, Doc? Tell me Beans is gonna be aight." There was a pleading look in Sin's eyes that the Doc had never seen in all the years knowing him. It almost made the Doc fearful to answer him. Sin quickly realized this and let the Doc go. Straightening out his shirt and apologizing. He placed a hand on the Doc's shoulder showing him that he meant no malice.

"No harm, no foul," The Doc quickly accepted.

"How is he?" Sin shifted right back to his concern for Beans.

"All things considered, I'd say he's very lucky. He took quite a few shots, bad ones. He lost an extreme amount of blood but I was able to remove the bullets and get the bleeding to stop. He's been sedated and I have morphine pumping through his IV for the pain but honestly Sin there is only so much I can do. You need to get him to a hospital. He needs to be in intensive care," The Doc said expressing his concern and expertise.

"No hospitals," Sin objected. "I need you to make it work here Doc. I'm depending on you." Sin buried his face into his palms then ran both hands down his face. "Can I see him?"

"Yes, right this way."

The sight of the tubes, IVs and machines made Sin feel like he was trapped in a recurring nightmare. No matter how hard he tried he just couldn't escape it. First his sister, now Beans, with all the money and power Sin still couldn't save the people closest to him. He turned towards The Doc who stood in the doorway. "Tell me what you need and I'll make sure you'll have it here within the hour. But absolutely no hospitals, you understand me?" Sin couldn't take any chances, he needed Beans out of harm's way and recovering peacefully while he figured this shit out.

"Yes, I understand," the Doc answered. He was fully aware of Sin's line of business. He understood the importance of being discreet. It was why they paid him the way they did. "Ok, let me make a list," he said disappearing out the room.

Sin slumped into a chair next to the bed and stared at

Beans. "You can't die my nigga," he said.

After about ten minutes the Doc stepped back into the room with a piece of paper and handed it to Sin. "This is gonna be a lot harder than the job I did for Ms. Ashleigh," he uttered as he exited the room. His words catching Sin's attention just as he made it to the door.

"Hold up Doc. Whatchu talking 'bout? What thing for Ashleigh?"

By Sin's reaction the Doc knew he had already said too much. "Oh it was nothing," he said trying to quickly dismiss it.

Sin stared at the Doc intensely and spoke firmly. "Listen, there is no reason on earth that my sister should ever have to come see you. She has no business being here—" Sin paused mid-sentence as a thought crossed his mind. He had been noticing something going on with Ashleigh as of late that he couldn't put his finger on. "Unless... was she pregnant Doc?" he asked.

"No, no. Nothing like that," the Doc assured him. "Quite the opposite actually. She came with her boyfriend. They needed to get rid of a body." The Doc said it so nonchalantly having done the deed so many times, he had become numb to it.

But for Sin it was a different feeling. This was his little sister they were talking about. Why would she need to dispose of a body? Was she involved in a murder? What had this new boyfriend of hers gotten her into?

"A body?" he repeated out loud in disbelief.

"Yes. Apparently the dead guy was the best friend of her boyfriend. He was extremely emotional but there was nothing I could do. The young man took a blast to the stomach and had lost too much blood. He was dead on arrival."

Sin stood silent for a moment, letting it all sink in. He needed to know more. "When was this?" he asked the Doc, pressing him for the details.

The Doc stared up at the ceiling trying to jog his memory. "A few months ago. The night of your brother's speech. I remember I watched it on TV."

"The same night my father was shot," Sin uttered. "The night my spot got hit," he recalled. "Aight thanks Doc," he said and turning his back as the man walked out. Sin pulled out his phone and dialed.

Kyrie answered on the second ring. "Yo," he said and Sin could immediately hear crying in the background. He didn't even have to ask Kyrie. He knew it was Egypt. Sin felt for the young girl, witnessing her twin's vicious death as they stood next to each other was a lot to deal with.

"Ashleigh's nigga still around you?" Sin questioned.

"Nah, we went our separate ways. Why what's up?" Kyrie could tell something was up just by the way Sin was talking.

"The night your spot got hit. How many niggas was it?"

"Two. I think."

"You said you hit one of em right? Where at?"

"In the stomach," Kyrie recalled. "I got him good too. Why?"

"Ashleigh brought Case to see the Doc that same night, with his man shot in the stomach. He didn't make it."

Kyrie couldn't believe he was just standing next to the nigga who tried to kill him. "Oh shit. This nigga trying to get in where he fit in. So he can do us all dirty."

"Exactly but I got something for him. He don't know we on to him. We gonna rock him to sleep. But that' for a later time. I need you to pick up some stuff and bring it out here to Doc for Beans," Sin told him.

"How he doing?" Kyrie asked.

"He alive," Sin said honestly cause besides that there was no good news. Sin ran off the list to Kyrie then hung up and dialed Ashleigh's number.

"Sin," she answered the phone frantically, "Are you alright?"

"Yeah but Beans got shot."

Ashleigh's heart began to race as she built the courage to ask her question. She was scared of the answer. "Is it bad?" she asked in a somber tone then closed her eyes as the words left her lips. She gripped her cell phone tightly, bracing for the response.

"Yeah it's bad," Sin admitted. "But he's alive. You know Beans is tough." Sin could hear her gasp on the other end of the phone and knew she was crying. "Ashleigh, I'm gonna ask you something and I need you to be completely honest with me," he said. "I know you went and seen the Doc a few months back with your boyfriend. Did you have anything to do with what happened to his friend that night?" Sin asked.

"Oh my God. No," she said. "When I showed up to his apartment I found his friend like that. I tried to help. So I took him to the Doc but it was too late."

"Why you didn't come to me about that?' he asked.

"I don't know," she replied.

"I think you should fall back from that nigga for a little while," Sin told her.

"Why?" she asked defiantly.

"You could've really got jammed up on some bullshit you ain't have nothing to do with" Sin told her.

"Case would never see me get caught up like that," she said.

"I mean what I say Ash. Stay away from that nigga. I ain't trying to go back and forth with you about it right now," Sin was direct and his tone was serious. He was making himself clear.

"Ok, damn," Ashleigh said then the phone fell silent for a few seconds. Finally, she spoke up again calling her brother's name. "Sin."

"Yeah."

"Beans not gonna die, is he?" she asked as her voice cracked a little bit.

"I don't know Ash but I gotta go," he told her.

"Ok," she said wiping tears away as she hung up.

CHAPTER 20

AGENT MOSLEY COULD TELL FROM the way the body was slumped over with the back of the skull missing, that Barkim had decided eating a bullet was his best and only option out. Maybe Barkim had decided to take his own life as a show of power. He had become so powerless in the final stages of his life, nothing more than Mosley's puppet. Maybe he wanted his last action in this world to be a totally selfish one. A display of defiance. Something that said, Only he ruled him. So he took his fate in his own hands. Thumbing his nose at Mosley and his plan to bring down Sin.

Mosley was used to seeing dead bodies. It was a

byproduct of his job. But this one felt different, Barkim represented his case. It too now seemed dead, without a person on the inside and potential star witness, what more did Mosley have. He shook his head just staring at the crime scene. Barkim had been dead in that room for days. Still the amount of blood was unreal. A pool the size of a small car had formed around Barkim. It was thick, dark dried blood. It was splattered on the wall as well. Barkim had made no doubt about his death. Mosley rolled him over. Barkim's mouth was still open, frozen from the bullet that had traveled through it and to his brain. Mosley felt no remorse, although he had played a major part in this outcome. This was Barkim's fault, a consequence of the life he chose. If there was any extra blame to go around, it belonged to Sin. He had killed Ali as a warning to Barkim. Mosley was sure of it, though he couldn't exactly prove it. Sin had proven to be just as smart if not smarter than is father and definitely was proving to be as difficult to catch. Mosley wanted him so bad he could taste it. He paced the hotel room, his frustration building with every step. At that moment he decided he would take Mason Holloway up on his offer. Missing persons wasn't his field of expertise but he would surely make some phone calls to make it happen. There was more than one way to skin a cat. After years of trying to bring the Holloway organization to justice, he had a willing ally inside the family. One he didn't have to plant there. All he had to do was find Bria Holloway and Sin would be served to him on one of the Holloway's expensive platters.

Mosley pulled out his phone and dialed. After three or four rings the phone was answered on the other end. "Hey, this is Special Agent Roe Mosley. I know it's been a while. I need to call in a big favor. It would help me on a case that I'm working on."

* * *

"FBI, Get down on the ground now!" a voiced yelled. "Get down now, FBI!" more voices quickly followed.

A swarm of red dots danced all over the house as agents in tactical vest and body armor appeared from everywhere. Bria could hear the sudden spurts of gunfire coming from all over the vast interior of the house, followed by agents shouting to one another that their areas were clear and secured. Bria could feel the momentum of the agents surging through the house. The closer they got, the more she felt an overwhelming sense of relief, knowing they were there to rescue her. She had never given up hope. She knew her parents would never stop looking for her. She missed them so much, even her little brother, who could be so annoying at times. She welcomed the chance to be annoyed by him again. It had been a long time since she had seen her family. She knew her mother had to be going crazy without her around. Who is keeping her company, she continuously thought to herself. Bria was well aware of how busy her dad could be and he sometimes would ignore her mother. It was okay, she made sure her mom always had her to talk to. But with her gone, her mom no longer had that. So once they were reunited, the first thing she would do was give her the biggest and tightest hug ever.

Bria could hear the sounds of the agent's boots marching down the hallway. They're almost here, she thought. It was almost over, she told herself. It was almost over and she was alive. She wanted to scream it to the Heavens. She had prayed and dreamed about this moment for months. She breathed in deeply, held her breath and then exhaled trying to calm the excitement she felt. But there was no way she could. This was truly the best day of her young life.

"Clear!"

"All clear!"

The agents were in the room next to hers. I'm next, she thought. Bria vaulted to her feet, adrenaline surging through her as she raced to the door. She snatched it open and ran into the hallway waving her hands. Suddenly there was a bright flash in the hallway followed by silence. Fear shot through Bria at the surprised look on the agent's faces. No one spoke but the sadness, repentance and disappointment quickly reached a deafening crescendo.

Bria could feel a burning pressure in her chest. She

looked down and saw the front of her shirt quickly turning crimson. She let out one last gasp, releasing her soul from her little body in that very moment. Her tiny legs gave out, her eyes forced themselves close and then a wave of light consumed her.

* * *

Agent Mosley stepped under the yellow tape that surrounded the large home and a quiet neighborhood, dressed in a grey suit and white shirt, his FBI shield visible on his hip. Marching passed a group of local, uniformed officers, he didn't stop to acknowledge their presence. This was an FBI crime scene, rendering them useless and they were now no more than bystanders with badges securing the perimeter. Mosley's heart felt as though it was lodged in his throat making swallowing a nearly impossible task. Nauseated and queasy from riding the rollercoaster of emotion had him sick to his stomach. The watery taste invading his mouth always preceded him vomiting. He had never been devoutly religious and rarely did he call on the power of prayer but Mosley had been silently doing so the entire ride over to the scene. This was definitely the biggest screw up of his career. He made his way through the house and went up to the room where Bria's body was. The two crime scene investigators who were gathering forensic evidence, stopped when they noticed him standing in the door.

"Agent Mosley," one of the CSIs said acknowledging his presence.

Mosley didn't reply to the greeting only nodded his head in both men's direction. "Let me see the body," he asked in a low and somber tone.

Mosley's head dropped into his chest as the sheet was removed off of the little body laying in the middle of room. His worst fears had been confirmed. It was Bria Holloway and she was dead. Mosley tried his best to remain as professional as possible turning his face away and exhaling to not let the tears forming in his eyes drop.

"Cover her back up," he demanded.

Mosley's eyes scanned the room and landed on a stuffed animal in the room besides a few dolls. It gave him a bit of relief to know the young girl wasn't being tied up or tortured while she was being held hostage. But the hospitable treatment poised a few new questions in his mind. It seemed like her captors had went out their way not to harm her. Sadly, the people who had been sent to rescue her had. Mosley lowered his head and stormed out of the room.

CHAPTER 21

SIN SWUNG HIS LEGS OUT of bed, letting his feet sink into the plush carpet of his bedroom, before burying his face into the palm of his hands. It was still early in the evening but he could tell it was going to be another sleepless night. They had become all too frequent lately. The news of Bria's death had rocked him in his soul. Sin was tortured by regret and pained by thoughts of what if. He kept asking himself the same question over and over. What could he have done differently to protect her. He had no answers and that tormented him daily turning him into a reclusive shell of himself. He had dropped out of sight. It had been over a week since anyone, family or friends, had laid eyes on him. He needed to be away from everyone to clear his mind, think things out and deal with his personal grief. No one could possibly understand what he was feeling. He had lost his daughter without ever really having her. Khari had robbed him of the joy of knowing Bria as his daughter and now he would forever be denied the opportunity. That was a hard pill to swallow.

Sin clicked on the lamp and picked up a photo off the nightstand. It was a picture of him and Ariane. It served as yet another reminder of all that had been lost during this war with The Commission. The picture was taken in Times Square on the night of their very first date. The smile on Ariane's face was so bright, her eyes were radiant and full of joy. Sin remembered the night like it was yesterday. He longed for the chance to look into those eyes once again, yearned to see her smile and desperately ached to hear the sound of her voice. He missed her sweet smell, her taste on his lips. Sin remembered what it felt like laying next to her, playing in her hair after they made love. He sat there in silence with a feeling of desolation, staring at her face then tracing it with his finger as he let a tear fall from his eye. He desperately wished he could have just one more moment with her, no woman had ever captivated him like Ariane had. The burden of guilt he felt was enormously heavy, weighing him down as he fought a losing battle to his grief.

He had buried his father, lost one of his closest friends, the woman he loved and now his daughter; all in a flash. A black cloud of death seemed to hang over him that he just couldn't seem to shake. A lesser man would have taken his own life by now. Put a gun in his mouth and squeezed. That would have been the easiest way out of the hell hole Sin found himself in. But what would ending his own life solve? Nothing. What needed to end was the war with The Commission. Sin felt responsible for too many deaths of people he loved. It had to end.

He placed the photo back on the nightstand, next to a picture of his deceased mother. He stood and strolled over to the window. From the view in his hideout in Jersey, he could see across the water to Manhattan. Staring out into the night at the city that never slept, the city lights illuminated the sky. Sin could see his reflection in the glass. He was shirtless, tattoos covering his chiseled frame, wearing only a pair of grey sweat pants. His hair needed to be cut and his beard had grown in full. He brushed the palm of his hand over his chin, barely recognizing himself. He shook his head and drew the curtains closed.

Just as he headed towards the bathroom, he heard a noise coming from the living room. He walked over to the nightstand, clicking off the lamp and grabbing the gun he kept under his pillow before creeping to the living room. His focus immediately centered on the front door noticing the knob jiggling. He heard it unlock, then the door opened. Cloaked by shadows, Sin stood mere inches from the intruder and snatched the person by the shirt, pressing the barrel of the gun to their forehead as soon as they stepped into his apartment.

"You got three seconds to tell me who sent you before I put a hot one in ya head."

"Sin, it's me."

"Cassie?" Sin asked recognizing the voice and lowering the gun to his side. "What are you doing sneaking in my apartment. You almost got bodied," he questioned flicking on the lights.

"First of all, I ain't sneaking. I got a key, remember?" she said waving it in the air. "This place is in my name remember. Ain't nobody seen or heard from you in over a week. I figured you'd be here."

"I forgot you got a key to this spot," Sin said turning and walking over to the couch. He plopped down and put the gun on the coffee table. "What you doing out here, by yourself, at this time of night?" he asked.

Although Cassie was no longer confined to a wheelchair, she still needed the help of a cane and walked with a noticeable limp. "I'm grown. I don't need anyone's permission to be out at night. Especially my little brother's," she reminded him. "Anyway, I been out all day looking for you. I almost forgot about this spot," she said moving gingerly over to him. "Bria's funeral is in a couple days," she informed him.

"Yeah, I'on know if I'm gonna make it," he said.

Cassie eyes grew hard with suspicion. "What's going on Sin? You didn't even take Ariane's death this hard. What are you hiding or hiding from?"

"Who said I'm hiding?" Sin replied instantly not liking her choice of words. He stood to his feet and walked over to his bar and poured himself a glass of Grand Marnier.

"Ain't nobody seen or heard from you in days. You got it all dark in here and shit," she said looking around. "Most of the liquor in your bar is gone and you look like shit," Cassie said walking over to him and grabbing his face.

"Fuck you," Sin shot back jokingly before sipping his drink.

Cassie laughed too. She was extremely brash but always honest, especially when it came to dealing with her brother. Sin could always depend on Cassie to tell him the truth. Checks and balances they called it. "Listen we're all hurting. Bria meant the world to everyone in this family. It's gonna be a while before any of us get over this. Hell, I don't know if we'll ever. But here's what I do know. You've worked too hard to let things just crumble cause you sitting up in here feeling sorry for yourself," she reminded him. "You can't just sit around here moping, thinking about if you made the right or wrong decisions. What's done is done. We all gotta live with the decisions we make. That's the game, daddy taught both of us that," Cassie said. "You got a business to run and that business requires your undivided attention. It's a lot of people depending on you and we all go as you go," she told him.

Sin looked Cassie straight in her eyes as he fought back tears. He wanted to tell her that Bria was his daughter. That's why her death hurt so much. But he couldn't, it was too much to explain. Maybe it was best to let the truth be buried with her. It was only important to him that Bria knew and now that would never happen, so it didn't matter. No matter how much he despised both Mason and Khari, they had suffered enough. He didn't want to ruin what was left of their marriage. And regardless of whether he wanted to hear it or not, Sin knew Cassie was absolutely right. She was speaking from the heart. Although he didn't need anybody to tell him how to handle his business, it was still good to hear it, especially coming from her. Sin knew having his mind preoccupied could cost him not only his growing empire or freedom but his life.

The strongest man isn't the one who can move the biggest boulder. It's the one who can swallow his anger and always keep in perspective who and what he's dealing with, Sin thought of something his father once told him. He gulped down his drink and sat the empty glass on the coffee table. He put his gun in the small of his back. "You right.

I'm gonna hop in the shower then we can head back to the city," he said.

"Now that's the Sin I know," Cassie spoke with pride. "And cut that nasty looking stuff off ya face while you back there. Bring my handsome brother back please," she shouted as Sin disappeared into the room slamming the door behind him. Cassie could hear him laughing from the other side of the door.

Using the darkness as a cover, an unmarked van pulled off the side of the road closely followed by another vehicle. The two cars drove deeper into the thickness of trees until coming to a stop at a clearing in the woods, illuminated only by the light of the moon. For what felt to her like a month, Ariane had been held in a small cramped space behind a locked door that only opened up enough to slide her food and water in. She hadn't been allowed to bathe but once or twice and was only allowed to go to the bathroom once a day. She hadn't seen the faces of the men who were holding her captive. She was forced to wear a blindfold anytime she was allowed beyond the locked door. But a few hours ago, the door was opened, a hood was placed over her head and she had been on the move in the back of the van ever since. Now her heart was pounding in her chest as they came to a stop. The thuds played so loud in her head, she swore her kidnappers could hear it. She knew being snatched from the cemetery wasn't random at all. Sin and his family was at war, hurting her would surely hurt him and her going missing would at the very least distract him. She just hoped that a kidnapping was all it was. The thought of what else could happen to her was enough to twist her stomach into knots. She had heard the loud explosion back at the cemetery and all she could think of was Sin being hurt or even worse. She had no idea that she was thought to have died in that explosion. She didn't know a memorial in her honor had taken place weeks ago. All she knew was that where ever Sin was, he was in pain and doing whatever he had to do to find her. She was only half right. Sin was suffering tremendously but he wasn't looking for her, only those responsible for her death. Ariane was dead and didn't even know it.

She heard footsteps in the van, then the hood was snatched off her head. "Where are we? What do y'all want?" she asked but no one answered her.

Suddenly the backdoors of the van opened causing her to jump from fright. A shadowy figure stood in the door staring at her. Ariane couldn't make out his face in the darkness and she didn't recognize his voice as he barked out commands to the other men. "Get her out the van."

Ariane began to kick and scream as two men grabbed her by the arms and legs and dragged her easily from the truck. "Get off of me!" she shouted.

The mystery man in the door just laughed.

"Why are you doing this? I don't have anything to do with nothing," she yelled. Still no one answered her. The mystery man just continued to instruct the men holding her, ignoring her pleas.

"Take her inside," he demanded and followed behind them.

As Ariane made it around the side of the van, she saw a cabin in front of her. It seemed to appear out of nowhere, just sitting in the middle of the tall trees and wilderness. There was nothing else around it. The lights from the two vehicles were the only thing that made it visible in the pitch blackness of the woods. Ariane tried fighting to get away but she was no match for the two powerful men as they forced her around the side of the house to a cellar door. They dragged her down the steps that lead to the basement Then tossed her onto to the cold concrete floor. She quickly stood, trying to make a run for it but was easily knocked to the ground by one of them.

"Be still," he warned.

"Aghh," she moaned, unable to brace her fall because her hands were tied.

"Not so rough fellas. She's precious cargo," the mystery man said with a hint of sarcasm as he stood in the cellar door.

His face wasn't visible to Ariane, only his silhouette and

she couldn't recognize his voice. "Who the hell are you?" she questioned.

"Think of me as your guardian angel," the man in the doorway replied sarcastically. "You should really be more careful about the company you keep," he said.

"Fuck you. If you're gonna kill me, just do it. Cause I ain't got shit to tell you," Ariane bucked.

"You're not gonna get off that easy," he promised her.

"That's a dirty little mouth, she got there," one of the other men said.

"Yeah," the man in charge said with a laugh. "We gonna have to do something about that."

"Fuck you, you sonofabitch. Sin is gonna find you and kill you," Ariane cried out.

"We'll see about that, won't we?" he teased. "Let's see how long that tough act last," he joked nodding towards the other men as they started to exit the room, the man in charge turned back to Ariane. "See you in a few days," he shouted then slammed the door to the cellar.

Ariane didn't realize she had been holding her breath until she heard the door slam and the clicking from the locks. It suddenly felt like there was no air in the room as it quickly became humid. There were no windows and only a small bit of light from under the door. She had already started to sweat. Ariane had remained tough for as long as possible but her emotions were now getting the best of her.

The way her heart was pounding, she felt like her chest was about to cave in. She had never been this scared in her life. Trapped and alone, her mind was racing and fear was pumping through her body. Ariane could no longer fight back the tears. She began crying uncontrollably but silently as she stared up at the cellar door.

CHAPTER 22

THE DARK COLORED DENALI CARRYING Sin came to a stop across from the Old St. Patrick's Cathedral on Mulberry Street. Sin peered out the window scanning the street. The driver of the SUV turned in his seat to face him.

"You want me to wait right here sir?" he asked.

Sin shook his head. It was after 12am. He knew a waiting car, idling outside of a church at that time of night looked too suspicious and would definitely draw the attention of any passing police car. "Nah. Spin the block a few times. I ain't gonna be that long."

"You sure you don't want me to go in with you?" the driver asked showing his concern.

"Nah, I'll be aight," Sin assured him patting the man on his back.

Sin exited the car cloaked in the dense fog that covered the street. He walked across the street and up the church steps before slipping out of sight. Once inside Sin was taken aback for a moment by the sheer size and beautiful architecture of the Cathedral. He made the sign of the cross over his head and chest out of respect before strolling down the aisle of the massive structure. All of the pews were empty as they passed, all expect for one. In a pew three rows from the front, sat Phil Catanzano, head of the family that bore his name. Well dressed, his suit was tailored and his shoes shined like new coins. Catanzano was one of Sin's father's closest criminal friends and one of the only ones that had remained loyal after his death.

"Sin," Catanzano said in a jovial tone seeing him standing in the aisle at the end of the pew. "It's good to see you again. How have you been?"

"I've been better," Sin answered honestly.

"I'm sure," Catanzano said. His brow wrinkling with a hint of sadness.

"I thought we agreed to meet alone. You don't trust me? That's no way to build a friendship," Sin stated pointing to the two random men near the front of the church, pretending to be deep in prayer.

A sheepish grin creased Catanzano's lips followed by a

big hearty laugh. He gave a nod to the men. They instantly rose to their feet and walked to the back of the cathedral. "Force of habit," he confessed. "Is that better?" he asked as his men disappeared.

Sin nodded his approval then slid into the pew next to the old Don.

"That was one hell of stunt you pulled, sending those body parts to Fat Tony. I would have paid to see the look on his face," Catanzano admitted with joy.

"Yeah but I see they still haven't gotten the message," Sin stated.

"Well that's what I wanted to meet with you about," Catanzano admitted. "I may have a solution to put an end to all your troubles."

"I'm listening," Sin replied.

"That thing at the inauguration was a bad look for everybody," Catanzano sighed before continuing, "These new guys are a bunch of wannabes, they have no real understanding of the way things are done. You don't just turn a New York City street into the wild west, in broad daylight, with thousands of innocent people around," he shook his head. "The police are going to be cracking down. Making conducting business hard on all of us. Now there is only so much any of us can do to make this go away. We can fatten the pockets of some people. Grease a few palms but the cops are not gonna just look the other way on this one. I can promise you that. It was a total embarrassment. Heads are going to roll," he explained. "We need to bring this war to an end, now. We don't need any more bodies on the news or blood in the streets. Or it won't be long before we're all sharing a cell. You understand?"

Sin shrugged but remained quiet.

"Your losing money fighting this war. The other families are too. I know it. I've been around long enough to know how these things go. It's no longer about who's right or wrong Sin. It's a business. Think about the business," Catanzano explained.

"War has never been about determining whose right or wrong, only who's left," Sin finally spoke. "I've never tried convincing myself that I'm the good guy in all of this. You shouldn't either. I do what I have to do, to get what I need done, done. We all do."

Catanzano smiled. "That's a good way to think." Looking at Sin brought back memories for the mafia boss. The young man was a splitting image of his father and just as smart, ambitious and straightforward. Catanzano folded his hands on his rotund belly. "What if I could set up a meeting in a neutral place. Somewhere you would feel safe coming. Where only the heads of the families would be allowed to attend," he offered. "I would provide the security and guarantee everyone's safety."

Sin had a plan of his own but he kept it to himself. The

mind was the best concealed weapon. He smiled and nodded agreeing to the meeting. At all cost he wanted to hide the thoughts that were controlling his brain. The surge of hatred that flowed through his body. He wanted to give no warning to anybody as to how he felt at the moment or what he was planning.

"Good, good," Catanzano said patting him on his back, happy that he decided to accept the offer. "We will all be better for it. There's a lot more money in peace than war."

"Let me ask you something. You know anything about an Agent Mosley?"

"Roe Mosley," Catanzano's voice boomed suddenly. "He's a hound dog. Once he has your scent, he doesn't stop. And he always had it out for your father," Catanzano chuckled a bit.

"What was his beef wit' my pops?" Sin fished for information.

"Marion never shared those details with me." Catanzano explained. "But it must have been something big because he never would let it go. He's after you now?" he asked.

Sin exhaled deeply. "Yeah. Is there any way around him? It has to be somebody I can pay to make him go away. Somebody has to have an outstanding gambling debt they can't pay or something. Whose retirement fund can I contribute to, to make this guy go away?"

"I don't know if money is the answer. If so, your father

would've done that years ago. It seems like it's more of a personal vendetta," Catanzano explained.

"Personal vendetta?" Sin questioned out loud as he gave it some thought. He rubbed his temples trying to jog his memory but nothing he had ever spoke with his father about provided any answers.

"See what dirt you can dig up on him. I wanna know everything about him. Where he eats, where he sleeps, if he gotta wife, kids, a mistress. I want to know it all."

"Now you sound like your father. He used to think I worked for him sometimes too," Catanzano chuckled at the way Sin have just given him an order. "I'm gonna give you a piece of advice. Your father was able to thrive in this business for so many years mainly due to his political connection," Catanzano informed him. "You should work on building those relationships. In this city nobody does anything without them. Now that Marion is gone, a lot of his old friends are trying to distance themselves from him, which means you too," he said. "Truth is, your father had a lot of dirt on a lot of people and most are happy that he is gone. They're hoping that their sins and secrets went in the ground with him," the mobster spoke truthfully. "Most don't feel the same sense of loyalty to you. Those that have remained loyal to your family, have decided to throw their support and weight behind your brother, Mason. He's viewed as the cleaner choice."

"Or the weaker," Sin responded.

"Either way, they aren't lining up behind you," Catanzano stated straightforwardly. "They're free agents again, available to the highest bidder. That means anybody with deep enough pockets."

Sin just nodded his head, processing all that he had been told by Catanzano. He reached inside his jacket and handed the Don an envelope stuffed with cash.

"What's this?" Catanzano said with a surprised look on his chubby face.

"For your time. Plus, I don't like favors," Sin said. "Set the meeting."

Both men shook hands then Sin stood to his feet, stepped out into the aisle and nodded towards the confessionals. Two of his bodyguards emerged from the doors and began to walk up the aisle of the church. Sin charmingly smirked at a surprised Catanzano and said, "Force of habit," then followed his men as they exited the cathedral.

CHAPTER 23

SIN STOOD AS STILL AS possible, staring out at the beautiful lake that rested at the edge of the Holloway Estate's backyard. The lake was a serene site, far removed from the main house and miles away from the hustle and bustle of the city and the ongoing war. The tranquil waters demanded you to step back a bit and enjoy the beauty life had to offer. As hard as he had tried to prepare himself for the possibility that Bria may not return to the family alive, the reality was a far greater pain then Sin could have imagined. He had remained stoic at the funeral watching as Mason shed tears. He found himself for the first time in life, feeling a bit of sympathy for his estranged brother. Strangely

Khari appeared to be numb to it all. She hadn't cried once during the funeral, even as they lowered Bria's casket into the ground and covered it with dirt. Khari just stared straight ahead with an empty look in her eyes, she seemed to be somewhere else in her mind. Sin suffered silently, the same way he was now. He had strolled to the lake needing a moment of peace in his life and the closer he looked at the view of the lake, the more relaxed he became. He could feel someone approaching and turned to see Cassie walking towards him with the help of her cane. She held a glass of wine in her hand and her face wore a stamp of grief.

"Beautiful view isn't?" she said.

"Yeah," Sin answered. "How'd you know where to find me?"

"This has always been your spot, since we were younger," she replied. "Whenever you came to visit, you would always duck off back here."

Sin nodded his head remembering the many days he had spent at that very spot.

"You ok?" Cassie asked. She knew her brother better than most and could tell something was weighing on him. "This is hard for all of us," she said.

"Yeah, it is but I'm good."

"I just wish we knew more about who was holding her in that house. The police killed all the men that were there, so there's no one to talk to. The house is owned by a dummy corporation."

"Another dead end," Sin said. He sighed deeply then went quiet for a moment.

"What's on your mind?" Cassie asked. She could tell by the look on his face that his mind was in overdrive.

"Just thinking about my next move. Catanzano reached out to me and I met up with him to talk," he informed her.

"About?" Cassie asked slowly sipping from her glass, peering out at the lake.

"He said he had a way to end the war, peacefully," Sin replied as a flock of birds flew off in the distances. He shifted his eyes from the lake to his sister.

"And you believed him?" Cassie asked turning to face her brother.

Sin shrugged his shoulders, "I thought it was worth hearing what he had to say."

"So, what did he say?"

"He wants to arrange a sit down between me and the heads of the other families. After the way everything played at the inauguration. He thinks the cops are gonna make life hell for guys like us. Nobody needs anymore dead bodies in the streets, especially innocent ones," Sin replied. "He said the meeting would be somewhere neutral and safe for all parties involved."

"What!" Cassie said with a confused look on her face. "No Sin. You can't go to a meeting with The Commission.

It's a set up. I don't trust it."

"Maybe. Maybe not," he said. "What other choice do I really have? No matter how many of them I kill. It's not gonna bring back the people I've lost. Not Pops. Not Ariane. Not Bria. Not Sheik. Not Cairo." He was sounding as if he was willing to accept his fate if that was the case. Cassie could feel his pain and she could see the heaviness in his shoulders. It was something he wouldn't dare let anyone else witness and she knew he hated that she could see it. Cassie's bond with Sin was unbreakable. They were as close as two siblings could be. There wasn't anything they wouldn't do for each other. They had proven it many times in the past. Now all Cassie wanted was to save him from himself.

"Sin, listen to me, please," she begged. "There has to be another way. You could call in a few favors from our out of town business partners. Stall for a while, give us time to recruit an army strong enough to win this war with The Commission," she pleaded.

Sin remained stubborn and steadfast in his willingness to meet with The Commission. "Reina has provided me with a strong enough army. That is not the problem Cassie. The Commission aren't losing love ones in this war though. I am!" he expressed. "This war has to end now. I can't keep allowing my love ones to die," he said wholeheartedly.

"And if they kill you?" she said with a hint of anger in her voice, not wanting to accept what her brother was saying.

"That's a chance I'm willing to take," he explained.

"Then what? Who would run the business?"

"You would. Beans would continue to help you," he said.

"Speaking of. How is he?" she asked.

"A lot better. I never seen a muthafucka recover as fast as him after being shot four or five times. "He'll be out of the doctor's care very soon."

"That's good," Cassie said with a smile. "Now back to this meeting Sin. I don't think you should risk it. Not alone at least. Can't we find out where it is gonna be held and get some men there?" she questioned. "Let's have a plan in place."

"I don't know," Sin shrugged without giving it much consideration.

Cassie sighed. "C'mon, Sin think. I can't even think about losing you."

"It was a time when we couldn't see this thing running without Pops but it did. And it would run without me too. I know you would make sure of that. But something has to be done, continuing this war will eventually collapse everything that Pops has built."

Cassie hugged her brother tight as tears formed in her eyes. She knew there was no changing Sin's mind. She squeezed him, unwilling to let go for a minute, knowing this could possibly be the last time they saw one another or spoke. "I love you Sin but your one stubborn man," she said sniffling away tears.

"I love you too Cassandra," he teased knowing she hated to be called by her full name.

Cassie released him from her embrace and saw the charming grin on his face. That was Sin, she thought to herself. Always there to make her smile and forget about all the bad going on in her life.

"C'mon, let's head back to the house," he said wiping her face and grabbing her arm to assist her.

As the two of them made it to the back of the house, Sin spotted Ashleigh quickly disappear around the side of the house.

"Go ahead, I'll be inside in a minute," Sin told Cassie.

"What's wrong?"

"Nothing, I just need to talk to Ash real quick," Sin helped Cassie through the door then walked around the side of the building. He saw Ashleigh puffing on a cigarette, her head was darting from side to side making sure no one saw her. Still he managed to creep up on her. "When you started smoking," he asked startling her.

Ashleigh began coughing and choking. "Sin, where'd you come from? Why you sneaking up on me like that," she asked between coughs.

"That's a nasty habit to pick up," he told her.

"Yeah well, there has been a lot going on for me to deal with. Daddy, Cassie, Bria. It's like a none stop thing with this family. Every time I turn around it's another funeral to attend. Although her voice was hoarse her words came out like she was on fast forward.

Sin remained quiet for a moment, just studying her mannerisms. She was constantly moving, seemingly unable to stand still as she stepped side to side. She was sweating and she kept pawing at her running nose. Sin knew the signs all too well. He had been around enough addicts in his time to know what was going on with her.

"Take your glasses off. Let me see your eyes?" Sin asked.

"Why?" she said like he had offended her.

"Just take your glasses off Ashleigh," he repeated.

Ashleigh remained defiant. "No," she told him then attempted to walk away.

"Give me these glasses," Sin said snatching them off her face in one swift motion. The look in her eyes nearly cracked his heart in two. Not his baby sister, he thought to himself. Her eyes were wide as a four lane highway and her pupils were dilated. "You been getting high!?" he asked sounding as if he was pleading for it not to be true.

Ashleigh lowered her head in shame. She could no longer face him or the truth.

"No. No. No Ash. What the fuck are you doing to yourself?" he raised his voice. "It's that nigga ain't it? He got you playing with your nose. He got you into all type of shit," Sin sighed and was furious. "I knew something was off with you. I been watching you all day. I'ma kill that nigga," Sin declared.

"No, Sin please," Ashleigh begged. "I'll stay away from him like you told me to. I promise. Just don't kill him," Ashleigh cried. Her pleas falling on deaf ears as Sin turned to walk away from her. She knew he didn't make idle threats. Ashleigh grabbed his arm, "Sin, I'm begging you. Don't kill him. He didn't force me to. But I'll get clean, I promise. I'll check into rehab," she offered.

Sin had fury in his eyes. All he could see was red. His nostrils flared like a bull ready to charge. Case was a dead man and there was nothing Ashleigh could say to change that. But Sin wanted her to get clean, so he'd agreed to not harm him if she checked in to rehab. "Ashleigh I'm gonna give you three days. If you haven't checked into rehab by then. I'm gonna tell the family about your little problem and I'm gonna kill ya man," he told her.

"Three days!? What am I supposed to tell everybody? Where will they think I've gone. My mother," she thought as tears ran down her face.

"You pack your bags and tell everyone you are going on vacation for a little while to clear you mind. That's your story," he said through his tightly clenched jaw.

"Ok," she quickly agreed seeing the anger in his eyes.

"Three days Ashleigh," Sin repeated handing her shades back to her then watching her walk away quickly.

Sin looked up into the sky and sighed in frustration then headed back around the house. He bumped right into Cassie's husband Elijah standing alone, smoking a cigar a few feet away from the back door. The two men made eye contact and Sin gestured towards him. Elijah approached Sin and the two of them began to walk.

"What's up? You got some information for me," Sin asked in a voice a little higher than a whisper.

Elijah exhaled a cloud of smoke. His eyes shifted from side to side, making sure no one was in listening distance before speaking. "Your brother Mason has been talking to that federal agent from the hospital."

"Mosley?" Sin asked.

"Yeah. I heard them speaking on the phone, in his office. A couple days before Bria was killed." Then he lowered his voice even more and said, "He offered to give you up, if Mosley found Bria."

Sin's brow lowered into a look of disdain. "This clown," he mumbled under his breath while shaking his head. "My pops worked so hard grooming this nigga, for him to turn into a rat. He probably rolling over in his grave as we speak." Sin wasn't surprised by Mason's actions. He always thought him to be a spineless coward, this was just more confirmation. Elijah was Sin's eyes and ears inside City Hall.

As a city official, Elijah was privy to very valuable information and as the brother-in-law of the mayor, he had unlimited access all over the building. Sin felt he couldn't trust Mason and wanted to know everything he was up to. Having Elijah kept Sin one step ahead of his brother.

"Oh and he's screwing his secretary. I'm almost one hundred percent sure of it," Elijah offered up another juicy piece of information that he thought could be helpful to Sin.

"This nigga ain't waste no time getting on his Bill Clinton shit," Sin said cracking a smirk then he began rubbing his chin, thinking of a play. "I need you to get me some info on that bitch," Sin demanded. "Her name, address, you know shit like that. Never know when information like that could be useful."

Elijah nodded eagerly. He enjoyed the stuffed envelopes Sin provided him for being a mole. Elijah was straight laced, not a law breaker at all. But through conversation, Sin recognized Elijah would be willing to bend a rule or two for some extra cash. So Sin took full advantage of it.

"Anything else?" Sin asked.

"Nah, that's it." Elijah answered.

"Aight," Sin replied. Then an awkward silence fell on the conversation. Elijah had a goofy look on his face. "What's up?" Sin asked.

Elijah rubbed his thumb and index finger together indicating his want for his money.

Sin laughed as he reached inside his suit and pulled out an envelope. “Here you greedy muthafucka.”

Elijah smiled. “You always say you don’t like favors,” he reminded Sin as he tucked the envelope away.

A loud crash followed by a scream caught both men’s attention. Sin pulled his gun from his waist and raced into the house to see what was going on. Elijah was right on his heels.

Khari tossed another bottle of wine across the room into the wall, showing her rage and hurt. She had finally snapped. A flood of emotions seemed to hit her all at once. Bria was gone. She was never coming back. Khari had enough of it all. The Holloway rules. The Holloway lifestyle. The Holloway way. She was tired of it. In her eyes, her daughter’s death was being treated like a farce. Khari was done with the charade and all the games she saw played in front of her eyes. The whole room fell silent as she started her rant.

“So all of you are going to sit here like my fucking daughter isn’t dead?” she said in a drunken, drug fueled babble. “Life goes on for the Holloway family, huh?” she said sarcastically.

By this time Sin and Elijah came running into the family room, Khari was a hurricane of rage and fury with tears spilling down her face. With one quick swing Khari knocked one of Emma’s expensive art pieces off the mantel above the fire place. Emma stood from the chair as the sculpture crashed to the ground, exploding into a thousand pieces.

“Ok, that’s enough Khari,” Emma raised her voice, quickly motioning to Mason with her finger. “If you don’t calm this crazy lunatic of yours down. I am going to have her bounded, gagged and carried out of here.”

“She needs a straightjacket,” Ashleigh mumbled under her breath but loud enough so she could be heard. She herself was high as a kite and found Khari’s outburst as a bit of much needed entertainment.

“Yes she does,” Emma agreed. “She needs to be institutionalized, Mason. She’s like the walking dead. She didn’t even cry at the funeral, now look at her. She is unstable, unpredictable.”

“And unapologetic,” Khari said as she knocked a painting off the wall.

“Mason!” Emma shouted.

“Mom please. You have to understand,” he said interjecting.

“I will not allow her to destroy my house. I don’t care what she is going through,” Emma barked as Mason instantly conceded.

“Khari, calm down,” he pleaded with his wife.

“That’s right. Do what your mommy says. Look at little Mason always following mommy’s orders,” Khari teased.

"You need to calm down right now," Mason demanded feeling uncomfortable as his wife embarrassed him in front of the entire family.

"Fuck you Mason. Why should I? Why should I calm down? Because I'm damaging your mommy's things? Fuck this," she screamed, knocking another piece of artwork to the floor. "And fuck her too. That is all you people care about is money and all the expensive things you have. What about what can't be replaced, like my daughter. Why isn't anyone worried about the fact that Bria is dead and she can't be replaced?" Khari fell to the floor in despair.

"You're an embarrassment," Emma seethed looking down at her. "No wonder my son cheats. You are so weak."

"Ma, that's enough," Cassie shouted.

Emma sucked her teeth, walked to the other side of the room and sat down.

Sin put his gun away and leaned up against the doorway, watching Khari's meltdown. He clenched his jaw tightly. He felt for Khari and wanted to walk over and pick her up off the ground. Although he resented her for all she had done, he couldn't help but to feel her pain. She was a mother who had just lost her daughter through extreme tragedy. There were no words that could give her comfort. Nothing in the world could mend her heart at that very moment. She needed to grieve and if breaking things and flipping out worked for her, he believed she should be allowed to do so, without judgement.

"Khari we're all mourning Bria's death," Cassie continued being the voice of reason. "She meant the world to all of us. She was our niece and my mother's granddaughter. This is hard for everyone. I couldn't imagine having to bury one of my boys. So I won't begin to pretend that I know what you're feeling. But you gotta dig down deep and try to pull yourself together. No one here is against you. We are here for you. We are all family," Cassie was trying to find the right words to comfort her sister-in-law and now found herself fighting back tears.

"Khari get up! Your embarrassing yourself," Mason rudely interjected. He strutted over attempting to pull her up from the floor, but she quickly snatched her arm away.

"Don't you dare touch me," she said. "Get myself together. Are you fucking kidding me? My daughter is dead. Oh I know," she said as her eyes grew wide. "I'm not handling it like a Holloway. I haven't seen one fucking tear drop from your eyes yet Emma." Then she turned towards her husband. "You're the weak one. You're a selfish son of a bitch," Khari spewed out venom with every word she hurled at Mason.

Emma sat down and grabbed her glass off the end table and took a sip. She started to interrupt but decided against it. A man had to be a man. Mason needed to handle this on his own.

"Me? You're the selfish bitch," Mason shouted losing his temper. "I did all I could to get our daughter back. What did you do but sit at home, complain and cry? You think you're the only one hurting behind this?" he said as he clenched his jaw tight.

Khari rose to her feet and was now face to face with her husband. "Have you really Mason? I sure as hell couldn't tell. You didn't seem that concerned if you asked me. Since the day Bria was kidnapped, you spent every day and night preparing to be mayor." The intoxicants were now controlling Khari's tongue and she didn't fight it, "Y'all were more worried about how he could look the part of the distraught father instead of actually being one. But you know what, it doesn't even matter. She wasn't yours anyway."

No one was quite sure if Khari meant to say what she had or if she had mistakenly let it slip out but suddenly an uncomfortable silence blanketed the room. The tension grew thick. It was like all the air had just been sucked out of the room. The faces of the Holloway family members told a story without the need for words. Jewlz eyes grew into big round circles. Ashleigh gasped and her mouth fell open in shock. Cassie's did too before she covered it with her hand. Elijah stared at no one in particular, not wanting to make eye contact. Emma had a devilish grin on her face that she hid by sipping her glass of wine. She stared directly at Sin, whose face remained unchanged.

"What did you say?" Mason's tone was unsettling to the room. Rage was building in him like a pot of water starting to boil.

"You heard me," Khari said. Despite the look on Mason's face she didn't flinch or felt rattled by him.

Mason's stomach was twisted in knots, his heartbeat quickened and beads of sweat began to form on his brow. "What are you talking about Khari. What do you mean, she's not mine?" he shouted grabbing her but she backed away quickly as he stalked towards her.

"Don't put your hands on me, Mason," Khari warned.

"Khari. Mason. Both of you calm down," Cassie interrupted by jumping in between them. "Mason you need to take your wife in the other room. It's obvious the both of you have some things to work out. But this isn't something you should do in front of everybody."

"No," Emma said. "We're all family here. There should never be any secrets amongst family." Her words were calculated. A subtle way to fan the flames, stoking the fire burning inside of Mason. Emma was so anxious for the truth to be revealed. Then everyone in the family would finally see Sin for what he truly was; an outsider. The love and admiration her children showed towards him was sickening to her and it was surely to fade once they all knew the truth.

"Not now ma. This is not the time for your antics," Cassie objected sternly, unlike the rest of her siblings, she never shied away from a war of words with Emma. Cassie loved her mother but she didn't have the same fear of Emma that the rest of the children had. They were frequently at odds but deep down Emma respected that Cassie was her own woman.

"No, I think everyone wants to hear what she has to say," Mason replied with his hands stretched out wide looking around at the rest of the family. He turned his attention back to Khari, there was fire burning in his eyes and before she could respond he began to hurl insult at her. "You drug addicted, slut bitch. I should've left your ass where I found you, in the gutter like the ghetto trash you are. You were never nothing more than a project bitch. How could you do this to me!" he shouted. "Bria," he paused looking up at the ceiling fighting back tears. Mason did not want to accept what she said as truth. He started to ramble, "She has to be mine. I know she is. How couldn't she be? Bria is not my daughter? Is that what you are saying to me?" Anger fueled his words and tears filled his eyes. For the very first time, in a long time, Mason was showing his wife that he cared. He was hurt beyond measure.

For a brief moment, Khari felt something she hadn't in forever, compassion. She saw the pain in her husband's eyes and it hurt her. She almost wished that she could take back her words. Khari didn't feel the sense of relief nor the gratification she expected. "I'm sorry but it's true."

"Your lying. You only trying to hurt me," he challenged.

"No Mason. I'm not. There is no way she could be yours," she spoke in a somber tone. "I was already pregnant when we met. I just hid it from you," she admitted.

"This is all too much. Mason please take Khari upstairs. You two need to talk about this." Cassie moved closer to her brother and rubbed his back. "You need to hear your wife out. This family is falling apart. We're all going through something but fighting, yelling and screaming at one another is not the way to handle it."

Cassie was trying hard to diffuse the situation but to no avail. Her mother fed off the dysfunction and Emma wouldn't be satisfied until the whole truth was exposed.

"Cassie, you really need to worry about your own marriage," Emma spewed as she rose to her feet. "Now Khari since you felt the need to air your dirty laundry in front of all of us. I have a question." The smug grin on Emma's face indicated that she was about to stir the pot as usually. "Do you care to share with us, who is actually Bria's father?" Emma's eyes were fixed on Sin as she spoke. He knew then that she already knew the answer to her question.

The whole room grew silent waiting for Khari to answer. Mason was unsure if he even wanted an answer to what his mother had asked. All he could see was flashes of Bria in his mind. All the time he had shared with her. The joy he felt hearing her first words and seeing her first steps.

How could she not be his? He felt so betrayed but there was another feeling there as well, guilt. He had used Bria as a pawn in his political game. He had gained from it but had lost so much as well. How could he judge Khari, when his sins were far more sinister and deeper than she could ever know. He had to forgive Khari in order to begin to forgive himself, something that would be much hard to do.

Khari shifted in her stance. Her mouth was dry as she tried swallowing. Finally, she spoke the name in a voice slightly above a whisper. "Sin."

You could hear the room gasp. Mason thought he had prepared himself for any answer she would give but he hadn't. "What!" he roared furiously.

Khari quickly darted her eyes towards Sin looking for him to say something. She just wanted him to save her from it all at that moment. "Sin please. Say something. Tell him the truth about us," Khari pleaded with him to come clean but she didn't need to beg at all. Sin wasn't going to shun Bria and he wasn't going to run away from the truth. Sin moved closer to the middle of the living room with his hands in his pockets. He knew this would've been a hard pill for any man to swallow, so he tried to keep it cool and calm. Although he never saw eye to eye with his brother, he would never wish this type of painful news on any man. It was worse than a bullet through the heart in his opinion.

"She's telling the truth. I know it doesn't lessen the

sting of all this but honestly I just found out myself," Sin spoke with an even tone. "I never knew Bria was my daughter. If I had, I would have—"

"You lying motherfucker," Mason quickly cut him off. "You expect me to believe this bullshit coming from the both of you. You've been fucking my wife this whole time." Mason shouted and lunged at Sin. Elijah immediately jumped in the way trying to stop the him. "I always knew you was a dirty nigga. I don't know why my father insisted on keeping you around. You will never be a part of this family."

Sin eyed Mason intensely. "In all the years you've been married, I've barely said more than two words to your wife and I haven't slept with her in longer than that," Sin told him. "I knew Khari long before you did. We're from the same neighborhood but the Khari I once knew, disappeared years ago. She traded it all for wealth and prestige," Sin explained, pointing around at the luxury that surrounded them all. "You can believe whatever you want. I really don't give a fuck. But the one thing you can believe is, if I knew Bria was mine, I would've never stood back and let her be raised by a nigga like you."

"Oh how noble," Emma chimed in clapping her hands sarcastically. "I see the home wrecker doesn't fall far from the tree. It's in your DNA. First your whore mother, now you," Emma relished the chance to throw dirty on Sin's dead mother's name. "Mason darling, relax, everything happens for a reason. Bria is gone now," Emma shrugged her shoulders, "God doesn't make mistakes."

Sin's entire body warmed with hatred, listening to Emma speak. The disregard for Bria was disgusting. Sin moved towards her aggressively. He wanted to choke the life out of Emma but stopped himself and exhaled deeply. "I've never encountered the type of evil that lives within you Emma and I've come across some of the worst muthafuckas this world has to offer. But never anything close to you. There's a special place in hell for people like you. Your day will come and I pray I'm there when it does."

"Don't talk to my mother like that you piece of shit," Mason yelled.

Emma found humor in Sin's threats. She felt victorious, having finally found a way to get under his thick skin. She enjoyed seeing his cool demeanor melt in front of her eyes. "Yasin your threats don't scare me. In fact, you should fear me more than I ever should you," she warned. "I've seen and dealt with far worst then you, young man. Marion always dreamed of the day I would accept his little bastard child who is nothing more than a bastard man now that your father is no longer alive. You can try your hardest to be a part of my family but you will never succeed. My late husband could roll over a million times in his grave and it still wouldn't happen. As long as I have air in my lungs you will always be an outsider, just the mistake that escaped the condom."

Sin stepped closer to Emma, they were now face to face, eye to eye. "Let me make this real clear to you. I don't need your acceptance or your approval. I never did. What you seem to forget is that the Holloway blood that flows through my veins is because of my father, not you. There will never be anything you can do to change that. The clothes you wear, the cars you drive, the life you live, all courtesy of my father. All this power and prestige was built on the same blood that runs through me."

Emma fumed, flaring her nostrils at the sound of Sin's voice and his display of self-confidence. "You have no idea whose blood all this was built on," she glared at him. Emma knew Sin wasn't easily intimidated. He was built strong, like his father. In her mind there was only one way to stop him. Sin would have to meet the same demise that Marion did.

"I thought I told you not to talk to my mother like that," Mason shouted before taking a cheap shot at Sin, landing a glancing blow to his jaw.

Sin reacted quickly, bull rushing Mason, taking him to the ground and pounding on him. Mason tried blocking as much as he could but blow after blow connected with his face, until he could no longer defend himself. Sin pulled out his gun and placed it to Mason's head.

"NOOOOOO!" Cassie yelled.

"Sin, don't..." Khari pleaded with him to spare Mason's life.

"Get off of him. Somebody get him off of Mason," Emma screamed.

Seconds later a group of bodyguards came rushing in, attempting to break up the fight between the two brothers. Sin stood to his feet, giving the guards a menacing glare. "Nigga, if you put your hands on me, I'm a bury you with this fuck nigga," he threatened. The men backed up, allowing Sin to get himself together, placing his gun back in his waist and straightening his clothes. He looked at the faces of everybody in the room. There was fear in his sibling's eyes; fear of him. He glared down at a bloodied Mason laying on the floor and gritted his teeth. "There will only be so many more times that Cassie will be able to save you," he said about sparing Mason's life. "Every day that you wake up, I want you to remember that you're only alive because I let you be." Sin meant every word he said.

"Get the hell out of my house," Emma barked, seething as she stared at Sin like flames would shoot out of her eyes. "Take that trash with you," she said pointing to Khari.

Unfazed, Sin didn't speak another word. He just marched straight towards the door.

Khari looked lost as she stood frozen not knowing if she should rush to Mason's aid or chase after Sin. Emma didn't give her a choice. "Khari get out of my sight. This is all your fault."

Khari searched the eyes in the room for sympathy but found none. She took off running behind Sin. "Slow down," she pleaded as he made it out the front door and to his car. "Sin, please— "

He turned on a dime. "Please what? Take you with me?" he shook his head. "I told you before there was nothing between us except for Bria. Now there is nothing." His lip curled and his eyes lowered into slits. "You're right where you belong. You're grimey ass fits in perfectly here."

Khari called out, trying to plead with him to stop but to no avail. Sin ignored all her cries and pleas, hopping in his car and speeding off. He felt for Khari, but he was too hurt and upset to care about whatever she was going through. Had she not lied to him about Bria, she might be still alive. Sin would never forgive her for that. He would have gone to the ends of earth to make sure his daughter was protected. Khari needed to understand that she had caused irreparable damage and now he was left to grieve over a child he never knew he had.

* * *

Khari just wanted the pain to stop. She felt like she was drowning and could see everyone else breathing around her but only she couldn't get the air. She raced back into the house, amidst the commotion still going on in the family room. Khari headed straight upstairs unnoticed. She went into the guest bedroom and threw herself across the plush mattress. The things Sin had just told her unraveled the last little string holding her heart together. Khari cried because she was hurting inside but mostly because what he said to her was the plain truth. She did belong right where she was. She deserved every bit of pain that dwelled inside of her. She sold her life for riches and ended up losing her morals, her dignity and her daughter. Now she was losing her mind. Khari had tried to convince herself of the possibility that her and Sin being able to rekindle what they once shared but now that was completely gone. He made that clear and every word stabbed at her heart with precision. Khari buried her face into a pillow and screamed as loud as she could. The muffling the pillow caused allowed no one to hear her cries. But what else was new, nobody ever heard her cries for help. She never seemed to matter to anybody, anymore.

"No, no, no. How can this be happening to me?" Khari questioned as she jumped to her feet and began pacing the bedroom floor. "This is not real. It can't be. I must be dreaming. Yeah, I am. I need to go back to sleep and when I wake up everything is going to be back to normal," Khari talk aloud, questioning and answering herself. She was becoming delusional. She felt alone, trapped in darkness. Although she still had her son, MJ, he was too young to understand or be there for her. Mason would surely leave now after this news, What self-respecting man with pride would stay? Emma would gloat in it for years to come and Sin would forever hate her with no remorse. Khari's life was not supposed to be like this and she was having a hard time accepting it. She had lost the desire to partake in life. "I just need to sleep," she kept repeating. Sleep was where she found peace, it was when she was awake that the nightmare occurred. Khari marched to the bathroom inside the guest room. She hurried and opened the cabinet looking for anything she thought could help take her pain away. She found it in a bottle of pain medicine prescribed to Cassie after her accident. The pills were exactly what Khari needed to rest peacefully and escape the world spiraling around her.

"Bria, mommy's going to take a little nap then we'll be together. I know I am going to see you." Khari was completely out of it. Her depression had put her in an unstable state of mind. Her thoughts were now clouded and her decisions were irrational. She emptied the contents of the pill bottle in her hand, swallowing them one by one and washing them down with sink water. Khari looked up at her reflection in the mirror and felt disgusted. She was ashamed of the woman she had become. She dropped the pill bottle in the sink and headed straight for the bed. After a few minutes she began to gag as the potency of the narcotic was too much on her stomach. Khari vomited hard and loud, then her head started to spin and she felt disorientated.

Within seconds her body went into convulsions and foam appeared around and corners of her mouth. This wasn't the peacefully death she had hoped for.

Etilda was strolling causally by the guest room when she heard a gurgling sound. Noticing the door was ajar, she peeked her head in. Shocked, she found Khari sprawled across the bed, her body in a violent seizure and her skin color now a purplish blue.

"Aaahhh! Senora Khari!"

Etilda's panic scream for help was the last thing Khari heard before the world went black.

CHAPTER 24

MASON ENTERED THE LOBBY OF the psychiatric clinic. One of the guards standing near the door pointed him in the direction of the reception desk. The young lady dressed in a nurse's uniform greeted him with a smile, when he approached. Mason stated his business and after having him fill out some papers, she escorted him to Khari's room. Mason followed the nurse up a short flight of steps and down a long hallway that only had doors on the left side. As they walked Mason admired the woman from behind. She was impressively built, although her face was not appealing to him. At the second to last door, the nurse used her key to open Khari's door. She motioned for Mason to enter then closed the door behind him.

Khari, dressed in an off-white robe with her hair braided into a ponytail, sat staring aimlessly out the barred window at nothing in particular. She didn't even turn her head to acknowledge her husband's presence in the room.

Mason's face showed pity. He reached out and stroked her hair then leaned over, kissing her cheek. "I came to bring you home," he said.

"I thought you hated me for what I did to Bria," Khari said.

"You didn't do anything to Bria," Mason replied turning her face away from the window and facing him.

"I killed our daughter," Khari was crying as she spoke. "I killed her with my lies and deceit. I always knew something bad would happen because of my secret. Now God is punishing me."

Mason kneeled down beside her chair. "No that's not true at all. Nobody blames you. Nobody will ever blame you." He rested his forehead against hers. The special bond they once shared now manifesting as sympathy between the two of them.

"I blame me," she explained, weeping without stopping.

"Don't," Mason pleaded with her. He stood up and straightened his clothes. "I promise you, from now on things will be better. I came to bring you home, so you can be around the people who love you. My mother has agreed to look after you while I deal with the duties of being mayor."

Khari looked up at him with tears running down her face. "No. I don't trust your mother Mason. She may have you fooled but not me. She has everybody fooled with her fake smile. It's all mind tricks." Her voice rose to a loud pitch.

"Nobody has me fooled about anything," he insisted. "I just need her help, looking after you while I work. The doctors say you need to have twenty-four-hour supervision. I have a city to run but I know you need me too. This is the only way for me to do both," he said. He wiped the tears from her face. "Please, just trust me." Mason was so convincing in his plea, but Khari knew all too well the many disguises Emma wore. She might have convinced her son that she would care for Khari with love and concern, but nothing she does is ever non beneficial for Emma. Khari knew with every inch of her body that Emma hated her and the truth of the matter was Khari shared the same sentiments towards her.

"Everything is going to get better, trust me. We are going to work on this. You and I, together as a family. I know I haven't been the most supportive but I promise I will work at it. We will work at it, ok?" Mason said lifting up her chin making eye contact with his distraught wife and looking for confirmation. He tried his very best to convince her that what he was saying would come to fruition, he wanted her to believe that what they had went through was reparable. Khari nodded her head in agreement forcing a half smile. She knew entering the Holloway estate she would be fighting more than an internal battle with herself. She now would be under Emma's clutch and supervision. For a mere second she wished the pills she swallowed would have ended her life. The last thing she wanted was to be anywhere near Emma. Mason grabbed Khari's sweater and placed it over her shoulders. He grabbed her bag already prepared and packed by the on duty nurse and they both headed for the door, for the very first time in a long time hand in hand.

* * *

"Let me out of here," Ariane cried out, pounding her fist on the cellar door. Her throat was sore from screaming at the top of her lungs and her stomach muscles ached. Without any access to daylight from windows, her days had begun to mix with her nights. She had no idea how long she had been locked away but it felt like forever. She had lost track of time and was slowly losing her mind. It was taking a heavy toll on her. The mental torture was unbearable and she felt on the verge of a psychotic break. Ariane pressed her back against the wall and slid down to the floor in a hunched position. Pulling her legs close to her chest, she rested her chin on her knees and rocked her body in place. It was the only thing she found that calmed her racing mind. She hadn't been able to think clearly about any one thing for any length of time. Her thoughts were scattered which left her with a sense of hopelessness. Ariane was all cried out. Her eyes were swollen, red and irritated, her hair was disheveled and her skin was dry and ashy.

Suddenly Ariane heard a sound that she hadn't in a while; the jiggling of keys as the locks on the door at the top of the steps began to unlock, one by one. She scrambled to her feet, barely able to keep her balance from the weakness of her legs. The door swung open, light flooded down into the room and Ariane shaded her eyes with her hands while squinting. There were footsteps on the stairs followed by a clicking sound, instantly the basement lit up. As the room brightened and things became clear, Ariane couldn't believe her eyes. She backed herself up against the cold wall in the basement, feeling as though she was hallucinating. The extreme isolation of solitary confinement had to be playing tricks on her mind. The man standing in front of her had to be a figment of her imagination, he couldn't be real.

"What are you doing here?" she asked. No longer was she afraid, Ariane was now enraged. "Is all this because of you? You're behind this? How could you do this to me," she shouted.

"Just relax Arianne. All of this is for your own good, your own protection. I wouldn't be able to live with myself if anything was to happen to you. You have to trust me on this."

Putting the voice with the face, she couldn't believe it was him. He was the silhouette from the other night. The man in charge. The person behind all of her suffering. "You thought kidnapping me and holding me against my will was the way to build trust?" she yelled.

"I didn't see any other way. It's my job to keep you safe. I am your father."

Agent Mosely stared at his estranged daughter with a look of true concern in his eyes. It had been an eternity since Ariane laid eyes on him. But his was a face that she could never forget. She hated him. By leaving her mother, brother and her when she was just a small child, Mosley had left a huge void in her life. With their mother in a constant drunken stupor, the responsibility to fill that void fell on her older brother. That burden of responsibility led him to the street which eventually took his life. Ariane had always blamed her father. Even after her brother's death he had chosen to keep his distance. Mosely blamed his son's choices for his death more than he did the people who actually pulled the trigger. He had no way of knowing that his son died defending Ariane's honor. Although Mosley kept away from his daughter, his watchful eye remained focused on her. He didn't want to risk losing another child, so he assigned Ariane her own personal watchdog to keep her out of harm's way.

"Ariane you've gotten yourself involved with someone so dangerous and something so big, you have no idea what or who you're dealing with," he told her.

"So this was all you? Kidnapping me. The explosion at the cemetery. Sin," she ranted then paused as thoughts of Sin flooded her mind. "Where is Sin? What did you do to him?" her voice crack with fear.

"Calm down. Nothing has happened to Yasin. Not yet at least." Mosley tossed some fresh clothes to his daughter. "Get dressed then come join me upstairs," he said before turning and walking out.

Ariane couldn't believe the turn of events. She had been kidnapped by her own father. What did he want with her after all these years and why was he after Sin, she thought to herself. She quickly got dressed and headed up the stairs to join her father. When she made it to the top stairs, she stood in a hallway.

"Over here," Mosley called out.

Ariane followed the sound of his voice. She found him sitting in the middle of the room at a round dining table for two. On top of a draping white table cloth sat two covered plates of food, a bottle of wine and a bouquet of daisies in the center of the table. Mosley sat with a smile on his face and his hand extended toward the empty chair, inviting her to take a seat.

"I took the liberty of ordering for you." His attempt at

humor was not well received. But Ariane was too hungry to object, so she took a seat. "It's been so long since we've shared a meal. I figured this was a perfect time. I remembered your favorite," he said.

Ariane removed the top off her plate. "KFC," she said. "This hasn't been my favorite since I was a child," she sucked her teeth.

"Forgive me, it's been a while," he stated the obvious.

"I want to leave," she said.

"That could be arranged but first eat your food," Mosley instructed her.

"What's stopping me from getting up right now and running out of that door?" she asked.

"You're free to try but how far do you really think you'll get? I have men all over, guarding this house. So let's talk," he said pouring them both a glass of wine. "There is so much that you don't know Ariane. I know you think you are in love with Sin but do you even know the type of man your dealing with? Do you know what he is involved with and what he is capable of," Mosely dropped a manila envelope on the table and slid it towards her causing the contents to spill out. On the table in front of her were pictures of Sin and his entourage. Ariane picked up a picture of Sin walking out of his car dealership. Tears came to her eyes, she missed his face, his lips, his smell, his touch. She picked up another picture, this was of him opening the passenger side door of the vehicle she test drove the very first day they met. Ariane's mouth fell open in shock and her heart skipped a beat. "You've been following me too?" she said.

"I've had someone following you for years. Just to keep you safe," he revealed. "Ariane, I've been building a case on the Holloway family since before Marion Holloway was murdered. Sin's father was the focus of my investigation but since his death, I'm certain Sin has taken over the organization."

Ariane sighed. "So you kidnapped me why? To get me to help you. I don't even know if what you are saying is true."

Mosley rose from his seat and walked over to her. He quickly searched through the pictures until he came upon two specific pictures. One of Ali's battered corpse and another of Barkim's dead body. "You ever seen these two men before?" he asked but continued before she could answer. "I know you have. They were Sin's friends. Two brothers, Barkim and Ali Simmons. He killed Ali because he thought Barkim was working with me"

"Well what happened to the other one?" she asked.

Mosley placed another more gruesome picture of Barkim's crime scene in front of her. "He killed himself, rather than to deal with what Sin would do to the rest of his family."

Ariane turned her head away, the pictures were too

brutal for her to view any longer.

"You see the things he is capable of," Mosely said to his daughter. "What do you think he'll do to you, if he ever thinks you've betrayed him?"

"Sin would never hurt me. He loves me," she explained.

"So use that to help me bring him down. Once and for all," he begged. "He trusts you. You said it yourself, he loves you right? He would never suspect you. I'm your father Ariane, your family. Family should stick together."

"Family," she repeated sarcastically nodding her head. "We haven't been family in a long time. You were always too busy for that, remember?"

"I know it's difficult for you to understand. This job can put the people you care about in harm's way," he tried explaining.

"Oh, so you abandoned your family for our own good?" she asked. "Where were you all the times I needed you? Where were you when Quan got killed?" The tears began to form in her eyes. Her father had no answer for her. "Just like I thought," she said. "You seem to do a lot of selfish things for everyone else's good. Abandoning your family, kidnapping me. Cut the bullshit," Ariane shook her head. "If you think I'm going to be the one that helps you bring down Sin, you're crazy. I would never betray him. If, and that is a big if, Sin is involved in whatever it is that you are saying, I know nothing about it."

"Why must you be so stubborn baby girl," Mosley called her affectionately. "He is a monster, a drug dealer on the highest level. Don't be fooled by his charming ways and handsome face. It's all an act. I'm just trying to keep you safe."

"I'm not in any danger," she proclaimed. "Here in this place, is where I don't feel safe. Now let me go!" Ariane yelled in frustration to her father.

"I'm afraid I can't do that," he said disappointed that she wouldn't help him.

"Sin will come for me, unlike you ever did. We both know he will. He won't stop until he finds me," she stated proudly.

"No he won't," Mosley stated flatly, almost mean in his tone. He didn't appreciate her measuring him against Sin, a drug dealing criminal. "He thinks you're dead," he informed her. Sin thinks you died in the explosion at the cemetery. Right now, he is in the middle of a war with The Commission over you. People close to him have died and will continue to die. You wouldn't be safe. Besides, what would he think if you just popped back up out of nowhere with this elaborate story, trying to explain away where you've been. Do you think he would trust you then? Do you think he will love you knowing your daddy is the Feds?" The thought made Mosley chuckle. Truthfully he would love to see the look on Sin's face when he found out. He was almost tempted to let Ariane walk out the door on that alone.

The news that Sin thought she was dead crushed all hope in Ariane. The air left her chest and she slumped in her chair. It explained why he hadn't come to save her from the pit of despair. But Ariane hurt more for Sin than she did herself. She could only imagine the pain he was in, the thoughts he must be having. The feeling of emptiness and unfulfilled love he must be dealing with daily. The guilt eating away at him, it probably kept him awake every night. It had drove him to wage war in her memory. In that moment, she had never loved him more and for that, she would suffer whatever consequences that came with it and she would do it happily.

"I'm not going to help you. If you want Sin, you will have to get him on our own." Ariane stood from the table, gulped down her glass of wine and grabbed a piece of chicken off her plate. "Thanks for dinner," she said as she turned and walked back into the darkness of the cellar where she was being held, slamming the door behind her. She sat on the floor and heard the sound of the door being locked at the top of the steps.

* * *

Ashleigh had hoped to find a stylishly luxurious like setting, where she would be receiving massages and getting her nails done. She had pictured the high-end rehab more like a resort than a place to heal and free herself from addiction. But there were no spa treatments, no fancy cuisines and really no luxury at all. Especially in her bedroom, it was quite basic, dormitory like, plain white covers and sheets on a twin sized bed. Ashleigh removed her designer shades from her face to get a better look at the cramped space she was expected to stay in. She turned her nose up, not impressed at all. She wheeled her luggage over to the bed and plopped down on top of the mattress, it was nice and soft. That was about the only thing she found appealing about the place so far.

"I'm not an addict. Why am I even here?" she uttered aloud. In her mind she was in full control, she could stop at any time, she just wasn't ready to yet. Cocaine made her feel alive when she felt dead on the inside. It numbed her when she felt pain. Nothing in her life offered that type of comfort. "Why did I agree to this?" she questioned then squeezed her eyes shut, fighting back tears that threatened to start. Ashleigh shook her head in disbelief, this was her reality for the next thirty days but she wasn't like the other patients there. They looked like addicts who needed the help. "I would never be like them," she told herself. Ashleigh was more elegant, more rich than all of them. She was the daughter of a boss, a queen in waiting. She was only there because of a promise to Sin not because she needed to be. "It was the only way to save Case's life," she told herself over and over. Ashleigh scanned the room, trying her best to get comfortable with her surroundings but she still felt out of place, even here luggage looked like it didn't belong.

She removed her oversized sun hat and sat it on top of her luggage. A conniving look came across her face and her eyes told of her scheming thoughts. This was when she favored her mother the most. "I know somebody in this place, snuck some drugs in here. At least some weed," she whispered only for her ears to hear. "Probably that blond hair, big titty bitch, I passed on my way in." Ashleigh sighed deeply, "If not, I'm gonna go crazy in this place." She laid back, looked up at the ceiling and banged both hands on the bed. "Arrgh." She let out a grunt of frustration. This was going to be a long thirty days.

CHAPTER 25

EMMA STOOD SILENTLY, HER arms folded across her chest as she watched Khari sleep. "Rise and shine, pretty girl," Emma sarcastically greeted as she pulled the drapes back allowing sunrays to invade the dark room. "Time to get up," she ordered.

Khari began to stir in the bed. She pulled the cover over her head trying to shield her eyes from the beaming sunlight.

It had been about a week since Khari was released from the psychiatric unit in the hospital. Mason didn't want to take any chances, so he drove her straight to the Holloway estates to be looked after. Khari was on suicide watch and needed full time attention, something he wanted to give her but wasn't able to do, due to his duties as mayor. Emma first dismissed the idea all together but after giving it some thought she accepted. She wanted Mason to be focused. Emma needed him on his A game, she knew he would be of good use once all her plans were fulfilled. His position would shield her from any prying eyes and allow her to conduct business without much scrutiny from the law. Emma believed Mason needed normalcy in his home life after Bria's death. If looking after Khari would alleviate some stress, she would go the extra mile to accomplish that for her first born child. She hadn't had to do much since Khari had been there, Etilda handled most of the duties. But today Emma had given all of her staff the day off, so she alone would have to tend to Khari.

"Oh no," Emma said pulling the covers back. "You need to get up, eat and shower. No more feeling sorry for yourself. Not on my watch. I am not here to be your nurse and I am certainly not Tilda," Emma said. She had quickly grown tired of hearing Khari's moans and cries all through the night.

Khari felt extremely sluggish and her head was spinning. No matter how hard she tried, she just couldn't find the strength to climb out of the deep hole of depression she was in or move much. In the last week she had only gotten out of bed to close the curtains after Emma ordered Etilda to open them or to drag herself to the bathroom. Even then, there were times when she hadn't made it and would soil herself or the sheets. Khari's mental break didn't explain why she felt so worn out. Physically nothing seemed right, that was unusual to her but nothing had felt normal since Bria's death. Unbeknownst to Khari, Emma had replaced her anti-depressant meds with the sedative Benzodiazepine and had a clueless Etilda feeding them to her day and night. It was one thing having to look after Khari but having to deal with her crazy theatrics was not an option for Emma. Keeping her drugged up and out of the way, Emma could show Mason how much of a non-factor his wife was. Khari couldn't be depended on, her mind had twisted around itself and she couldn't find her way out. Mason needed his mother more than ever now.

Khari forced herself to sit upright in the bed. She pulled her knees to her chest and rested her chin on them still keeping her eyes closed.

"My God it smells horrible in here. A grown woman like you should be ashamed and embarrassed to be giving off this type of body odor. And you're supposed to be the first lady of this city," Emma looked down at her with a despairing expression.

Khari remained silent. She had no fight left in here. No energy to respond to Emma's remarks.

"Here you need to eat something. Tilda said you haven't been eating," Emma said picking up a tray off the nightstand. "You're starting to look a little frail and sickly. You're going to resemble a bag of bones, standing next to my Mason. Here I made it myself."

A look of concern furrowed Khari's brow. Although it was just a half sandwich and soup, Khari like everyone else in the family, knew Emma couldn't cook. "I'm not hungry," she shook her head, which seemed to boil Emma's blood some.

Emma slammed the tray back down, spilling the soup. "Look what you made me do" she yelled. The elevation of her voice made Khari coward a bit, her nerves were fried making her a jittery mess. Emma walked over and snatched the covers off the bed. "Come on get up. Enough is enough."

"No," Khari replied, snatching the covers away from Emma, pulling them back on to herself and turning her back. "Just leave me alone," she pleaded. The pain in her voice evident.

Emma was disgusted by how weak and useless Khari was. She couldn't believe she had allowed her son to marry such a worthless waste of air and space. "I know what you want," Emma pulling a bottle of pills from her robe and shook it like she was ringing a dinner for a dog. Khari rolled back over to face her. Emma smirked, she had to remind Khari who was really in control.

"Now Mason is going to stop by later on to check on you. He is bringing us dinner. I'm gonna need for you to pull it together by this evening. Do you understand me?" When Khari didn't reply Emma shook the pill bottle again. "Do you understand me?"

"Yes," Khari said sitting up, eager to get her hands on those pills.

"Emma disappeared in to the bathroom and returned with a glass of water. "Here," she handed Khari the glass then extended her other hand. There were two pills in her palm. "You can rest for now but," Emma pulled her hand away as Khari reached for the meds. "Ut, Ut, Ah. You can rest for now but I want you showered, smelling good and look as decent as possible later on tonight. I know you don't expect any comfort from your husband looking like that." Then she gave Khari the pills.

Khari quickly popped them in her mouth and downed the water. She handed the glass back to Emma then turned her back once again as she laid down.

Emma sucked her teeth. "Pitiful," she said as she walked out the room and closed the door.

Khari waited a few seconds then leaped from the bed and walked into the bathroom. She didn't know what it was but every time she took those pills, she felt like the living dead. They made her zoned out and sleep for what felt like days at a time. She opened her hand and dropped both pills in the toilet. "Not today bitch," she said. Khari had deceived Emma with her sleight of hand. She couldn't mourn Bria properly with all the drugs she was being fed, she just seemed to mentally check out while on them. Khari flushed the toilet then headed back into the room. The house seemed so quiet, not even the usual noise of Etilda singing Spanish tunes as she worked throughout the house. Khari slowly cracked the door and stepped out into the hallway. She began walking towards the steps that lead to the kitchen downstairs but stopped short of the steps when she heard Emma's voice.

"You convinced me to trust you but you didn't deliver. I gave you the perfect opportunity to kill my husband and you failed. So I had to do it myself."

Khari's mouth fell open in disbelief hearing Emma admit to killing her own husband. Her wicked ways extended far beyond Khari's scope of imagination. She had never witnessed a viler person than Emma Holloway. The woman had no morals at all.

"My husband became weak over the years. As he grew older, he grew soft. If this had been 20 years ago, would I have been able to get rid of him so easily?" she questioned.

"No, you wouldn't have."

Khari's heart nearly stopped when she heard the mysterious voice of a man. The entire time Emma spoke Khari had assumed she was on the phone. But her co-

conspirator was in the house. Khari listened more intensely trying to recognize the voice but it was one she had never heard before.

"Do you feel any remorse?" the man asked.

"Remorse? You can't be serious," Emma laughed. "I loved my husband but he loved himself more. He killed my entire family without thinking twice about me. Then took over my father's empire. Or don't you remember?"

"Of course I remember. I'm the one who told you, all those years ago. But that's a long time to hold on to a secret like that," the man said.

"I'm a patient woman," Emma said sinfully her evil eyes gleaming.

"And I'm a patient man. I've waited a long time to have you all to myself," the man's voice was filled with charm and confidence.

"And so have I my love," Emma's tone became seductive momentarily as she smiled. "But I want back what is mine," she reminded him. "I won't allow his bastard to take over what rightfully belongs to me. Now we've lost the one piece of leverage we had over him with Bria. That kidnapping was a disaster. The little girl was not supposed to die. Now are you gonna kill Sin or do I have to handle that myself too?"

"In due time my love. Everything is going according to plan. You just have to trust me," he assured her.

"I just want him dead," Emma pouted falling into his

embrace. It was the rare glimpse of the innocent and beautiful girl she once was.

"Shhh," he warned her as he kissed her lips. "Not too loud, what about you daughter in law."

"We have nothing to worry about. She is asleep and won't be waking up anytime soon. I've had her popping sedatives like Tic-Tacs," Emma revealed. "I have a few hours to fill," she flirted.

"Are you sure?" he asked.

"Even if she did overhear anything. Who would believe her?" Even Emma's giggle sounded sinister. "She's bat shit crazy. She tried to take her own life. She's strung out on the drugs. Everybody knows it. You think they are going take the word of a suicidal junkie over mine?"

Khari stood at the top of the steps with tears pouring down her face, cringing at Emma's words. Her stomach was in knots. She knew Emma was evil but she never knew she was cold enough to do the things she had heard her admit to. "You sick, evil bitch. Never in my life have I encountered someone like you. You lying, murdering bitch. Not only did you kill your husband but you are the reason my daughter is dead," Khari whispered to herself like Emma was standing directly in front of her. Khari's head began to spin and her mouth was dry. It was the withdrawal eating at her. She stumbled backwards almost losing her balance as she turned and headed back to the room.

Khari had never felt such shame and self-loathing. She gently closed the door to the room and leaned against it. "What have I become?' Khari asked herself. She was so distraught. This had to be a nightmare.

"She's going to pay for this," Khari promised. She was serious and meant every word. From the accumulative effects of the drugs, she didn't have the physical strength to do any harm to Emma. But Khari made a vow to get clean and restore her mind to its rightful state. The only way to honor Bria's memory was to seek proper justice. How would she convince Mason that his mother was truly a monster, when he was her puppet? "But Bria was his daughter, he had to believe her," she thought to herself.

Under her condition and with her track record, it would be hard pressed for anyone to believe her story. But if they didn't then Emma will have gotten away with the unimaginable. She had harmed her own family.

"I need to find a way to get out of this house, I have to get to Mason, I need to let him know what is going on," she spoke frantically in a whisper. "No, no, Sin," she said like a light going off in her head. "I need to get to Sin. He will listen to me. He knows how evil Emma is. He has to believe me. He has to listen. I'll make him listen." Although she knew he hated her deep in his soul, Sin was her only hope. Khari prayed he would help her. She put all her faith in the fact that maybe, just maybe, somewhere deep, down inside of him, Sin remembered what they once shared and how real it was.

Khari walked to the bathroom and turned on the shower before stepping out of her clothes. Looking at herself in the mirror, she saw a woman who for years had been surrounded by pure evil, manipulation and corruption. She had been broken, glued back together and broken again. Never in her life did she ever imagine she would be going through such tragedy. She had lost her daughter and slowly her mind followed. She had tried to escape from all the pain, anger and deceitfulness by taking her own life. She had failed and as she stared in the mirror she was thankful she hadn't. Khari now wanted to live more than ever. It was time for her to take her life back. And through revenge was how she would seek it. Emma had to answer for what she had taken from her. And only blood answered for blood in Khari's mind.

The bathroom began to fill with steam. Khari jumped in the shower and let the water run down over her face. She imagined washing away all of her demons. She was determined to start a new, rebuild what had been broken within her. With or without her husband or Sin. She had MJ to live for.

Lost in her thoughts, Khari never heard the footsteps entering the bathroom. She wasn't alone and she had no clue. Suddenly as she reached for the shampoo she was jolted back as a something wrapped around her neck and restricted her air supply. Khari tried to scream but only a faint sound escaped. Her breathes were quickly becoming shorter and harder to come by. Khari clawed with her fingernails trying to pry the cord from around her neck. Every attempt was unsuccessful, she was no match, easily being overpowered. Bright red lines appeared in her bulging eyeballs. They looked as though they would pop out at any minute.

"No, please. Not like this. I don't want to die yet," her final plea was merely a thought in her head. Khari twist and turned, knocking down the shower curtain, fighting tooth and nail for just another single breath. But it wasn't meant to be, her air supply had been cut off and whatever breath she had left in her lungs was no more.

"Lord forgive me for my sins," was the last thought Khari had before drifting into a forever sleep. Khari's killer lifted her lifeless body up, tying the cord around her neck before swinging the cord around the shower head and securing it tightly. Khari's body leaned forward then slumped over as her naked body hung freely. Her death had been staged perfectly, a clear suicide.

About a half hour later, Emma walked over to the kitchen counter and poured herself an oversized glass of wine. She took a sip, enjoying the robust flavor then picked up her cell and dialed 911. When the operator answered she put on an award winning performance. The devastated mother-in-law. Her deceit could be so believable when she needed it to be. Immediately following the call to 911, Emma placed a call to Mason's office at City Hall. He answered on the third ring. "Get over here now. There's been an accident with Khari," she cried into the phone before hanging it up. Emma sipped her wine once again then headed up the long flight of steps. There would be news reporters and cameras arriving soon. She had to look her best. This would definitely be the biggest story on the nightly news.

* * *

Lil Smoke knocked tentatively then stuck his head into the office. "You busy. Can I talk to you for a minute?" he asked.

"Yeah, come in," Sin said.

Lil Smoke stepped inside and shut the door behind him. Sin could tell by the look on his face that something was bothering him. That was made more clear when the young man flopped down into the chair with his shoulders slumped as he stared at the floor.

"What's on ya mind?" Sin inquired.

Lil' Smoke leaned back in his seat and sighed. "I don't know if I'm cut out for all this," he said.

"For what?"

"For all this working eight hours a day type shit. This some sucker shit," Lil' Smoke confessed. "Ain't no real money in this."

"That's your problem," Sin expressed to him. "You wanna start at the top. You wanna start off being the boss. It don't work like that."

"Why not?" the young man asked arrogantly.

Sin laughed. He could remember a time when he wasn't so patient either. Where they came from was ruled by fast money, Lil' Smoke was no different. "Listen to me. There's plenty money to be made right here," Sin said pointing out at the showroom floor. 'Sky's the limit. If you work hard and learn the business, by the time you're my age, you'll have more money than you could even imagine."

"No disrespect but I ain't trying to wait that long. You didn't and neither did my father," Lil' Smoke reminded him.

"You ain't me tho, you ain't ya pops either, just cause they out here calling you by his name. He put in a lot of work to get that name. That's a path you don't have to take."

"Speaking of," Lil' Smoke said. "You and Beans were there the night my father died right. How come y'all never talk to me about it?"

"Because it's nothing to really talk about," Sin said. "The situation got handled. It serves no purpose to dwell on the past. Holding on to a bunch of bad memories. I just try and remember all the good ones and move on."

"Was my father really like they say he was?" Lil' Smoke asked.

Sin nodded. "Your pops was a live wire. Me, him and Beans came up together during a really rough era. You really had to be who you said you were to move how we was moving," Sin reminisced.

"Was that what got him killed. Being a live wire, moving too reckless?" Lil' Smoked asked.

Sin was silent for just a moment as he gave it some thought. Then he said, "There's no way to say for sure. Smoke was just unlucky. It could have been anyone of us that night."

Lil' Smoke caught the false note in his voice. He knew there was something Sin wasn't saying but before he could press any further Sin switched subjects.

"You wanna make five hundred dollars? I got a job for you," Sin said snapping his fingers. "And you don't have to wash no cars," he joked.

"Yeah I'm with it," Lil Smoke said still a little disappointed at the change in topic. But five hundred dollars sounded good to him. "What I got to do?"

Sin grabbed a pen and wrote down an address. He passed it to Lil' Smoke. "You remember the nigga from the parade, Case? I need you to lay on his crib and call me when you see him."

"Aight," Lil' Smoke said without any hesitation just as a knock at the door interrupted them.

Both men looked up to see Kyrie and a fresh out the

hospital Beans enter the office. A wide smile spread across Sin's face as he stood to greet Beans.

"Oh shit, look at you," Sin said. "You look good for a nigga that should've been dead."

Beans laughed. "I'm back and ready to get to it. Niggas tried to take me out. They gonna have to answer for that. Now what's this I hear about you going to a meeting with—."

"Hold up, Slow down, my nigga. I'll fill you in on everything in a few," Sin said cutting an excited Beans off then nodding towards Lil' Smoke. Beans immediately stopped talking.

"Lil' Smoke, what's up?" Kyrie said.

"What's up Ky," Lil Smoke answered then turned to Beans. "What's up Beans? Good to see you're alright."

"Thanks," Beans said dryly then the room fell silent.

"I'm gonna go take care of that for you," Lil' Smoke said to Sin as he stood from his seat. He nodded to Kyrie then looked at Beans harshly as he exited the office, slamming the door behind him.

Beans sighed deeply, shaking his head as he took a seat.

"What?" Sin asked with his head in his pockets and a smirk on his face.

"You know what," Beans said, inconspicuously running his fingers across the scar in his face. He never understood Sin's need to fulfil a promise to their former friend that had snaked them. "So this shit with the Italians, Kyrie was telling me about, when is it supposed to go down?"

"Tonight. In a few actually," Sin said checking his watch.

"Where is it?"

"I'm waiting on the call from Big Phil to find out."

"What?" Beans' voice rose. "What made you agree to that shit? You must've lost ya mind while I was laid up, recovering."

Sin just shook his head and laughed. "You know I never go into anything blind, deaf or dumb. I got it all under control," he said with confidence.

Beans remained unsure. "I don't trust that shit. It just don't feel right to me. Niggas having secret meeting locations and shit."

"Yeah, shit sound funny to me too," Kyrie chimed in with his thoughts. "You really feel you can trust Catanzano to make sure everything is straight? You said all the other families are united right? Shit they might try and murk both of y'all tonight."

"2 for 1," Beans quickly agreed. "That's how I would do it."

"Keeping the meeting's location a secret until the last possible moment was Phil Catanzano's idea," Sin explained. "He organized the sit down and guaranteed the safety of every man involved. If no one knows where the meeting is being held, that makes it virtually impossible for anyone to violate the temporary peace treaty in place. Catanzano knows that if anything happens to any of the men at the meeting, he himself would be killed or at the least risk going to war. The last thing he wants is more war."

"So whose supposed to be at this meeting," Beans asked.

"Just the heads of all five families. No underbosses, capos or hench—"

Sin's phone began to ring interrupting him mid-sentence. He looked at the phone then looked back up at Beans and Kyrie. He recognized the number, "This Catanzano right now," he said as the room fell silent. He picked up and Phil Catanzano spoke briefly on the other end before quickly hanging up.

"What'd he say?" Beans leaned forward from in his seat with anticipation as Kyrie did the same. They looked like they were waiting on the winning lotto numbers to be read to them.

"He said Foxwoods, in an hour," Sin answered grabbing his coat off the back of the chair.

Beans stood up, "We gonna follow you, just to make sure everything cool."

"Nah, y'all stay here and wait for me to call. I got this," Sin insisted then dapped each of them as he exited his office.

CHAPTER 26

LIL' SMOKE SAT ON THE bench directly across the street from Case's building, smoking a blunt. It had just begun to get dark and the once packed block had started to slow with foot traffic. Smoke had been waiting for Case to appear but he had yet to show his face. Sin had him on the lookout with strict instructions to call as soon as he spotted Case. After talking with Kyrie, Sin was sure that it was Case that had been robbing his spots out in Brooklyn. He couldn't let that go unpunished, on top of the fact that Case had turned Ashleigh into a full blown cokehead. He had to be dealt with. Sin didn't tolerate any form of disrespect and Case had done that and more.

Lil' Smoke inhaled deeply, sucking as much smoke as possible into his lungs before exhaling. His head was filled with so many conflicting thoughts. He thought the weed would help with the stress but all it did was make him think more and analyze things deeper. Was Barkim really telling the truth about what happened between Sin, Beans and his father? Lil' Smoke had no way of knowing the truth, after all Barkim had snitched, his word only couldn't be trusted. He had betrayed his whole team, clearly he wasn't above misleading Lil' Smoke for personal gain. But what was he really trying to gain, besides just wanting Sin dead? Why after all these years was he just telling him this? And why doesn't anybody else know about it, or do they? Lil Smoke kept thinking to himself. But something about what Barkim said rang true to him. No matter how much he tried, he couldn't deny it. Smoke felt it in his gut but he wanted to believe that Sin would never do anything like that. Sin had been looking out for him for as long as he could remember but could it have truly been because of his guilty conscious? Smoke knew that the rules of the streets were played different, it was a dirty game. He had heard all the stories of friends turning on each other for that mighty dollar. Barkim had been right about one thing, Beans never really messed with him. Even when Smoke was younger he couldn't remember a time when Beans showed him any type of love or attention. After his father's death Beans never came around to see his grandmother the way Sin did. "Maybe that was how he dealt with his guilt," Smoke told himself. When it came to Beans something inside of him wanted what Barkim said to be fact.

Lil' Smoke took the last pull off the blunt as a car pulled up in front of Case's building and came to a stop. At first he thought about abandoning the mission. Sin would just have to find another way to get Case without his help but then he quickly reconsidered. Smoke brushed the ashes off his pants and pulled the phone out his jacket. He dialed Sin's number.

"What's up?" Sin answered, picking up on the second ring.

"He just pulled up and went in the house," Lil' Smoke replied. He knew Sin understood exactly who he was talking about.

"Ok. Cool. Stay there and let me know if he makes another move. I'm 'bout to send somebody through there," Sin told him.

"Alright bet," Lil Smoke answered.

"You did good," Sin declared.

"Told you I was ready to step up. I just needed my shot," Lil Smoke boasted proudly. "I'm ready to get put on."

"We'll talk later," Sin said.

"No doubt," Lil Smoke replied before the phone hung up.

* * *

Sin scrolled down his phone and pressed send. He navigating through traffic as the phone began to ring.

"Yo, everything good?" Beans answered with excitement in his voice.

"Yeah. You still with Kyrie?" Sin asked.

"Yeah, why?" Beans asked.

"That nigga at his house right now," Sin said.

"That nigga who?" Beans asked.

"Ol' boy Ash was fucking with, Case" Sin explained. "Tell Kyrie and Egypt to go through there and take care of that," he ordered.

"I don't know if it's a good idea to send the twin wit him," Beans told him.

"Why, what's the problem?"

"Kyrie was just saying she still fucked up behind her sister. I think she should sit this one out," Beans explained. "I'ma go with him."

"Nah my nigga. I can't let you do that. You still recovering. You're not healed up yet. Just let Kyrie go, tell him to bring some of Reina's men with him."

"That'll take too long. We together already. Nigga, I'm going," Beans insisted.

Sin heard the excitement in Beans' voice and decided he wasn't in the mental state to argue with him. He was focused on meeting with The Commission. "Alright my nigga. Be safe tho," he said.

"I should be telling you that. I still think you going to that meeting dolo is a bad idea," Beans said. "You walking into a room full of enemies and expecting to walk out alive. I told you I don't trust none of those muthafuckas."

"Everything is gonna go smooth," Sin said with confidence.

"I hope you're right. Your life could depend on it," Beans reminded him.

Sin quickly changed subjects not interested in hearing what could be his grim reality. "Y'all go take care of that business and we'll talk later," Sin told him before hanging up.

* * *

"I hate these fake ass Harlem niggas. I don't even like coming through here," Kyrie said as he drove through the streets in Case's neighborhood. He didn't fuck with anybody from that side of the city and rarely did he ever leave Brooklyn.

"Nah, it's thorough niggas out here," Beans warned, keeping his head on swivel, taking every precaution possible. "That's why we gotta do this shit smooth. We taking a risk just by coming to the next nigga's hood, you feel me?"

"I feel you," Kyrie said reaching under his seat, grabbing his gun and putting it on his lap. "But I ain't never slippin'. I'm wit' the shits. I wish one of these fuck niggas would try something." Kyrie was young and unafraid. At just 19 years old, he was already a vet in the streets.

The two of them pulled onto Case's street and parked. The block was not as busy as the rest of the city. Beans quickly scanned the street up and down looking for Lil' Smoke. "Where is this lil' nigga?" he asked shaking his head. "I don't know why Sin trusted his ass to handle this."

"I remember y'all used to have me doing shit like that. Being a lookout, watching for TNT and the niggas trying to rob," Kyrie reminisced.

"Yeah, I remember that too but he ain't like you was," Beans replied.

A smirk creased Kyrie's face. "It ain't like he was going in there with us. He did his job," he expressed.

"Still, he was supposed to stay around 'til he saw us," Beans sounded irritated, his frustration with Lil' Smoke was clearly getting the best of him.

Kyrie had begun to notice a trend when it came to Beans' interaction with Lil' Smoke. For some reason he didn't take to the young man the way Sin did. "Why you always so hard on the lil' nigga," Kyrie laughed. "Wasn't his pops ya man and shit?"

Beans didn't immediately answer, letting the question linger in the air. He checked his gun making sure it was off safety then chambered a round before sticking it back into his waist. "C'mon let's go take care of this nigga," he said reaching for the door only to be stopped by Kyrie.

"Yo, you sure you feeling up to doing this?" he asked showing his concern for Beans health. He had shed a ton of weight since getting hit up by the bullets at the parade. His movements were a bit slower and to Kyrie he looked a little off his square. "You know I can handle it by myself, right? Ain't no thing. I'll be in and out. You know I'll never speak on it," he looked at Beans sincerely. Out of respect, Kyrie was offering him a chance to sit this one out. He understood Beans wasn't fully recovered.

"Nigga, I taught you how to do this. I'm good, trust me." Beans smiled then winked. For him this was personal, although he would never admit it to anyone. He wanted to be the one who delivered the bullet to Case. Beans was feeling Ashleigh more than he led anybody to believe. The back and forth she had been doing between the two of them had built up so much tension, it was bound to explode. From the beginning it only was going to lead to gunplay. Even if she was too blind or selfish to see it. She was playing a deadly game that up until now hadn't resulted in any bloodshed but that was all about to change. Beans didn't like Case from the first time he laid eyes on him. He didn't take to new nigga easily. If everything went according to plan this would be the last time anybody ever laid eyes on him. "C'mon," Beans said pulling his arm away from Kyrie, pulling his hood over his head and opening the car door.

Kyrie did the same, exiting the driver's side then both men made their way up the sidewalk and quickly ducked into the alleyway on the side of Case's building.

"Come here, look," Beans whispered pointing up at a small foggy window in what appeared to be the bathroom of Case's apartment.

"What?" Kyrie whispered back to him.

"That window right there. You see it? It's cracked open a little. You see the steam coming out of it?" Beans asked pointing at the window. "Nigga probably in the shower or something. We can go through the window and murk the nigga. I'm telling you we catch him off guard. Easy money. He won't even see it coming," Beans said with certainty.

"You ain't in no condition to be climbing up no fire escape and shit, my nigga," Kyrie stated. "You sounding out of breath from just walking up the block."

Beans glared at Kyrie for a moment then looked up at the window. He sighed deeply in frustration, coming to the realization that it would be physically impossible for him to make it up the fire escape. "Aight, you flyin' solo then," he said. Then Beans laid the whole thing out for Kyrie. They couldn't afford any fuck-ups or mishaps, this had to go right.

"Go in there, body the nigga and come out. Straight like that, no bullshittin'," Beans stressed to Kyrie.

Once up on the fire escape, Kyrie tried lifting the window as quietly as possible. Down below in the alleyway, Beans looked on impatiently as Kyrie slowly cracked the window open. He was anxious. His heart started to pound faster in his chest as adrenaline raced through his veins. Beans didn't like having to sit on the sidelines. He was used to being on the frontline, in the mix, handling this type of thing. He greatly wished it was him going through the window of the apartment with gun in hand right next to Kyrie.

Back up on the fire escape Kyrie looked down at Beans, nodding, signaling the window was open. He pulled out his gun and climbed through the window. A thick cloud of steam filled the bathroom making it hard for him to see. The sound of the running water drowned out any noise his feet made as he moved across the bathroom floor approaching the shower with his gun aimed, ready to kill. Through the slight separation in the curtain, Kyrie could see that the shower was completely empty. He looked back over his shoulder and could see that the bathroom door had been left ajar. Kyrie wanted to get a peek out the door to see if he could locate Case's whereabouts in the house. He moved closer to the door but with the loud rain of the shower Kyrie was unable to hear the footsteps coming down the hallway.

Not until it was already too late and the footsteps were right on him. The bathroom door came flying open and Kyrie fired twice.

CHAPTER 27

ARIANE SAT ON THE FILTHY cement floor and looked around the basement helplessly. Her face was covered in dirt and dried tears. She had stopped crying hours ago and now she just wore a defiant scowl on her face. Her once welcoming smile had been replaced by a sneer and her bright eyes were dark with anger. Ariane stared down at her dirt stained hands and tried to make sense of what had happened. She couldn't believe the lengths her father would go to close a case. Kidnapping her was the lowest of the low. If there was ever a chance to repair their relationship, it had now crashed and burned. Ariane could never forgive him. "What kind of father does this to his daughter?" she spoke aloud to herself. Then her thoughts turned to Sin, she fought hard to keep the tears at bay. She really missed him. She wondered where he was and what he was doing. Ariane wondered if he had moved on by now. She prayed that he hadn't, just the thought allowed a few tears to escape. There was a scrapping noise in the room. Ariane was using the concrete floor to sharpen the leftover chicken bone. She had purposely swiped the piece off her plate when she had dinner with her father. Ariane was quick on her feet. Her mind was always working. Now it was in overdrive. She needed to get the fuck out of there.

With the chicken bone now as sharp as needed, Ariane tested it out by pricking her index finger and was satisfied when she saw a trickle of blood appear. "Yeah, muthafuckas," she said, excited about her work.

Her father had vastly underestimated her. Losing her brother, had made her tough. Ariane was forced to survive with no one there to protect her. Her survival skills would be the only thing that would get her out of that basement. With no windows or much light, she had no real sense of time. But she had somehow managed to figure out a way to tell when they would come to bring her food. They should be here soon," she told herself.

Her thoughts were interrupted by the sound of the cellar door opening. One of the guards entered the room.

Sliding herself against the wall closest to the door, Ariane folded over clutching her stomach and appearing to be writhing in excruciating pain. Ariane contorted her body, squirming and twisting. "Ahhhhh! Help me please!" she began to cry, laying it on thick.

"What's your problem?" the scowling man mumbled while standing over Ariane.

"I can't take the pain, my stomach it hurts, where is my father? I need my father," the tears just seemed to flow down her face.

"He's not here. Get up, I'll take you to the bathroom upstairs," the man said.

"I can't get up it hurts too bad. I need help," Ariane pleaded.

The guard groaned in anger. He didn't want to help her but he knew Agent Mosley would have his head if anything happened to his daughter. Finally, after a few seconds passed, he bent over to help Ariane on to her feet.

As soon as he lifted her by the arm, Ariane used her free hand to pierce the side of the agents face with the jagged bone. He screamed in agony, releasing her arm and grabbing his blood soaked face in pain.

"Ah! You little bitch," he shouted.

Ariane dashed towards the daylight of the open cellar door. She was blinded momentarily by the sun. It had been months since she felt the sun on her skin. Her eyes were sensitive to the flood of light after being locked in darkness for so long. She squinted and shaded her eyes with her hand doing her best to focus on her surroundings. All she saw was big tall trees on every side of her. To her great surprise there were no other agents in sight. Her father had manipulated her into thinking the place was constantly guarded by a group of men.

"Hey get back here," Ariane heard the agent call out to her from behind as he emerged from the cellar still holding his face.

Ariane made a run for it. She was disheveled with no shoes and no idea of where she was. "If I stop. I'm dead," she repeated to herself as motivation to keep on moving. Her legs were weak, her lungs were on fire and her heart was beating so hard that it hurt. Still Ariane refused to stop. If she could just make it to civilization she could flag down help. She could hear the swoosh of cars passing by at a high rate of speed, in the not so far distance. Ariane kept running as fast as she could until she saw the passing headlights through a break in the trees. Her mission was to make it out of there and to Sin. He thought she was dead. She needed to let him know she was alive and well. She had to warn him about her father. Her legs threatened to give out just as she emerged from the bushes and out into the road. Ariane froze like a deer in the bright beam of headlights and a blaring horn. She was in the middle of traffic on route 9A.at her direction as she didn't notice she was in the middle of traffic. Her mouth was dry and her heart was beating rapidly. She looked all around expecting agents to pop out of everywhere and grab her up to take her back. But none did.

Ariane was startled when a man grabbed her arm. Caught off guard and afraid she jumped back screaming "No! Get off me. I not going back."

"Easy ma," the guy said with his hands up in defense as he stepped closer to her. "Are you injured?" he asked looking at her tattered clothes. "Have a seat right here on the side of the road. Let me get you some help."

"I'm ok," she insisted refusing to sit down. "I just need a ride into the city," Ariane pleaded.

The guy shook his head at the mystery woman standing in front of him. He didn't know what was going on with her but he felt sympathy for her. Her whole appearance was off and she looked like she needed his help. "Look Ma, I could drop you wherever you need to go. You look like you need the help and I ain't tryna see you out here stranded."

She knew it was a risk getting in a car with a stranger but anything beat where she had just been. "Where are we?" she asked wanting to know her location.

"You in Westchester. Where you need to go?" he replied.

"Brooklyn." Ariane said as she walked to the guy's car and got in. She was tired and hungry and in need of a hot bath. She hoped that Sin would be home. She needed to explain all that had happened to her. The explosion, her father, everything and she prayed he would understand.

CHAPTER 28

THE SUN HAD GONE TO rest and the moon had taken its place in the sky. It was something about the darkness of the night that Emma always loved. It hid the sky's flaws, its imperfections, the way she always wished she could hers. A breeze blew through her hair as the sounds of the ocean soothed to her soul. The crashing waves like a classical symphony playing in the air. Emma sat on the white chaise lounge chair admiring the beautiful view from her summer home in the Hamptons. She didn't frequent the vacation home as much as she would like too but when the time called for it, she gladly answered. With all that was going on in her family, she needed a little break to enjoy the simple pleasures of self-indulgence. To the naked eye, one would think Emma was unfazed by it all. The violence, the betrayal, the deception. Those things had become second nature to her but it didn't make them any easier. She had long lost count of the sleepless nights, unfinished meals and grey hairs. The life had certainly taken a toll on her. She concealed it all behind a venomous smile, an impeccable sense of style and the occasional bottle of hair dye. Sacrifices were necessary, decisions had to be made, this game that wasn't for the faint of heart or the average person. But then again, growing up a kingpin's daughter then becoming a kingpin's wife wasn't for the average person either. Emma was bred for the life more than some men were. Kill or be killed, it was survival of the fittest. Emma planned to outlast all of her enemies and be the last one standing.

The thought of her children crossed her mind. Everything she had done in life was for the betterment of them. She felt accomplished that Mason was in office. Although he was dealing with the death of his wife and daughter. Emma knew he was seen as a sympathetic figure to the public. That would surely keep him in office for both terms. She would help him rebuild his inner strength. Mason was her most prized possession and valuable too, but he was also her weakest child. She would have to get him back in order, Emma needed to get him focused and ready to do what he was put in office for and that was to clear any stumbling blocks that might trip up the family business.

Emma thought about Cassie and how smart she was, she smiled at the thought of her late husband's admiration for their daughter. Both Emma and Marion knew Cassie was special, she was a rare gem. She had all the potential to be a leading force in the family, and she indeed was. Emma only wished her daughter would be more open to her advisement at times. Cassie wasn't as influenced as Emma would like her to be. If she could get her eldest daughter to side with her they would surely be unstoppable.

Consumed with her thoughts, Emma never heard the footsteps slowly approaching her from behind as she sat in the chair. She was unguarded, free and felt nothing but the wind blowing at her back. The shadowy figure slowly stalked towards her quietly, being certain not to make their presence known. Emma reached down beside her to grab her glass of champagne. As she drank from her glass, she felt the moon's light shining on her back disappear and a large shadow replaced it. Emma went to turn around but before she could, a hand reached down and touched her shoulder. Startled, her muscles tensed up then relaxed for the soothing sensation of being massaged. Emma knew those hands all so well. She closed her eyes and welcomed the strong hands on her delicate skin.

"How long have you been standing behind me?" Emma

said.

"Not long, my love."

"I've missed you. I'm glad you decided to meet me here tonight. It had been a while since you held me in your arms. You were spectacular as usual," Emma complimented him on the love session they had just shared before she found sanctuary out on the beach.

The love affair between Emma and Andres Santos had been going on for years. Emma loved Marion, but she also loved Andres, the likelihood of Emma and Andres getting married would have been high had Marion Holloway not walked into her life. Andres fell in love with Emma from the day he laid eyes on her and she knew it. She always did but the confirmation came when Andres revealed to her the truth about her father and uncles' deaths. Marion Holloway, the man that claimed to love her was responsible. He had killed her father and taken his seat in the throne. Andres wanted to kill Marion but Emma pleaded for him not to, for her children's sake. Andres understood Emma's love for Marion and he knew she would never leave him. So he continued to supply Marion with drugs out of his loyalty to Emma. He knew Marion would provide a comfortable life for Emma. Andres always assured Emma there would be peace between him and her husband for as long as she wanted it to be. He never pressured her or hurt Marion because he understood Emma's feelings for him. They were equivalent to the ones he himself had for her. Andres promised her that he would wait and whenever she was ready to erase her old life and start anew with him he would do any and everything in his power to make that happen for her. Tonight was that night. By nights end The Commission would be no more, Sin would be dead and New York would be in their sole control.

"Are you sure we're discrete here?" Andres whispered in Emma's ear and gently kissed her cheek.

"Yes we are," she rubbed his hand gently and affectionately.

"The last time you said we were safe, your daughter in law overheard us talking. I had to get rid of her, that wasn't a part of the plan. I don't want you to have to lose any more family members," Andres expressed freely.

"She was never family. Khari, was a liability, she would have eventually done something else to earn herself a one-way ticket to hell," Emma expressed coldly. "Trust me my love, no one knows we're here, we're safe" Emma assured.

"Mi Vida, you're always safe with me, never forget that," Andres reiterated.

"Is everything done?" Emma asked in a sweet voice. Emma didn't show her soft side to many, Andres was one of the few. He played on a different level. He was a boss bigger than even her late husband. Emma was attracted to power and his gave her a euphoric feeling when she was around him.

"It will be soon," Andres said reaching into the pocket of his robe and retrieved his cell phone. He dialed a number and by the second ring a voice greeted him.

"Hola Papa"

"Mi hija, it's time to sever ties with our friend Yasin. Give the order," he commanded.

"Ok Papa. No problema."

Andres hung up the phone and combed his finger through Emma's hair. "It's done my love."

Emma smiled. She would finally have back in her possession what was rightfully hers. It had all been worth it. She was going to sleep peacefully tonight. But not before she thanked the man who helped make it all happen.

"Let's go inside," she whispered to Andres. "Good news like that is cause for a celebration and I have a few ways in mind on how I would like to celebrate," Emma flirted.

"You lead the way" he replied with lust in his eyes. Andres finally had the woman he loved all to himself. He had waited years for his turn, secretly jealous of Marion because he had Emma's heart. The thought of Emma loving only him, made Andres smile. Him as the king and her as his queen, all felt right. Little did he know Emma was a woman who was temporarily pleased. In her mind, she was king. In due time all would know and all would feel it and be force to acknowledge it. No exceptions.

* * *

"Ok Papa. No problema," Reina Santos said as she hung up the phone. She had been anticipating the call for weeks. On her father's orders, Reina had placed her men around Sin, guarding him and posing as his hired guns. They were to protect him until she gave the word to kill him and everyone in his organization. Sin had been so pre-occupied with the war against The Commission that he had unknowingly opened the door for his own demise by accepting Reina's help. The phone call from Andres Santos had just sealed Sin's fate. For years Andres Santos had encouraged Reina to do whatever necessary to get close to Sin. He used his daughter's beauty like a weapon, knowing one day he would use it to rid himself of Marion's bastard son. Andres felt Sin would be his only challenge once he killed The Holloway leader. The other children were the least of his concern. They could easily be controlled by Emma and made to believe whatever she told them. The plan was flawless. All except for one thing, Reina had developed deep feelings for Sin and didn't want to kill Sin.

To Reina, falling in love with Sin was like the first couple seconds on a rollercoaster ride. At the beginning she thought "I can't believe I'm doing this, maybe this isn't such a good idea." But at some point, she realized it was too late to back out. Then every twist and turn became more exciting than the last and she started to let go and trust her heart. In time, Reina started to believe that what she felt was real but still she could never go against her father's wishes.

As her car pulled to a stop, a tall Cuban bodyguard climbed from behind the wheel. He walked to the rear of the car, opened the door and reached inside. Reina took his hand and emerged from the backseat of the Mercedes with a joint in her mouth. She tossed it to the ground and snuff it out with the heel of her shoe as her bodyguard shielded her from the sudden downpour with an umbrella. Reina quickly marched towards the door of the Botanica where they practiced Santeria. Once inside, she brushed the beads of water off that had formed on her coat before making her way to the back office. She took a seat behind the desk then dialed a number in her phone. The call was picked up by one of her top lieutenants.

"Pull all of the men off of Sin and his people. Effective immediately," she commanded. Reina quickly hung up the phone. Her heart was pounding. She had just signed Sin's death certificate and she couldn't help but feel an intense sadness. She pulled a large, white candle from inside her desk, lit it and closed her eyes as she began to chant a protection prayer.

* * *

Agent Mosley stood with his arms folded and a look of

frustration on his face as he stared around the empty cellar that once held his daughter. He kicked up some dirt on the floor as he flew into a rant.

"You are a Federal Agent of the United States government. How could you be so incompetent? You fucking imbecile. You just put this whole case in jeopardy!" he shouted at the agent holding the bandage over the deep gash in his face.

Mosley sighed deeply as he put his hands on top of his head. "Get out of my sight right now before I have your badge."

The agent lowered his head in shame, turned and walked out the basement.

Mosley thought quick on his feet. Everything was not lost. There was one card he had yet to play. He pulled his phone from the inside pocket of his suit jacket and began to pace as he dialed a number. After a few rings the call was picked up on the other end.

"Hello, Agent Cole Spencer, this is Special Agent Roe Mosley. I'm going to need to see you in my office tomorrow morning. I want to know everything you have on Yasin Kennedy and the entire Holloway organization."

"Why so urgent and sudden?" Agent Spencer questioned. "I'm getting pretty good intel. Why pull the plug now?"

"Oh, I'm not pulling the plug. There has been a change

in circumstances. Which calls for a change in our plans. I'll discuss all this with you tomorrow morning, 9 AM sharp," Mosley told him.

"Ok sir, no problem," Agent Spencer said.

* * *

"Ok sir, no problem," Elijah said into the phone then hung up, quickly making the secret phone disappear into the nightstand just as Cassie emerged from the bathroom door dressed in a blue, satin and lace baby doll.

"Were you just on the phone?" she asked.

"Yeah," he waved his regular cell in the air and shook his head. "Nothing to worry about though. Just some work shit," Elijah said playing his role.

"This late?" Cassie had a suspicious look on her face.

"Yeah, unexpected meeting in the morning. You know how that shit goes," he said, his words filled with deceit.

"I get a little scared when either of our phones begin to ring. Lately it's been all bad news," she said.

"Yeah but let's not dwell on that tonight," he said staring at her with lust in his eyes.

"Damn," Cassie pouted.

"What?" Elijah asked full of concern.

A devilish smile appeared on Cassie's face. "Now I feel bad that I'm about to wear you out, seeing how you have an early morning meeting" she flirted.

"You sure about that?" Elijah said with a handsome grin then stood to his feet and dropped his boxers.

"Hmm," Cassie bit her bottom lip seductively as she admired her husband's naked chocolate body.

CHAPTER 29

THE MEETING WITH THE COMMISSION was being held in Connecticut. Foxwoods Casino it was considered the largest on the east coast. Although millions of visitors strolled through its doors every year, few had never seen the underground portion hidden deep below the grounds of the massive structure. Most weren't even aware of its existence. Phil Catanzano was, and this was where he decided the men would met.

Sin walked through a pair of smoke glass doors and was immediately met by two hulking bodyguards who began patting him down. After they were done, he was quickly escorted down to the underbelly of the casino. At the end of a long hallway Sin was met by another one of Catanzano's goons.

"You're the last to show. They've been waiting for you," the man said, seemingly annoyed by Sin's tardiness to the meeting. The bodyguard stepped aside, pushing open the double wooden doors, behind which the heads of The Five Families all sat around a large, conference table. Expensive paintings decorated the walls of the room and a European crystal chandelier hung above the table. Sin identified all the men in the room, in a single glance. Seated at the head of the table with his fingers interlocked in front of him, Phil Catanzano stared directly at Sin, offering a welcoming smile and a respectful nod as he entered the room. Facing Sin, on the far side of the table, were Joey Barboza and Tommy Black, leaders of two of the five New York families. On the near side of the table, Dom Brigandi was pouring himself a drink. Beside him sat an empty chair, purposely left open for Sin. At the opposite end of the table Fat Tony Martello flicked the thick ash of his cigar as he looked up at Sin, showing his irritation at his late arrival to the meeting. The way he fidgeted in his chair, it was clear that sharing a room with Sin made him feel uncomfortable.

"Pardon my lateness gentlemen," Sin said looking around the room again, as if to reassure himself of what he was seeing. There were half empty glasses of liquor on the table, along with burning cigars in the ashtrays. Sin had purposely been a few minutes late but by the amount of ashes in the ashtrays, he could tell that the meeting had been going on for quite a well.

The bodyguard that led Sin in, pulled the chair out for him and Sin took the seat in between Brigandi and Catanzano.

"Glad to see you finally decided to join us," Tommy Black made a wisecrack as Sin sat down. Sin didn't acknowledge it or entertained him and the room grew silent.

Once the door to the room had been closed, Catanzano cleared his throat, pushed his chair back and stood up. "Gentlemen, I've asked you all here today so that we could put an end to this war once and for all and avoid any more trouble in the future. In this room sit the most powerful men in New York. In order for us to remain that way, things like what happened at the Mayor's inauguration can never happen again." To those in the room Catanzano's words didn't feel or sound natural. They were stiff and predetermined.

Sin quickly spoke up, "Perhaps there are men in this room, who were responsible for my father's death." Sin stared into the eyes of each Don for an equal amount of time. "Maybe one of you are responsible for the car bomb that killed someone very special to me. Maybe all of you were behind the hit at the parade. But if peace can be made here today between us, to avoid me losing any more of my loved ones, then I'm all for it," Sin said humbly.

"Listen, there's a lot of money to be made if we all keep our heads and cooperate with each other like businessmen and not like animals," Catanzano said looking over first at Fat Tony then at Sin. "You have a lot of territory under your control, Sin. Maybe you would be willing to relinquish some of it in order to forge some peace," Catanzano offered a solution. Between the men in the room there wasn't a sound, all waited anxiously for Sin to respond.

When he didn't Fat Tony spoke. "Listen let's cut all the monkey business," he said pun intended. "You're at a disadvantage here. Your losing this war. It won't be long before we kill everyone that is connected to you. Give up the territories or suffer the consequences," Fat Tony threatened.

"Hold on gentlemen," Catanzano interjected, "there's been too much killing already. Some of it had to be done," he said looking over at Fat Tony, referring to the death of Mike Di Toro. "And some of it didn't. Bloodshed only makes trouble for guys like us. As the oldest Don here and the one who has controlled his family the longest, I've seen a lot but I've never seen war determine whose right or wrong, only whose left. So I think it is in everyone at this tables best interest to see if we can all agree to ending this war." Catanzano said then leaned back in his chair, folding his arms over his chest as he waited for a response.

Sin looked around the table at the faces of the other

members. He saw smirks and smiles. All the Dons looked excessively pleased as a result of the power play that had been made by Fat Tony. Their looks told Sin one thing. That they had discussed the matter before his arrival and maybe even prior to this meeting. The other thing it told him was that Catanzano had to be in on it. He must have succumb to the pressure from the others. The threat of war against his family was too much. The other families were united. They would crush him. The only way to survive was for him to align with them. Marion had always told Sin that's what Catanzano lacked in power, he more than made up for it in brains. This was a smart move, even Sin had to admit it.

"So tell me something Phil," Sin turned to his father's old pal. "What they give you for setting me up?" he asked.

Phil Catanzano shook his head then let out a hearty laugh from his gut confirming Sin's suspicions.

"So what was it money or did they promise not to wipe you out along with me and my organization?"

"You're smart kid. I must admit. You're almost as sharp as your dad was. The things is, just like him, you failed to see the bigger picture," Catanzano bragged as he stood from his seated position. "Nobody gave me anything to set you up. I did all this on my own."

All of Catanzano's bodyguards suddenly drew their guns, aiming them at the men seated at the table. The smiles left from the faces of the Commission members as Catanzano's smile widened.

"You see gentlemen; the most powerful man isn't the one who can do the most work. It's the one who is smart enough to get others to do that work for him. I set this war in motion long ago," Catanzano confessed. "Who do you think gave Mike Di Toro the idea of becoming Capo di tutti capi, boss of all bosses? Me. He was strong, his family powerful. I knew he would take the bait and knock off the other families," he explained as he began to circle the room. The power he felt was intoxicating. "I tried to get your father involved too but he was smart, he didn't take the bait at first. But eventually he couldn't resist either going to war with Di Toro. I just sat back and watched everybody fall to the waste side. Patiently waiting for a day like today. Now I have you all exactly where I want you and after tonight I will be the boss of all bosses." To the shock of the other bosses, Catanzano had outsmarted them all as he unfolded his master plan.

Around the table, the bosses looked to each other, watching for reactions. Not a face at the table gave away a thing, though Fat Tony could barely hide his unhappiness at the turn of events. He looked as if some physical harm had come to him. Suddenly he rose to his feet and jabbed his finger forcefully on top of the table as he spoke, "You double crossing bastard. We were just supposed to kill this mouliyan here. I'll see you in hell," Fat Tony shouted.

"Sit down," Catanzano told him then waved his hand to one of his goons. The man hit Fat Tony at the base of his neck with the butt of his gun.

"Argh shit," Fat Tony squealed in agony as he crumbled back in his chair.

The members seated around the table began to stir. Tommy Black was next to speak up, "How do you expect to just kill all of us and get away with it? There are cameras everywhere in this casino. Even in the hallway out there," he pointed to the door.

"Why do you think I picked this place to meet. I have full control. Every camera you passed on your way into this room had been turned off. None of you are here, including me," Catanzano said. He had truly planned everything down to the smallest detail.

Sin stood from his seat. "You know Phil when this all started, I wasn't quite sure which one of you was pulling the strings," Sin said. "Then I thought of something I once read and it made everything crystal clear."

"What was that?" a curious Catanzano asked.

"A good enemy will accompany you on your journey, but you will never reach your destination with him," Sin said nodding his head. "You were too eager to help. That made you obvious. It's gonna be fun watching you die."

"I think that you are mistaken my friend. You are in no position to decide life or death," Catanzano told him.

"Nah. I think you've overestimated your power and underestimated mine," Sin replied. With just a head nod all the bodyguards turned their weapons on Catanzano, who nearly choked at the realization that his own men where on Sin's team. "I anticipated that one day it would come to something like this. So I've been paying your men double what you have for some time now. Great investment, huh? How you think I got in here with this?" Sin pulled a gun from the small of his back, aimed it at Catanzano and fired. The shots hit the mobster square in the forehead, sending him slumped back into his chair, dead. All the other bosses jumped at the sound of the gunshot. "It's a new day," Sin informed the rest of the Commission members. "And you muthafuckas is old news," he said with a bright smile. Sin backed away from the table and walked over to the door. On his way out, he nodded to the bodyguard for a job well done. As the doors closed behind him, gunfire erupted in the underground conference room. The Commission was no more.

CHAPTER 30

THE SHOTS FROM THE GUN seemed unreal at first, like Kyrie was dreaming but with his eyes open. He instantly knew it was a mistake, something that wasn't supposed to happen but it was pure instincts that made him pull the trigger. But now it seemed like a glitch in time that needed to be redone. Everything moved in super slow motion as he watched Ashleigh's white robe turn crimson as she stumbled back a few steps. Her body slumped against the wall. The towel in her hand dropped to the floor. Ashleigh looked down at her blood stained robe, the look on her face was one of nonbelief and pure shock. She collapsed to the floor, landing on her back, staring up at the ceiling as her breath faded away.

Out in the alleyway, Beans heard the shots and walked to the front of the building to wait for Kyrie to emerge out the front door. He limped heavily as he moved but still at a steady pace. The sound of gunfire was a frequent occurrence in that neighborhood, especially at that time of night and nothing on the block seemed disturbed as he looked around. No one reacted to the shots. There was no one peeking through there curtains. No calls to 911. No screams, shouts or any signs of panic. After a few seconds had passed with no signs of Kyrie, Beans anxiety began to kick in again. "I knew I should have handled this myself," was his first thought instantly followed by concern. Maybe Case had gotten the drop on the youngster and the shots he heard where from his gun, he thought. Beans smoothly pulled his gun from his waist and hobbled for the steps. Suddenly his phone began to ring with Kyrie's number showing on the screen. Beans hesitated momentarily before answering, unsure of what was going on. Whatever it was, didn't feel right to him. Finally, he answered but didn't say anything, holding the phone out in front of him, halfway between his ears and his eyes. Almost certain that Case's voice would come barking from the other end at any moment but what Beans heard was more surprising. Kyrie speaking in a way that was impossible to understand.

"What the fuck was she doing here? Aw man Beans. This is not good. I fucked up. Oh shit. Sin is gonna kill me," the young G spoke in spurts of jumbled clusters, filled with so much emotion.

"Hold up, slow the fuck down!" Beans demanded. "She who? Fucked up how? What the hell are you talking about Ky?"

"Ashleigh!" Kyrie shouted into the phone.

* * *

Sin had a tight grip on the gun in his lap as he drove past the line of police cars with their sirens blaring, racing in the opposite direction towards the casino. They were sure to find the massacre that he had beautifully orchestrated. Sin drove straight back to the city without stopping. During the ride, he reflected on everything that had happened over the last year or so. Losing his father, his woman, his friends. Finding out about Bria then losing her too. It all seemed to hit him at once. There was a flood of emotion but there were no tears this time. He would have to deal with those loses for years to come. Tonight he felt a sense of relief. The war with The Commission was truly over. He took a deep breath and enjoyed the ride.

A while later he pulled on to his block. He couldn't wait to take a shower and get in his bed. It had been so long since he had enjoyed a good night of sleep, he looked forward to the opportunity to do so. As he pulled to the curb and parked his phone began to ring. He ignored the call and cut the car off, taking the keys out the ignition. Immediately his phone rang again, this time Beans name flashed on the screen. He answered it, interested in finding out how the business he sent them to handle had went.

"What up," he said but was greeted by the sound of Beans sobbing on the other end. It was a sound he had never heard from Beans in all the years he had known him. Sin was instantly alarmed. His brow lowered, "What is it my nigga?"

"It's Ashleigh. She's dead," Beans cried out sitting on the floor of Case's apartment, covered in blood as he cradled her in his arms. He let the phone fall from his hands, dropping it to the floor next to him. He pulled Ashleigh into his chest, kissing her on top of the head and continued crying without interruption. His tears weren't a show of his weakness, they were from rage. Beans had never been in love before and it wasn't until the moment that he held Ashleigh's lifeless body in his arms that he realized he had been in love with her.

"What!" Sin shouted as if he hadn't heard him correctly. "What the fuck happened? Beans! Yo Beans!" he called out to him hearing the phone drop to the floor. Sin could hear him crying in the background. Why was Ashleigh there? She was supposed to be in Florida, in a rehab, Sin thought to himself in a cloud of confusion. Now outside the car, Sin turned to look over his shoulder as he heard footsteps coming across the street. It alerted him, he was always alert. It was how he had stayed alive for so long. Catching a glimpse of the person walking towards him didn't alarm him but it did surprise him. So surprised he asked, "What are you doing here?"

The person didn't respond nor extend their hand to greet him. It was at that moment that Sin knew what was about to happen. His brain was processing so much information that he couldn't react. He saw the gun appear, so small it seemed harmless. He saw the stiffness in his killer's face. For the first time Sin understood the looks on the faces of the men he had killed. The absolute bewilderment in their eyes when they realized that life was about to end. He understood that feeling now and knew today was the day, he would finally have to pay for living the life he chose. In his mind he smirked, although it never showed it on his face, he thought to himself that this was exactly the way he would've done it. It was a brilliant plan, he had to admit, he never saw it coming.

Sin dropped the phone and lunged forward reaching for the gun. At the same time the killer came forward to meet him.

BOOM! BOOM! BOOM!

Three bullets entered Sin's body, forcing him to stumble backwards and crumble to the ground.

* * *

Ariane was a nervous ball of energy. She kept bouncing her leg as she sat on the couch in Sin's living room dialing his number over and over again. He was notorious for not answering numbers he didn't recognize and it was driving her crazy at the moment. The nice gentleman who had given her a ride was kind enough to leave her his cell phone but as of yet it hadn't done her any good. The giddiness she felt reminded her of the first time she and Sin kissed. Ariane smiled as she thought back on them. She craved his presence and couldn't wait for him to walk through the door. The way he looked at her made her feel like the most beautiful woman in the world. Her love for him was reflected in the strength she showed to escape from her father's clutches. It filled her with a warmth and vigor like nothing else. It made her feel a happiness and lust for life like she never had before. Sin made her feel like they could weather any storm.

Ariane heard his car door slam and all the little hairs on the back of her neck stood at attention. Then she heard the shots and immediately bolted for the door. "Oh God. No," she cried, fearing the worst. She raced through the door and down the steps. Her heart pounding so hard that it hurt. Finally, she reached the bottom and burst through the door. Ariane lost her breath. Wavering for a moment as her heart stopped and she trembled seeing Sin stretched out on his back, shot, in the middle of the street. Ariane became immobilized by fear. Unable to move, she began sobbing, watching in horror as the person with the gun stalked towards a wounded and incapacitated Sin.

From his back, Sin looked up at Lil' Smoke standing over him, aiming the gun at his head. There was no mercy in his young eyes, only blind fury and vengeance. "You killed my father." It was more of a declaration then a question. His words were violently intense and it was clear that he was on the edge.

Sin tried to speak but couldn't. Blood was quickly filling his lungs making each breath a challenge. He slowly nodded his head. Admitting the bitter and severe truth, giving the young man the answer he was seeking. Then he waited for the final bullet to crash into his skill.

Lil Smoke now had tears running down his face. His emotions were all over the place. He hesitated momentarily, seemingly reflecting on the death of his father and the man laying on the ground at the other end of his gun. For as long as he could remember Sin had been like a father figure to him. The person he looked up to and wanted to be like even more than he had his father. All he heard was stories about Big Smoke, he was a myth to him. Sin was real, someone he could see and touch, a living legend to him. But Lil' Smoke now felt like the kid who just found out Santa Claus wasn't real. He had gone too far to turn back now. He had watched

Ashleigh not Case pull up in front of the building and enter Case's apartment a few hours earlier. He knew exactly what he was doing when he placed the call to Sin. He knew what it would lead to, he hoped for it. He didn't care that Ashleigh's blood was on his hands. He wanted Sin to feel the pain of losing someone close to him. Now he sought his final and ultimate revenge. "I'm just taking back what's rightfully mine," he said as he curled his finger around the trigger.

The loud scream of a woman made him look in the direction it came from. Taking his eyes off the target as he squeezed the trigger.

BOOM!

The bullet barely missed Sin's head as it slammed into the ground. Lil' Smoke behaved like a skittish horse, taking off running as he saw Ariane racing towards them.

Ariane's knees hit the ground hard as she hovered over a barely conscious Sin. "Help," she called out. "Somebody help me, please!" her desperate screams echoed through the streets. This was the other side of love. This is what made it so dangerous. It was the most destructive force anyone could every invite in. In order to feel it, Ariane had to allow it to become a part of her. Sin had removed the armor from around her heart. He tore down the walls she had spent years building. He touched the very center of her being. A piece of him had entered Ariane's core and become a part of her. Now the pain she felt watching him cling to life resonated deep within her essence. Every other pain could be deflected by her armor but not the pain of love and the thought of losing Sin. The hurt originates from the deepest, most vulnerable place inside of her. Because that's where her love for him lived. The regions in her heart had never felt pain like that before. "Sin don't leave me please," she begged as tears streamed down her face.

In his mind Sin knew he had been shot but oddly enough, he felt absolutely no pain. He felt serene and peacefully relaxed. It was like he was being lulled to sleep and covered with a heavy, invisible blanket of death. He was at death's door, clinging to consciousness but he felt comfort like he wasn't alone. There was a sense of being surrounded by something familiar that washed over him and in that moment he felt safe. Then he heard Ariane's voice call out to him. He opened his eyes and saw her face. She was so beautiful just like he remembered. It was as if God had sent her to encourage and welcome him into heaven. Sin felt this infinite vastness, but also the absence of time. He was going to be with the woman he loved again. He wasn't scared to die now. He would have eternal happiness with Ariane. Knowing he was about to die Sin wouldn't have wanted anyone else to walk him into the other side, besides Ariane. If this was how he was going to transition he welcomed it.

"No!" Ariane shouted as she watched him close his eyes

once again. “Come back to me,” she screamed while shaking him. It was like Ariane’s heart had been ripped from her chest leaving her bloody and wounded.

About the Author

Raised in Peekskill, NY, Ty Marshall is an undeniable talent with a highly skilled pen. Discovered by New York Times Selling Authors Ashley & JaQuavis, his ability to seamlessly weave authentic depictions of the street with great storytelling sets him apart from the pack. He is widely considered one of the rising African American authors in the country. Ty has independently released several titles which include: Keys to the Kingdom, 80's Baby and Eat, Prey & No Love. He also released a ebook through St. Martins Griffin entitled Luxury & Larceny. Ty is a proud husband and father that currently resides in Atlanta, Ga.

www.TYMARSHALLBOOKS.com